Offensive Language

CW01433039

Also available from Bloomsbury

Antagonism on YouTube, by Stephen Pihlaja
Linguistic Inquiries into Donald Trump's Language, edited by Ulrike Schneider
and Matthias Eitelmann
The Art of Political Storytelling, by Philip Seargeant
The Discourse of Online Consumer Reviews, by Camilla Vasquez

Offensive Language

Taboo, Offence and Social Control

Jim O'Driscoll

BLOOMSBURY ACADEMIC
LONDON • NEW YORK • OXFORD • NEW DELHI • SYDNEY

BLOOMSBURY ACADEMIC
Bloomsbury Publishing Plc
50 Bedford Square, London, WC1B 3DP, UK
1385 Broadway, New York, NY 10018, USA
29 Earlsfort Terrace, Dublin 2, Ireland

BLOOMSBURY, BLOOMSBURY ACADEMIC and the Diana logo are trademarks of
Bloomsbury Publishing Plc

First published in Great Britain 2020
This paperback edition published in 2022

Copyright © Jim O'Driscoll, 2020

Jim O'Driscoll has asserted his right under the Copyright, Designs and Patents Act, 1988,
to be identified as Author of this work.

Cover design: Rebecca Heselton

All rights reserved. No part of this publication may be reproduced or
transmitted in any form or by any means, electronic or mechanical, including
photocopying, recording, or any information storage or retrieval system, without prior
permission in writing from the publishers.

Bloomsbury Publishing Plc does not have any control over, or responsibility for,
any third-party websites referred to or in this book. All internet addresses
given in this book were correct at the time of going to press. The author and publisher
regret any inconvenience caused if addresses have changed or sites have
ceased to exist, but can accept no responsibility for any such changes.

A catalogue record for this book is available from the British Library.

Library of Congress Cataloging-in-Publication Data
Names: O'Driscoll, Jim, author.
Title: Offensive language: taboo, offence and social control / Jim O'Driscoll.
Description: London, UK; New York, NY: Bloomsbury Academic, 2020. |
Includes bibliographical references and index.
Identifiers: LCCN 2020027553 (print) | LCCN 2020027554 (ebook) |
ISBN 9781350169678 (hardback) | 9781350193321 (paperback) |
ISBN 9781350169685 (ebook) | ISBN 9781350169692 (epub)
Subjects: LCSH: Taboo, Linguistic. | Politeness (Linguistics) | Obscene words. | Swearing.
Classification: LCC P305.18.T33 O46 2020 (print) | LCC P305.18.T33 (ebook) |
DDC 306.44–dc23
LC record available at https://lccn.loc.gov/2020027553
LC ebook record available at https://lccn.loc.gov/2020027554

ISBN: HB: 978-1-3501-6967-8
PB: 978-1-3501-9332-1
ePDF: 978-1-3501-6968-5
eBook: 978-1-3501-6969-2

Typeset by Integra Software Services Pvt. Ltd.

To find out more about our authors and books visit www.bloomsbury.com
and sign up for our newsletters.

Contents

Preface

Sometimes when I attend a seminar or session at an academic conference, the presenter begins by warning us that the presentation involves the examination of language regarded as in some way offensive: for example, it contains swearwords or explicit sexual references. Quite frequently, the warning is couched as an apology. I always feel offended by this warning. Who does the speaker think I am? I'm a linguist and linguists are not (or at least shouldn't be) afraid of words. And anyway this is an event for specialists, not the general public.

Nevertheless, I can understand why the warning, even an apology, is so often issued. There is something visceral about encountering those offensive words or references. By forewarning them of what is about to come their way, the speaker gives listeners the opportunity to make sure they have, just in case they haven't already, a 'face' (see section 2.2) ready for it. Indeed, so visceral are those words and references that their occurrence can be discomfiting even for the presenter who is already prepared for them. Once when I was giving a presentation, the technology through which I intended to play back a video recording of a song with, by all conventional standards, some extremely offensive lyrics, failed to work. As a result, I had to 'sing' the song myself. I found this embarrassing, far more so than if I had been able to play the recording, not because I'm a terrible singer (although I am) but because of the words coming out of my mouth. (Why? The question of the position of the person who simply reanimates someone else's words is taken up in Chapter 11.)

Given these considerations, I hereby proffer two sequential apologies to the reader of this book. Apology 1: I'm sorry if you find some of the material herein hard to stomach – I do not mean to discomfit you. Apology 2: I'm sorry if that first apology offended you – I did not mean to misidentify you.

I think I can identify three distinct motivations for writing this book. And I think the earliest was the colloquium on swearing and linguistic impoliteness, chaired by Neal Norrick, at the Sociolinguistics Symposium in Berlin in 2012. We had a great time and there were many excellent papers delivered. But I came away with the distinct feeling that while we all knew what we were talking about in the round, it often seemed hard to pin down exactly which part of this field, and what characteristics of it, we were talking about at any one time. I particularly felt that exactly what was meant by 'swearing' needed to be excavated. What has emerged from these efforts can be found in Chapters 3–6 of the book and explains the appearance of the word 'taboo' in its subtitle.

The second motivation is a wish to develop impoliteness scholarship. Quite clearly – and as will become clearer as the text progresses – this book owes a huge debt to Jonathan Culpeper's (2011) authoritative monograph *Impoliteness: Using Language to Cause Offence*. Indeed, if we accept Culpeper's suggestion of 'impoliteness' as an umbrella term for a certain range of behaviour, it might feasibly, and only slightly misleadingly, have had that word as its main title (and I will be quite happy for that same umbrella to shelter this book in library classifications). But for greater accuracy in reflecting my focus, I have chosen 'offensive language'. The causing of offence is just one of the two defining characteristics of Culpeper's (2011: 23) technical definition of impoliteness and it is this characteristic alone which this book addresses.

The third motivation is the zeitgeist. As Smith et al. (2010: 1) observe in their study of 'incivility', "Books on freefalling manners have long replaced those about etiquette on bestseller lists" and "What makes our age distinctive is … the intensity and form of the anxiety" about a supposed breakdown of civil society. They give examples of the recent criminalizing of what they call 'everyday rudeness' as a reflex of this anxiety. My more particular motivation here arises out of my perception of this anxiety reflected in reactions to the use of language. There is an awful lot of offence-taking around these days. It seems that, in public and semi-public life at least, the range of what language counts as offensive (and, indeed, subject to legal sanction) is getting increasingly wide. At the time of writing, in the country in which I live (England), hardly a week goes by without some item in the news about somebody getting into hot water for something they said. Such a development runs up against free speech and poses questions for this principle. It also suggests the exertion of an increasing amount of external control on people concerning the kinds of things they feel they can acceptably say, hence 'social control' in the subtitle. I felt strongly that it needed to be examined. This is not, by the way, the first time this phrase has appeared on the cover of a book about the use of language. It was suggested to me by Sarangi & Slembrouck's (1996) excellent study of the discursive power exercised by modern public bodies, *Language, Bureaucracy and Social Control*. I am grateful to them for offering an exemplar of the satisfyingly ringing tone it can have as the last item in a three-part list.

Motivation for writing a book is one thing; actually writing it is another. Many, many people have helped me to get it done. I have attempted, but probably not always succeeded, to express my thanks to those who have helped with particular matters at relevant points in the text. But there are two groups of people to whom I owe a more general debt of thanks. One comprises my fellow core members of the Linguistic Politeness Research Group, Bethan Davies, Karen Grainger and Andrew Merrison. To them, thank you for much stimulating discussion. The other group comprises my colleagues in Linguistics at the University of Huddersfield. Quite apart from their willingness to offer expert help on particular points whenever I asked for it, they have been wonderfully tolerant of the times when I may not have been fully pulling my weight and have picked up the slack ungrudgingly. So to Tom Devlin, Matt Evans, Erica Gold, Liz Holt, Lesley Jeffries, Dan McIntrye, Louise Nuttall and Hazel Price, thank you! My wife, Lynne, has been likewise tolerant, except much more so. More importantly, it was she who first drew my attention to many of the incidents which have furnished the material for the case studies in this book. Perhaps most importantly of all, she has always known when to suggest I should be stopping for a break and when to tell me I should just be getting on with it. To her, thank you doesn't cut it.

Finally, I am especially grateful to those who have made time to read through a draft manuscript. I have benefited greatly from the meticulous attention to detail of, and numerous helpful suggestions from, Maria Sifianou and Anne-Marie Simon-Vandenbergen in particular, but also Daniel Stanley, Matt Butler and one anonymous reviewer. I have attempted to incorporate some of their suggestions into this final version. (I only wish I had the time and ability to incorporate all of them.) Whether these attempts have been successful is for the reader to judge, and the judgements must attach to me, not to them or anyone else mentioned above.

Part One

Offensive language and why it matters

1

Introduction

1.1 What this book is about

I must have been five or six when I first encountered the adage:

Sticks and stones
may break my bones,
but words will never hurt me.

It might have been my parents or it might have been a teacher. The intention was clear, though. Although literally an assertion, it was advice given by grown-ups for children to use as a motto, a resource for preserving their self-esteem in the face of verbal attack (and, of course, for grown-ups to preserve the peace). I have a memory of kids reciting it as a riposte to the person who had insulted them. The motto (sometimes with 'names' instead of 'words', sometimes with 'can never' instead of 'will never') was widespread in mid-twentieth-century London. A brief internet search suggests it is well known throughout the English-speaking world.

However, a moment's reflection shows us that it is advice which we human beings – not only children but also the grown-ups themselves – find very difficult to take to heart. While it may offer some solace in moments of personal crisis, it does not work as a statement of fact. Indeed, there is some evidence to suggest that the opposite may be truer, that the sticks and stones are actually less hurtful than the words (Kinney 1994, Culpeper 2011: 4). The author Stephen Fry is of the same opinion and has amended the adage to read "Sticks and stones *may* break my bones, but words will *always* hurt me" (my italics). And he goes on to provide a reason: "Bones mend and become actually stronger in the very place they were broken and where they have knitted up; mental wounds can grind and ooze for decades and be re-opened by the quietest whisper" (Fry 2011: 101).

Fry is of course referring only to words experienced as hurtful in the first place, and arguing that these are *more* hurtful than the sticks and stones, not that any particular (string of) words is always hurtful. (See also Jay 2009a.) That words *can* hurt, that what people say sometimes triggers negative reactions in those who hear it or see it, is obvious to any scholar of language-in-use, simply because language is our major means for constructing, maintaining and modifying not only personal relationships, not only our sense of self as a social being but also our understanding of the world in which we live. And what people say can sometimes run counter to these constructions.

These negative reactions can vary in type and intensity. If an offending utterance impacts on the recipient's sense of self, it can vary from the mildly affronted to the mortally insulted; if it impacts on his/her projected self-image at a particular moment (face – see section 2.2), it could leave him/her feeling anything from fleetingly embarrassed to utterly humiliated; one which is incongruent with the recipient's understanding of his/her relationship with its producer can cause the former to feel anything from obscurely disturbed to deeply hurt; if the utterance impinges on the recipient's sense of security (as in threats, menaces, harassment or more), his/her reaction can vary from the slightly uneasy to the terrified. This book is about such utterances.

By referring to 'utterances', I mean to emphasize that this book is about something more particular than the language used in situations of conflict. This latter is a field which has long been of interest to scholars of interaction (e.g. Grimshaw 1990) and has since been widened to encompass the language surrounding large-scale conflicts. The founding of a journal dedicated to this field (Garcés Blitvich & Sifianou 2013–) and a recent edited handbook on language in conflict (Evans et al. 2019) are testament to increasing interest in it. This study, though, is focused specifically on offensive *language*, on things that are said which either can cause or have caused offence. It does not address the trajectories of conflicts per se. On the other hand, a full understanding of an offending utterance and its effects necessarily involves a consideration of the wider context. As such, this study may be seen as a contribution to just one area of this field.

1.2 Potential offence and actual offence

This book, then, is about stretches of language, of any length or duration, which can – and sometimes do – engender one or more of the negative reactions outlined above. When talking about such stretches collectively and in the abstract, I refer to *offensive language*. But the distinction between 'can' and 'do' is crucial. When talking about stretches of language which can cause offence, I use the umbrella term *taboo language*; when talking about what has actually caused offence on a particular occasion, I refer to an *offending utterance*.

To take the latter first: my working definition of an offending utterance is:

> An utterance which, when performed, is experienced by its recipient(s) as deleterious to (one or more aspects of) their sense of self and/or wellbeing – that is, it makes them feel, mildly or extremely, discomfited and/or insulted and/or hurt and/or frightened.

By thus defining such an utterance not as something that its producer does but rather as the post-facto, felt experience of its recipient, I sidestep (for now, but see next chapter) two of the abiding concerns of (im)politeness scholarship – intention and evaluation. The experience *may* include perception of the producer's intention to offend and it *may* lead on to moral evaluations such as 'gauche', 'insulting', 'impolite' 'rude' or 'outrageous'. But neither the perception nor the evaluation is necessary for the offence to have been caused. The former can intensify the experience; the latter is a rationalization of it. (See Vangelisti & Young 2000, who also find an interaction between the two.) In the analysis of particular cases, I am still interested in these perceptions and evaluations because, when expressed in words, they provide evidence that offence has indeed been taken and how much. But they are not definitive. What defines an offending utterance is simply the negative experience. (For a fuller account of this conceptualization of offensive language and discussion of its relation to impoliteness theory, see section 2.1.)

Taboo language, on the other hand, is not about language used on a particular occasion but rather about particular linguistic items, abstracted from time, place and participants. However, the distinction being drawn here is not simply that fundamental to linguistics between language use and language system. There is nothing inherently (i.e. system internally) offensive about any particular string of sounds or letters. What makes them potentially offensive is the value accorded them in a particular language community; certain words, phrases and propositions have become associated with offensiveness so that their articulation indexes it. Therefore, the attempt to define this kind of language must make reference to society's dominant values, and I suggest

> any (string of) words whose production is transgressive of polite social norms.

(Chapter 3 explains and develops this definition, and discusses its ramifications.)

Another way of seeing this distinction is in terms of Austin's ([1962] 1975: 94–108) differentiation of locutionary, illocutionary and perlocutionary acts. When someone produces a string of words, they usually contain some propositional content made up of the sense of the words, the sense created by their grammatical relation to each other, and what the words refer to in the context of their utterance. This is the locutionary act. By being uttered in a particular context, they have a certain communicative force (e.g. a warning or a request or an expression of emotion). This is the illocutionary act. Finally, by being uttered, they have a certain result (e.g. the warning is heeded, the request is denied). This is their perlocutionary effect. Potentially offensive (taboo) language is a matter of locution. Actually offensive language (an offending utterance) is a matter of perlocution, often affected by the offended person's perception of the illocutionary force of the utterance.

1.2.1 A banned TV advert

As a spectacular example of the distinction between potential and actual offence, consider this scene from a Dutch TV advert.[1]

> A prototypical nuclear family get into their car. The father gets into the driver's seat, the mother gets into the front passenger seat. The two children, both girls, one around 11 years old, the other around 8, get into the back seat. The man is wearing a jacket and tie, the woman an expensive looking blouse done up to the neck. She has neatly styled short hair. Everything about them shrieks bourgeois respectability. As soon as they get in, they buckle up with their seat belts. When the man switches the engine on, a song is immediately heard on the audio system. The first line of the song heard goes
> "I wanna fuck you in the ass",
> which is then followed by a pleasant rhythmic jingle. The man and woman look at each other blankly. Then comes the second line, which is
> "I wanna fuck you in the ass",
> again followed by the jingle. The music is of the anodyne pop genre and the man and woman smile in vague appreciation of it. So do the two girls in the back. By the third iteration of
> "I wanna fuck you in the ass",
> and jingle – there are no other lyrics – the woman is enthusiastically moving her head from side to side in time with the rhythm, the man is tapping out the rhythm on the steering wheel and the girls in the back are also happily swaying to the music. They drive off with the same lyric ringing agreeably in their ears once again.

In this scene, four people encounter an utterance which anybody with any competence in English would recognize as conventionally highly offensive. It contains taboo words ("fuck … ass"), taboo reference (to sexual congress, moreover of an unorthodox kind) and a taboo propositional content (that "I" perform this act whose reference is taboo on "you"). In our terms it is undeniably taboo language. And yet this lyric, even when repeated several times, did not cause offence to any of those who heard it, even though they appear to be precisely the kind of people most likely to be offended by it. The reason for them not taking offence, it turns out, is because they don't understand enough English: as the car drives off, words inviting viewers to learn English at a certain language institute appear on the screen.

Actually, in the real world this advert *did* cause offence, to the body overseeing advertising standards in the Netherlands, and it was banned.[2] But the characters in the storyworld who encountered the lyric did not take offence; in their world, it did not qualify as an offending utterance.

The above is a fictional example, but it serves to point out vividly the obvious necessity of making a distinction between potential and actual. As it illustrates, whether the use of taboo language is offending depends on context, especially participants. Culpeper (2011: 116) has an example concerning the strongly taboo English word 'cunt' being happily used as an everyday form of address and reference. A similar example comes from when as a young person I lived in a house in London with several other young adults. One of our number was a student from Kurdistan who, because of the circles in which he normally moved, had learnt the mildly taboo English word 'shit' as pure denotation. So when our very respectable landlord visited us once, and a rather formal, stiff encounter ensued, he felt no compunction about raising the matter of the cat 'shit' on the conservatory roof … and it became an offending utterance.[3]

1.3 The rest of this book

The chapters which follow contain numerous case studies and examples. The analytical aim in each case is to enquire into what was found, or could be found, offensive. That is, what is it exactly about the language used in a particular utterance which has this effect? What features are implicated?

Part II of the book (Chapters 3–6) examines use of taboo language – language which *can* cause offence. Studies of language which has this potential have often displayed confusion and vagueness about their scope, as witnessed by the vast number of different labels attached to it (swearing, cursing, profanity, offensive language, abusive language ...). So in this part, using *taboo language* as a cover term, I first explain the definition given above and then make use of some very elementary pragmatic categories to distinguish between *taboo words*, *taboo reference* and *taboo predication*. While more than one of these aspects of taboo are often in play at the same time, I show that they are all in principle separate analytical categories; each can occur in isolation and each thus has the potential to cause offence all by itself.

Part III (Chapters 7–10) contains a series of case studies where offence *has* been caused. We know this because we have access to the responses which followed the offending utterance. Many of these cases took place in the public domain. They have become what we might call 'language incidents'. The cases studied cover a wide variety of settings and the full gamut of severity of offence: at the personal level from an obscure feeling of having been insulted to a feeling of real fear for one's safety; at the group level from a perception that the offender's use of language is improper to one that it is a threat to social harmony and public order. The responses to the offending utterance also vary in intensity. Most of the responses in these case studies involve the exercise of power, so that the offender suffers some kind of substantive negative consequence. These consequences range from a mere metaphorical rap on the knuckles from a superior at work (as in section 8.2), through more general social opprobrium and financial penalty (as in section 8.4) and loss of position (as in sections 8.3, 9.1, 10.1 and 11.1) to criminal conviction (see Chapter 9 and section 10.2). And again, in each case examined, the question asked is: what exactly is it about the utterance in question that incurred a particular negative consequence for its producer? Just what is it that people and/or institutions found so awful about these instances of language use?

The concluding two chapters (Part IV) draw on what has been discerned from the analyses in earlier chapters to consider more generally what is commonly regarded as socially un/acceptable and thus the flavour of public life in the early twenty-first century. Some principles for dealing with offensive language, both analytically and publicly, are suggested.

The analyses of examples and case studies are conducted through the application of, and some opportunistic cherry-picking from, an array of linguistic-pragmatic approaches. Chief among these are (im)politeness theory, face theory, speech act theory and its development in the notion of pragmatic acts, and a largely Goffmanian conceptualization of context. Use is also sometimes made of concepts from conversation analysis, critical stylistics, emancipatory pragmatics and that of discourse analysis more generally. Chapter 2 discusses the main theoretical apparatus and outlines how they are to be used in the analyses which follow. And at the start of Part III, before the analyses of cases of actual offence are conducted, some more theoretical issues germane to these are considered.

In the course of this 'proving' of various approaches, some of their rougher edges get knocked off and some modifications to them can be – and are – suggested. However, theory-tweaking is incidental to the main thrust of these investigations, which is to determine what it is about each utterance which caused the documented response to it, how the precise response was motivated (and even whether it was justified), and what both tell us about current social attitudes, especially those of the powerful. This is an exercise, then, in the application of theory. No new theory emerges, but a new *approach* to offensive language does, one which involves both how we study it and also how it should be received in public life.

1.4 The need for this enquiry

Incidents as a result of what someone said and how they said it are legion in the news these days and get their sayers into varying degrees of hot water. In any society which values the principle of free speech, these immersions need to be critiqued. "It was wrong to say that" or "I don't like that kind of language" is not enough. *How* was it wrong and how much? *Why* don't you like it? And when it is wrong, what kind of sanction, if any, can be justified? A principled way needs to be found of distinguishing what is merely embarrassing from what is reprehensible from what is censurable from what – maybe – should be criminal from what should be better shuddered off as just plain nasty. Such a search involves legal and political issues beyond the purview of this book (or, indeed, the competence of its author), but since the data and cause of all such cases are the language that someone used, a linguistic approach should have a substantial contribution to make in this effort.

It could be argued that the two main parts of the book – the taboo language part and the actual offence part – are only tenuously related. But I argue there is a link and it is a socially significant one (and that therefore the distinctions drawn in the former are more than a mere exercise in typology for its own sake). It is this: when a piece of language is rated taboo, whether for its form, its reference, its propositional content or a combination of these, it goes unexamined by participants. There is little or no reaction to *what* was said, only to *that* it was said. In some contexts, this reaction is a warm feeling of relative intimacy (as when taboo words are used as an enactment and celebration of social solidarity). In others, it might be one of mirth (as when taboo reference appears in a situation licensed for entertainment and comedy – see section 5.2 for an example). But when the situation does not allow such latitude and participants react negatively, the taboo utterance gets condemned out of hand. A snarl-word label (foul-mouthed, vulgar, racist, sexist, terrorist, hate-speech …) is attached to it and/ or its perpetrator and social sanctions often follow, the infraction being not so much the content of the language but rather the fact that it was animated at all.

There is some evidence to suggest, some of it in this book, that as the twenty-first century unfolds, the territory of taboo language is expanding. While this development may be a reflection of Stephen Pinker's (2011, 2018) convincing thesis that we human beings generally behave more benignly towards each other than we have ever done before, the consignment of more and more utterances to the 'taboo dustbin' constitutes a threat to free speech, one of the principles which has facilitated this social improvement in the first place. It does so directly but also indirectly, in that a general perception of constraints on what can be uttered in public (often characterized by those who so perceive as 'political correctness') can lead to a backlash, with a consequent dumbing down of public discourse. (I point in the last chapter to a glaring contemporary example.) To counter this threat, it behoves us, as scholars of language use, to resist the urge to cast forcefully aside offending utterances lest, in our knee-jerk reactions to them, we risk losing sight of precisely what it is that we find offensive. Even when these utterances seem deeply unpleasant – in some cases transparently so – we need to examine them forensically, if necessary holding our noses as we do so. Some of the cases examined in this book fall into that category.

Theoretical and analytical apparatus

This is a book about language. Although it tends to focus on language's larger chunks (lexis, syntax and discourse rather than phonetics, phonology or morphology), it is in principle open to evidence from any area of the language system. Nor does this study confine itself to any specific domain of language use. In these respects, its general theoretical orientation can fairly be characterized as pragmatic; that is, not the study of a well-defined area of language or language use but rather a perspective on language use generally (Verschueren 1999). It is also characteristically pragmatic in its focus not just on bits of language but also on the people who produce and receive those bits. Offence, after all, requires people to be offended. And bearing in mind that it is also an affective phenomenon which, by definition, occurs in situ, I think this work can be positioned a little more specifically, within that subdiscipline of pragmatics which, following an original coinage by Leech and/or Thomas in the early 1980s, has come to be called sociopragmatics.[1] (See, for example, Haugh et al. forthcoming for a collection covering the field.) The concepts which comprise the section headings in this chapter, in that they focus principally on the meso level of context, fall fairly comfortably under this umbrella term (see Culpeper forthcoming).

Nevertheless, use is often made of at least two of the conventional pillars of what Leech and/or Thomas, in order to distinguish it from sociopragmatics, termed pragmalinguistics – the study of the encoding of speaker meanings and intentions and the linguistic resources. One of these, speech act theory, turns out to have a particular relevance to some of the cases examined in Part III of this book and is discussed in detail in Chapter 7. The other is Grice's (1975) theory of implicature, an attempt to explain how people manage to understand utterances whose intended meaning is not made explicit. This rests on the positing of a number of 'maxims' of conversation (i.e. expectations about its conduct) which interlocutors assume will, ideally, be followed, so that when they are clearly *not* followed, it can be inferred that something 'else' is meant (this something being an implicature[2]). Reference to these maxims and their 'flouting' is sometimes made in the analyses because a necessary prelude to taking offence at an utterance is to derive some sense from it.

Some of this study (Part II) is not about utterances which people *have found* offensive on particular occasions, but rather about utterances which people *can*, often do, and so on a particular occasion *might*, find offensive. That is, it is about language in the abstract. Nevertheless, the understanding of such, only potentially offensive, language requires the investigation of attested, situated examples. Therefore, the concepts, theories and approaches discussed in this chapter include those which pertain to the analysis of interaction as it happens, as these are also needed for the understanding of what *could* happen.

2.1 Offence, impoliteness and related concepts

An obvious place to start in marshalling concepts, theories and approaches which can help with the study of cases of offensive language is with studies of impoliteness. These studies began emerging a few decades ago as an offshoot of the developing field of politeness studies. Following the work of Lakoff (1973), Leech (1977 [1980: Chapter 4], 1983: Chapters 5–6) and Brown & Levinson ([1978] 1987), a whole new field of study into the affective aspects of interaction was opened up to scholars of language-in-use. It was Brown & Levinson's work which made the biggest impact and it was this work to which, until the advent of what became known as the 'discursive' approach to the topic (Eelen 2001, Watts 2003, Mills 2003), most immediately subsequent studies addressed themselves and/or used as a basis for empirical research. One reason for the size of its impact was that it offered a specific and detailed scheme to explain why people say the things they say to each other in particular ways. Indeed, to this day, in that it attempts to predict what people will say in a given situation (specified chiefly by interpersonal relationship and cultural milieu), it remains the only true theory, in the strict sense of the word, of interpersonal linguistic behaviour.

However, around the turn of the century, and taking off from the simple observation that what Brown & Levinson describe has very little to do with what most people understand by the word 'politeness' (or the nearest lexemes in other languages), not to mention the fact that these people vary greatly in *exactly* what they understand by it, so that what they regard as polite or not polite is a matter of discursive struggle, scholars in the field have largely given up on prediction.

Building on a distinction first pointed up by Watts (1989, 1992) between first-order concepts (lay concepts, therefore both culture-specific and infinitely variable) and second-order concepts (technical, definable and potentially universal), they have turned the focus of attention away from explaining *why* people say what they say towards the *effects* of what they say – not so much what *will* be said but what *has been* said. One of the aims in doing so is to incorporate lay understandings (first-order) into any theory-building (second-order) that might emerge. This shift in temporal perspective involves a concomitant shift in personal perspective – away from that of the producer of an utterance towards that of its recipient(s).

This more recent emphasis has brought to the fore several troubling issues concerning the use of the term 'politeness' as the most suitable circumscription of the overall field of study. The first of these arises from the first/second-order distinction; it may not be clear enough at any one time whether the focus of discussion (or simply the referent) is a culture-specific concept or a technical, universal one, a risk of confusion which is all the greater because 'politeness' and its equivalent lexemes in other languages tend to be highly salient in any culture.

The second issue with the term 'politeness' arises partly for the same reason and is especially relevant because of the aforementioned desire to focus on first-order understandings. This is the relatively narrow range of affective interpersonal behaviour which this lexeme-or-its-equivalent tends to connote – mostly mundane aspects of manners and interpersonal conduct between acquaintances and strangers but not close friends or intimates. I remember an indicative occasion when walking around the city of Basel with a group of fellow conference participants. We were all carrying our conference shoulder bags, which had the words '5th International Symposium on Politeness' emblazoned in large letters on them. At one point, I noticed some onlookers commenting amusedly on our bags. I think those words were the cause of the mirth. 'Politeness' to them meant a trivial aspect of interactive behaviour unworthy of the serious discussion which presumably took place at an academic conference. And anyway, what about rudeness?

And this last observation is the third reason for misgivings about 'politeness' as an umbrella term for the field of study – the fact it calls to mind only the supportive kind of interpersonal behaviour: what about when people are *not* 'polite'? This positive valence for 'politeness' is not intrinsic: the study of the phenomenon of heat, for example, is presumed to include its absence. Nevertheless, to avert this possible misunderstanding, the form '(im)politeness', and sometimes its alternative 'im/politeness', began to appear at the start of this century (including in the titles of some of the successor conferences to that one in Basel in 2010!). However, this form still appears much less frequently than 'politeness' in the title of journal articles. (The statistics for use of these terms can be found in Culpeper et al. 2017a, whose edited volume also has '(im) politeness' in its title.)

In any case, this rather tortuous neologism only works in written form and does nothing to address the other two above-mentioned issues of cross-linguistic and connotational baggage carried by 'politeness'. In response, other terms intended to cover more or less the same field of human behaviour have been proposed: one is 'relational work' (Watts 1989, Locher & Watts 2005); another is 'rapport management' (Spencer-Oatey 2000, 2005), both of which have had some uptake; beyond language study, in sociology, anthropology, politics, behavioural sciences and practice-based disciplines, the term 'civility' seems to be popular (see e.g. Fyfe et al 2006, Griffith et al 2011, Balibar 2016, Thiranagama et al 2018). All of these, of course, have their own diverging emphases, and arguably do not completely overcome the problem of positive valence. The term 'interpersonal pragmatics' has also had some success, as witnessed by an edited volume (Locher & Graham 2010) and a journal special issue (Haugh et al. 2013) of that title. This last term, containing the technical 'pragmatics', has the advantage of denoting a scholarly field of enquiry, and thus clearly separates it from lay understandings, but arguably widens the field beyond the purely affective focus originally intended.

It is with this terminological cauldron in mind, and the reorientation of the field (whatever we call it) outlined above, that we need to view impoliteness studies. These started off as a reaction to the absence of any account of hostile, antagonistic or aggressive interactional behaviour in early theories. Early examples are Lachenicht (1980) and Austin (1990). Most notably, as one strand of the myriad critical reactions to Brown & Levinson's model, Culpeper (1996) proposed and described a mirror image of their hierarchy of 'politeness super-strategies' ([1978]1987: 60, 68–71) with instead of, for example, an account of the possible exponents of 'negative politeness' ([1978] 1987: 129–210; and see section 2.2. below), an account of those for realizing 'negative *im*politeness'. In doing so, this paper went along with the pre-facto, production perspective of politeness theory at the time. Succeeding works also give the speaker's intention a central role in characterizing impoliteness (e.g. Culpeper et al. 2003, Culpeper 2005, Bousfield 2008: 72) and/or use it as a means of drawing a technical distinction between rudeness and impoliteness (e.g. Bousfield 2008: 73, Terkourafi 2008). At the same time, all but the first of these do at least make reference to the hearer's reception, in that his/her *perception* of the speaker's hostile intention is part of the definition offered: Culpeper (2005) sees this as one possible origin of impoliteness; Bousfield (2008: 72) sees it as a condition for impoliteness to be 'successful'; Terkourafi (2008) sees it as the defining feature of rudeness (in contrast to mere impoliteness). And Locher & Watts (2008) see the perception alone as the defining feature of impoliteness.

The progression to a more fully recipient-oriented definition of impoliteness comes with Culpeper (2011). This follows Terkourafi's (2001: 120–7) view of (specifically) politeness in relegating the recipient's perception of the producer's intention (never mind the actual intention) to an 'exacerbating' factor, and it is within this definition that I situate my study of offensive language, so I quote it (almost) in full.

> Impoliteness is a negative attitude towards specific behaviours occurring in specific contexts … Situated behaviours are viewed negatively – considered 'impolite' – when they conflict with how one expects them to be, how one wants them to be and/or how one thinks they ought to be. Such behaviours always have or are presumed to have emotional consequences for at least one participant; that is, they cause or are presumed to cause offence. Various factors can exacerbate how offensive an impolite behaviour is taken to be, including for example whether one understands a behaviour to be strongly intentional or not.
>
> (Culpeper 2011: 23)

This definition, then, specifies two defining constituents of impolite acts. These are that they (1) conflict with H's expectations, beliefs or desires concerning interactive behaviour and (2) "cause or are presumed to cause offence". The first of these follows from the emphasis on evaluation in a hearer-centred approach to (im)politeness (see above). Expectations, in particular, relate to social norms and can be studied empirically (e.g. Tayebi 2016). This book, however, is focused firmly and exclusively on the second of these constituents. It is a-theoretical with respect to the notion of impoliteness per se. That is to say, I make no attempt to define, refine or develop this concept or related notions such as rudeness and inappropriateness. Nor do I discuss or entertain discursive struggles as to what constitutes impolite behaviour. Rather, I explore what it is that causes an offended reaction, and in the process discuss not only what constitutes offence but also what kind and degree of offence. However, this eschewal of impoliteness as a topic for theoretical discussion does not mean that I ignore assessments of impoliteness entirely. When these are articulated, I see them as rationalizations of the offended reaction and in the analysis of particular cases of offence, when they are available, I use them first as evidence that offence has indeed been taken and second as pointers to the cause, nature and/or degree of offence.

2.1.1 A definition of offensive language

Notice that Culpeper's use of the word 'offence' in his definition of impoliteness appears as a paraphrase of "emotional consequences", necessary in order to make clear that the 'emotional consequences' are negative ones. Following this lead, my definition of offensive language is expressed in terms of felt experience. However, I feel there is a potential problem with the word 'offence' within this definition. If it is interpreted as referring to its everyday English usage (arguably encouraged by its functioning in the definition as a paraphrase), it tends to limit the field to, or at least foreground, behaviour which has relatively trivial consequences, evoking images of someone of brittle ego *taking* offence when perhaps others would not. And perhaps it is no coincidence that, as Culpeper et al. (2017b) observe, the impoliteness literature has neglected non-conditional threats and incitement. These are two kinds of act which can have very *severe* emotional consequences. They are definitely within the purview of my understanding of offensive language, which I wish (as no doubt intended in Culpeper's definition) to encompass all possible degrees of negative emotional consequence. Offensive language is a scalar phenomenon. Accordingly, my working definition is

> any word or string of words which has or can have a negative impact on the sense of self and/or wellbeing of those who encounter it – that is, it makes or can make them feel, mildly or extremely, discomfited and/or insulted and/or hurt and/or frightened.

The adjectives at the end of this definition are intended to cover the full gamut of severity of a particular kind of negative emotion. For instance, 'discomfited' is intended to encompass everything from slightly, fleetingly embarrassed to utterly humiliated and 'frightened' everything from obscurely uneasy to genuinely terrified. It is by removing references to potential from this definition and referring to an act of producing language on a particular occasion rather than a string of words that I derive the definition of an offending utterance given in Chapter 1.

These definitions (both offensive language and an offending utterance), then, restrict offence to felt experience on the part of the offended. In doing so, they exclude the fact that taking offence is usually understood to involve also the overt registering of this felt experience (see Haugh 2015b, Haugh & Sinkeviciute

2019: 197–203), this latter being in any case a necessary data component of any study of offend*ing* language because it is how we know that offence has been taken in the first place. They also exclude the fact that, for British English at least, corpus evidence indicates that the use of the term 'offensive' normally includes a moral judgement (Culpeper & Haugh forthcoming). I do not wish to deny these facts, and for this reason would not want to advance the definitions given here as suitable for the study of offence per se. But I use them here because this study is about offensive *language* and I want (a) to be as inclusive as possible about what could or does offend and (b) to direct attention, initially at least, to the linguistic exponents which could or have offended. The responses to these, and evaluations of those responses, come into play as part of that focus.

2.1.2 Conventionalized impoliteness formulae

The inclusion of "has or can have" and "makes or can make" in the above definition is there to distinguish between the actual and the potential (see section 1.2) which is basic to this study. It is a mirror of "have or are presumed to have" and "cause or are presumed to cause" in Culpeper's definition of impoliteness above. I infer the intention of this inclusion of the 'presumed' category is to allow for the same kind of distinction – impoliteness not only as an assessment of a particular occasion of language use but also as an assessment of strings of words in the abstract. Following a discussion of the extent to which impoliteness is inherent in language which arrives at a 'yes-and-no' answer, Culpeper (2011: 119–26) adapts Terkourafi's (e.g. 2001, 2002, 2005) work on conventionalization in politeness to draw up an inventory of conventionalized impoliteness formulae for English by checking in a large corpus of modern English for the statistical frequency with which particular expressions, when used, are interpreted as impolite (Culpeper 2011: 126–39). Thereby, we have empirical support for the identification of certain English expressions as especially likely to be assessed as impolite when used. His inventory comprises expressions which:

1. predicate, refer to or imply something derogatory about a participant (comprising his categories of insults, pointed criticisms, unpalatable presuppositions in questions and condescensions);
2. aggressively enact domination over the addressee (categorized as message enforcers, silencers and threats);
3. indicate strong dislike of the addressee (by dismissals and negative expressives)

The basic idea behind conventionalized impoliteness formulae is that by virtue of people's experience of the regularity of their occurrence in particular co-texts and/or metadiscourse around (im)polite language, they come to be associated with impoliteness in people's minds. They become, as he puts its elsewhere (Culpeper 2012: 1150), "semantically tagged for context". As such, they can become prepackaged expressions which are readily available as a means of causing offence and, by the same token, are comparatively readily interpreted as offensive.

These formulae have an obviously close relation to my notion of taboo language, which I have defined (Chapter 1) as

> any (string of) words whose production is transgressive of polite social norms,

but they are not the same thing. Culpeper's (2011: 42) remark that "Taboos are less a matter of mediating an individual's self and more a matter of social conventions" points to the nature of the difference, which results in taboo language being both wider and narrower than conventionalized impoliteness formulae. It is wider in that, while the latter foreground the interpersonal, taboo language also includes the impersonal. The potential of Culpeper's formulae to cause offence is their indication of a negative appraisal of and/or aggressive linguistic behaviour towards an addressee or other participant. It is notable that, with a couple of exceptions involving third-person reference to a person who is present, all the listed formulae have 'you' in there somewhere (either explicitly or implicitly in a bald imperative). Taboo language, on the other hand, does not necessarily require a target to be present. It can occur even when nothing is predicated of any participant. For example, it would be difficult to find a place in Culpeper's inventory for the lyrics of the TV advert example in section 1.2.1. This features a respectable family in a car listening to the song lyric "I wanna fuck you in the ass". In its transitive structure it is closest to his 'threat' category, but the problem is that the 'you' is not present in the car and anyway the tone of the music accompanying the lyric suggests it is an expression of a wish rather than threatening. And yet if those car passengers had been able to understand English after all, we can be sure they would have been very embarrassed and quite possibly outraged – i.e. offended. (The fact that the advert was banned shows that some people who *did* understand the content *were* offended. And as banning involves the exercise of power by a socially constituted authority, it also points again to social conventions.)

On the other hand, taboo language is also narrower than conventionalized impoliteness formulae. All of Culpeper's English-language examples are proved by the corpus evidence to have high potential to cause offence. But this fact does not automatically qualify them as taboo language. To take examples from his insults category, I would not include "You are such a disappointment", "You can't do anything right" (his 'personalized negative assertions') or "Your stinking breath" (from his 'personalized negative references') as automatically taboo. Such utterances are obviously likely to be hurtful and judged extremely unkind but they do not in themselves transgress polite social norms. (For an account of what is meant by 'polite social norms', see section 3.2.) Likewise, his 'message enforcers'; such as "you got that?" and 'dismissals' such as "get lost" predicate stark domination of and a low opinion of the addressee and may therefore cause that person to feel severely affronted and/or disparaged but are not widely recognized as the kind of thing you cannot say in polite circles. (In fact, all the above utterances *can* become taboo, but this requires very particular participant relationships and roles – see Chapter 6). In summary, while acts of impoliteness which use these formulae often contain taboo language and taboo language is often deemed impolite, neither is constitutive of the other.

2.2 Face and facework

Face is a concept pertaining to the image of themselves which people project in interaction. It will be noticed that in the above discussion and in my definition of offensive language, just like Culpeper's definition of impoliteness, I have avoided mention of this concept. This avoidance has taken some care because in the most well-known politeness theory (Brown & Levinson [1978] 1987) face is a central component. In this theory, it is the reason why people typically perform speech acts in particular ways – they wish to maintain each other's faces and a very large number of acts intrinsically carry threats to face, so that they usually get performed in ways which mitigate this threat: for example, in English requests, not "Give me five pounds" but rather "Give us a fiver, love" or "Sorry about this but do you think you'd be able to lend me five pounds" or even "Oh dear, I'm out of cash". A simple search on Google Scholar will reveal that the lexemes 'polite' and 'face' have been almost routinely yoked together (see O'Driscoll 2011: 21–2 and 2017: 90). And in fact, most of the producer-oriented attempts at a definition of impoliteness cited above refer to 'face-attack'.

My reason for having so far avoided 'face' has much to do with the distinction between first-order and second-order concepts outlined above. While first-order notions of (im)politeness, whatever name it goes by, are salient in every culture, first-order notions of face have very varying degrees of salience in different cultures and even when they have high salience are not necessarily linked consistently to notions of (im)politeness (see, for example, Hinze 2012, St André 2013, Sifianou 2013). Face – or more specifically facework (i.e. the term denoting behaviour relevant to face) – and (im)politeness are not the same thing, and the value of considering face in its own right has been argued by, among others, Arundale (2013), Haugh (2013), Kádár & Haugh (2013: 50–2) and O'Driscoll (2017). So, in this work here, in keeping with more recent approaches to (im)politeness (e.g. Eelen 2001, Watts 2003, Haugh 2007, Kádár & Haugh 2013, Haugh 2015) and with the first element of Culpeper's definition of impoliteness (see above) in mind, I reserve the lexeme 'polite' to refer to more or less conscious evaluations of behaviour; that is, to people's beliefs about what is or isn't polite. In other words, I use it in a first-order sense.

In contrast, I will be using the term face and the accompanying term facework – things done or said which have or could have an effect on face – very much in a second-order, technical sense. I use as a starting point, and follow throughout the general spirit of, Goffman's ([1955] 1967a) essay *On Face-Work*, which begins by pointing out that in any encounter a person

> tends to act out what is sometimes called a *line* – that is, a pattern of verbal and nonverbal acts by which he expresses his view of the situation and through this his evaluation of the participants, especially himself. Regardless of whether a person intends to take a line, he will find that he has done so in effect. The other participants will assume he has more or less wilfully taken a stand ... The term *face* may be defined as the positive social value a person effectively claims for himself by the line others assume he has taken during a particular contact. Face is an image of self delineated in terms of approved social attributes.
>
> (Goffman [1955] 1967a: 5; original italics)

I follow this conceptualization by seeing face as the best self-image ("positive social value") which a person can realistically project ("effectively claims") given the 'line' that s/he appears to have taken ("others assume") within an encounter ("particular contact"). It therefore refers to an identity radically contingent on the circumstances of interaction and is more specific than identity in general, which is not confined to interaction. The usual sociological variables (age, gender, ethnicity etc.), as well as a person's individual reputation, are of course involved in the composition of his/her face because they are part of his/her line, but the importance of each depends on the situation and the ongoing interaction. Numerous attributes make up my own self-image (not all of them positive) but in any one encounter some will be more relevant than others and some will have no relevance at all. And while I am largely in control of my own self-image, I can hope only to influence my face because it is dependent on those with whom I am interacting. I make these observations to emphasize that face is not just a fashionable word for identity or self-image but something particular made up – but only partly – of both. (For a suggested list of all the ingredients contributing to face, see O'Driscoll 2011.) What makes it especially relevant to offence as conceived in this study is that it is strongly "associated with attributes that are affectively sensitive" (Spencer-Oatey 2007: 644; see also Goffman [1955] 1967a: 6).

It is also worth noting that every interactant has face. It is not something only possessed by people who are oversensitive about their dignity. It is an inevitable consequence of the circumstances of interaction. Face is real simply because linguistic interaction, for very practical reasons, cannot be a Joycean cacophony. If, when encountering another person, we all insisted on expressing everything passing through our minds and/or on recounting our entire personal history, we wouldn't be listening to each other and nothing, interpersonal or transactional, would ever get done. There just isn't time to express everything we are thinking and feeling or to inform other interactants of everything we believe they don't already know about us. Instead, we have to make situationally influenced choices about what to say. So do our fellow participants, and we are all forced to act on impressions. From these impressions are derived our faces.

I also follow Goffman and more recent face theorists (see, for example, Arundale 2020) in regarding face as primarily a result of interaction, rather than, as Brown & Levinson do, as a desire which interactants bring along with them to it. This means that I see a threat to face not as a property of speech acts but rather as something which occurs in ongoing interaction, albeit perhaps caused by what can be identified as a particular speech act. When this threat is not averted by appropriate facework, when what gets said has a negative effect on someone's face which cannot be brushed off and which therefore discredits the line s/he has been taking, I refer to face-*damage* instead. This post-facto perspective also means that, in contrast to Brown & Levinson's apparently pessimistic view of interaction where the best that can be hoped for is that faces do not get damaged (see, for example, Fraser 1990: 235, Nwoye 1992: 311, Werkhofer 1992: 180), it is possible to speak not only of face-threatening acts and face-damaging acts but also of acts which enhance face (e.g. Bayraktaroğlu 1991, Sifianou 2001, Leech 2014). It is, though, the former two – threat and damage – which are of particular interest in this work.

Much of the scholarship on face in the last thirty years has been a matter of discussing what face is made of and possible types (see O'Driscoll 2017 for a review). The most well-known suggestion in this respect is Brown & Levinson's ([1978] 1987: 61–2ff.) notion of it comprising positive and negative aspects. Although this claim has been much criticized, the notion of negative face in particular,[3] it has proved to be remarkably resilient in that many of the alternative proposals of the constitution and constituents of face bear a resemblance to these two (see O'Driscoll 2017: 105–7). Here, I retain these concepts for my analysis but with the narrower meanings suggested by O'Driscoll (1996, 2007, 2011) whereby they both refer solely to the dimension of relative social distance – positive face is the appearance of togetherness, of belonging with others; negative face is the appearance of being an independent, autonomous individual. But obviously there is more to a person's face than appearing to be one of the gang and one's own boss. The salience of other components will always be situation specific but I wish to advance here two features that are crucial for several cases I examine in this work and which I suspect are often salient. They are both perhaps suggested by Lim & Bowers' (1991) notion of competence face. One I will call interactive face. This is simply that part of one's line whereby it is assumed one is interactively competent, able to hold one's own in an encounter in the most basic sense that one can follow and adapt appropriately to the interpersonal trajectory of talk. Failure to do so results in what Goffman ([1955] 1967a: 8) calls being in 'wrong face'. The other pertains to that part of face connected to an individual's competence with regard to his/her societal role, which is very salient in many situations. This has been called professional face (Márquez-Reiter 2009, Schmitt & Márquez-Reiter 2019). Given a certain role in society and by the situation, a major part of face is invested in that role and failure to live up to it may well cause significant face-damage.

2.3 Context

It is a truism that in order to understand an utterance fully and accurately, we need to take context into account. The challenge for the analyst is to find a practical way of ensuring that all possible contextual factors are considered. This was the motivation behind Hymes' (1974: 53–62) well-known S-P-E-A-K-I-N-G mnemonic for circumscribing all the components of linguistic interaction. Although sometimes referred to as a model, this is actually just an inventory of all the factors which can affect what someone says, what they say and how they say it. There is no attempt to relate the factors to each other or order them. Another, simpler, itemizing of aspects of context, also from twentieth-century US sociolinguistics, came from Fishman's (1972) concept of domain, essentially a particular configuration of three factors – participants, setting and topic (in other words, who, where-and-when and what) – which determine which language members of a bilingual speech community would use on any one occasion.

Both of these approaches are geared towards understanding why people say what they say in the way that they say it. That is, they are geared towards understanding the producers of language. My focus here, though, is on understanding the reactions of recipients of language. From this perspective, I find it useful to see context as comprising two aspects: *background* and *immediate*. The former is what participants bring along with them to an encounter; the latter, often known as 'situation', pertains to the circumstances of the encounter itself.

Background context includes both the personal and interpersonal histories of each participant in interaction. The former is understood to be the totality of their experience, which therefore includes not only their knowledge of the world but also the norms of behaviour and its interpretation, both generally and in certain kinds of situation, inculcated from a particular culture or cultures (see Culpeper 2008: 30–1), differences in which are often appealed to when analysing miscommunication across cultures. The latter is the aggregate and tenor of participants' previous encounters with each other. In addition to this interpersonal experience, there is also the knowledge that one or more participants may have about (an)other participant(s) beyond their encounters. Finally, there are the wider sociopolitical circumstances. This last factor is obviously relevant in the public domain, especially if the topic pertains to politics (see, for example, the analysis in section 10.1), but it can even be relevant in comparatively private encounters. When I compare with students two ways for a job applicant to answer the question "Why do you want this job", the response which emphasizes the applicant's urgent need for a job is generally deemed unwise in a western cultural milieu. But it was once pointed out to me that if the interview was taking place against a background of 50 per cent unemployment, it would not be such an unpolitic thing to say after all.[4]

There are obvious factors involved in immediate context such as setting, topic and participants. But for my purposes here, three concepts are crucial. These are described below.

2.3.1 Activity type

An abiding aspect for understanding and interpreting what takes place when people use language with each other is their understanding(s) of what sort of thing is going on. This has been variously termed by Goffman 'definition of the situation' (1959: 15), 'social occasion' (1963) and 'frame' (1974). I will use the term 'activity type', which Levinson defines as "a fuzzy category whose focal members are goal-defined, socially constituted, bounded, events with constraints on participants, setting and so on, but above all on the kinds of allowable contributions" (Levinson [1992] 1979: 368). This aspect is crucial because, as Levinson avers, it gives us an insight into the kinds of things that participants, normatively, can say and can't say. Note, then, that although activity type is a concept delineating an aspect of immediate context, participants' understandings of it are conditioned by their cultural and situation experience (i.e. background context).

2.3.2 Footing

A particular activity type also entails some of the characteristics of participants, such as their number and individual roles. This is the second crucial aspect of immediate context. For this, I use Goffman's (1981) concept of footing, which he describes as "the alignment we take up to ourselves and others present as expressed in the way we manage the production and reception of an utterance" (Goffman 1981: 128). His exposition of this concept includes two others by which the notions of speaker and hearer are deconstructed. One of these is *participation framework*, which identifies, as well as a person speaking, a number of different interactive alignments. A first distinction here is between ratified participants and unratified ones. The former are people who, as he describes them elsewhere have all "jointly ratified one another as authorized co-sustainers of a single … focus of visual and cognitive attention" (Goffman 1964: 135) and are "open to each other for talk or its substitutes" (Goffman [1955] 1967b: 144). At any one moment, when there are more than two people so ratified, not all of them may be being directly addressed, so they can be divided into addressed and unaddressed. The other, unratified type of participants feature only when the encounter is taking place in an open environment so that it is accessible to them. Such *bystanders* are aware of the encounter and that talk is taking place. Sometimes, though, they can be in a position to understand what is being said, and thus become *overhearers*. It is also possible for the ratified participants to be unaware of people who may be deliberately listening in. These are *eavesdroppers*.

Along with this itemization of the various roles involved in receiving utterances, Goffman identifies three separate roles involved in producing them, which he calls their *production format*. The *animator* role is to make the words physically manifest and accessible, for example by vocalization or typing on a keyboard. The *author* role is to choose the words used. The *principal* role is that of being accountable for what is said. In ordinary casual conversation, all three roles are performed by the same person. But we do not have to look far to find other formats (e.g. spokesperson at a press conference, a person taking an official oath, an actor on stage performing). Moreover, there are many cases where one or more of these roles seems to be shared between people, and in this respect of particular interest for this study is the principal role – when offence is taken, who does the finger point at? This issue and others are complicated by the phenomenon of embedding, by which what is said involves a figure "who belongs to the world that is spoken about, not the world in which the speaking occurs" (Goffman 1981: 147). This is the case whenever someone reports what someone else (or even themselves) has said, so that we have a production format at two levels. And in fact, in everyday speech, it is quite common to incorporate words which are not 'freshly' authored but taken from somewhere/someone else (e.g. an adage, a mocking re-enactment) or to 'put on an accent' which is not our own.

The above outline refers principally to operational, moment-by-moment participant roles. Footing also involves the social capacity in which a participant is presumed to be acting. This distinction has sometimes been conceptualized as that between discourse role and social role respectively (e.g. Sarangi & Slembrouck 1996: 66–71, Halvorsen & Sarangi 2015). While the former pertains to utterances and ongoing talk, the latter pertains to the activity type (and therefore also points to features of background context). The former is interpreted, and assessed for acceptability or otherwise, in the light of the latter (see Davies 2018, O'Driscoll 2018 for examples). When the 'fit' is perceived as wrong, offence can be taken.

There are in fact many subtle permutations of the precise footings of ratified participants (addressed or unaddressed), unratified participants (bystanders, overhearers and eavesdroppers) and speakers. Numerous additional categories of participant have been suggested (e.g. Levinson 1988, Clark & Schaefer 1992, Scollon 1996, Dynel 2010, Haugh 2013). For my purposes, though, the basic Goffmanian typology suffices, especially if the various categories are seen not as boxes into which the analyst needs to place each participant but rather as reference points by which the precise footing of each can be described. This perspective is in any case recommended by the observable fact that in what they say and do, participants frequently negotiate between these various points, both for themselves and other participants. (For a more detailed argument to this effect, and a more comprehensive account of participant roles in general, see Holt & O'Driscoll forthcoming.)

2.3.3 Co-text

Both the 'not-fitting' phenomenon and the negotiation phenomenon mentioned above bring us to the third aspect of immediate context crucial for this study: the words around the words being examined. In a general sense, this concept is important because "a context is not just one possible world-state, but at least a sequence of world-states. Moreover, these situations do not remain identical in time, but *change*" (van Dijk 1977: 191–2; original italics). Participants constantly shift their precise footings. For our purposes, it is important to note that this shifting includes the producer of language. How an utterance gets interpreted by participants, and how an analyst can interpret it, is often heavily conditioned by what the same producer has said before it. Part of this foot-shifting is what Gumperz (1982) called 'contextualization cues'; that is, the invoking of a different contextual frame (including activity type) to that which, it has been assumed, has obtained up to that point. Some of the cases examined in this book involve a failure or refusal to 'pick up on' the apparent redefinition of the situation which such cues propose.

2.4 Analytical procedure

In the many examples and case studies which feature in the rest of this book, I start with an outline of their context. For the sake of space and relevance to the issue at hand, I do not systematically itemize all elements of context every time before proceeding to analysis. Background context is most suitably described beforehand but many aspects of immediate context are often more conveniently picked up during analysis. Of these, footing, and particularly participation framework and production format, are nearly always relevant in detecting what was or could be found offensive. This is the case despite the fact that many of the situations examined do not involve face-to-face, embodied communication, which is what Goffman's exposition centres around and largely assumes. Attempts to apply and adapt his framework to technology-mediated communication are discussed in Chapter 7.

As regards analytical method, I often employ the practice known in stylistics as textual intervention (Pope 1995), whereby one part of the data – a word, phrase or clause – is replaced with a different word, phrase or clause and the alteration in the overall effect of this replacement is examined. The idea here is that by imagining what *could have* been uttered in the circumstances in place of what *was* uttered and then considering the effects of this replacement, we have a standard of comparison with which to arrive at a better understanding of the effects of the 'original'. Most often, textual intervention is a paradigmatic exercise. I sometimes stretch the practice somewhat by considering the effect if one part of the data were simply removed.

Part Two

Potential offence: Taboo language

Taboo language

In this chapter, I discuss the nature of taboo language; that is, roughly, language use which has the potential to cause offence by virtue of it being normatively unacceptable. (Whether it does actually cause offence, how, how much, why, whether the taking of offence is justifiable and what might be an appropriate reaction to it is the subject of the third part of the book.) In the face of what emerges as confusion as to what exactly is and isn't taboo language (section 3.1), I attempt to pin down exactly what it is that we are talking about and to offer a valid definition. I then identify three distinct types of taboo language in terms of three distinct features of it which can cause offence.

3.1 What we are talking about: a review of the literature

Notwithstanding the observation that the topic can be considered inappropriate for discussion in an academic environment (Jay 2000: 10), and not infrequent comments about the comparative lack of academic attention to the matter (e.g. Johnson & Fine 1985, Stenström 1991, McEnery & Xiao 2004, Murphy 2009, Beers Fägersten 2012, Stone et al. 2015), studies on words and/or aspects of language use that are considered in some way socially unacceptable have in fact become numerous. They have been undertaken in the fields of psycholinguistics, sociolinguistics, pragmatics, communication studies, media studies, philosophy, psychology and law. But it is perhaps indicative of the distaste generally felt about such language – or at least distaste about talking about it – that in these studies it goes by a large number of different names.

The works cited in Tables 1–3 below are the result of an informal survey of the main headings of the titles of academic books or articles on this subject. It is very far from being exhaustive, being compiled from whatever I have come across in the course of my enquiries plus a comprehensive trawl through the impressive list of references provided by Beers Fägersten & Stapleton (2017b) and the list of references in Allan (2019a). But it suffices for my purpose here.[1] As can be seen in Table 1, easily the most common descriptor (47 cases in my survey) involves the lexeme *swear*, which usually appears as the activity of 'swearing', but sometimes appears as 'swearwords', occasionally as the verb 'swear' and once as the plural noun 'swears'. The lexeme *taboo* is also very commonly found (30 cases), most frequently as a premodifying adjective but sometimes as a premodified noun or as a noun all by itself (see Table 2). However, as Table 3 shows, there are numerous other choices (49 cases).

Table 1 Informal Survey: The *Swear* Lexeme in Academic Titles

'swearing' (37 cases): Andersson & Trudgill 2007, Beers Fägersten 2012, Beers Fägersten & Stapleton eds 2017b, Bergen 2016, Berger 2003, Bowers & Pleydell-Pearce 2011, Cavazza & Guidetti 2014, Cressman et al. 2009, Dewaele 2010, 2016a, Drange et al. 2014, Dutton 2007, Dynel 2012, Finkelstein et al. 2016, Hughes 1998, 2006, Jay 2018, Jay & Janschewitz 2008, 2013, Johnson & Lewis 2010, Leaver 2011, Ljung 2011, McEnery 2006, McEnery & Xiao 2004, Mercury 1995, Mohr 2013, Montagu [1967] 2001, Murray 2012, Nelson 2014, Salmani Nodoushan 2016, Shakiba 2011, Stapleton 2003, 2010, 2019, Stephens & Umland 2011, Stone & Hazelton 2008, Vingerhoets et al. 2013
'swearwords' (6 cases): Beers Fägersten 2007, 2014, Dewaele 2004b, 2005, Goddard 2015, Rathje 2014
'swear' (vb.) (3 cases): Dewaele 2004a, Rassin & Muris 2005, Thelwall 2008
'swears' (1 case): Kapoor 2016

Table 2 Informal Survey: The *Taboo* Lexeme in Academic Titles

'taboo [word/terms/lexis]' (16 cases): Allan ed. 2019a, Colbeck & Bowers 2012, de Klerk 1992, Dewaele 2004b, Gonzalez-Regiosa 1976, Harris et al. 2003, Hoeksema & Napoli 2008, Janschewitz 2008, Jay 2009b, Jay & Jay 2015, Jay et al. 2008, Napoli & Hoeksema 2009, Napoli et al. 2013, Rosenberg et al. 2017, Stenström 2006, Valdeón 2015
'taboo [language/intensifiers/expressions/comedy]' (5 cases): Christie 2013, Crisafulli 1997, Davies 2016, Kehayov 2009, Mirus et al. 2012
'[verbal/linguistic/word] taboo' (5 cases): Agyekum 2002, Holzknecht 1988, Keesing & Fifiʔi 1969, Pedraza ed. 2018, Simons 1982
'taboo' (unmodified) (4 cases): Burridge 2006, 2010, Krajewsky & Schröder 2008, Ouidade & Obermiller 2012

Table 3 Informal Survey: Other Lexemes in Academic Titles

'**obscenity/obscene language/obscene words**' (10 cases): Baudhuin 1973, Blumberg 2017, Feinberg 1983, Harrison & Hinshaw 1968, Johnson & Fine 1985, Mulac 1976, Seizer 2011, Stepka 1997, Stone 2007, Strub 2013

'**expletive(s)**' (9 cases): Bailey & Timm 1976, Bayard & Krishnayya 2001, Blakemore 2014, Daly et al. 2004, Hughes 1992, Millwood-Hargrave 2000, Oliver & Rubin 1975, Van Lancker & Cummings 1999, Wajnryb 2005

'**curse/cursing/curses/curse words**' (9 cases): Ainsworth 2016, Goddard 2015, Jay 1992, 1996, 2000, Jay & Jay 2013, Jay et al. 2006, Kushner 1999

'**offensive language/offensiveness**' (7 cases): Archard 2014, Dewaele 2016b, Kaye & Sapolsky 2004, 2009, Sapolsky & Kaye 2005, Sidiropoulou 1998, Zimmerman & Stern 2010

'**profane language/profanity**' (6 cases): Adams 2016, Coyne et al. 2012, LaPointe 2006, Mabry 1975, O'Neil 2002, Selnow 1985

'**bad [language/words/English]**' (4 cases): Adams 2002, Andersson & Trudgill 1990, Davis 1989, Fleming & Lempert 2011

'**dirty word(s)**': Griffith 2006, Jay 1980

'**vulgar language**': Ginsburg et al. 2003

'**forbidden words**': Allan & Burridge 2006

The search which has produced this collection of descriptors is inexhaustive not only because it is not a comprehensive survey of sources but also because it excludes many other related terms which crop up in the literature. Some of these straddle the boundaries of this field: for example, the technical-linguistic term 'dysphemism' and the general word 'slang'. It also omits metaphorical characterizations such as 'verbal dynamite' (Dewaele 2017). More importantly, it has omitted terms which denote some more specific language use to which there can be negative reactions, such as 'blasphemy', and lexemes denoting directed aggressive verbiage, such as 'insult', 'verbal abuse' and 'epithet', or pejorative lexical items such as 'slur' (of which more below). I have also omitted lexemes which in general usage indicate a negative judgement, such as 'rude' or 'impolite'. Had all of these been included, the list would have been much, much longer. But it is enough to indicate that what exactly constitutes the field – its extent and its boundaries – is not at all clear.

That there appears to be no single agreed term does not in itself matter as long as it is clear in any one case exactly what it is that is and isn't being addressed. However, a perusal of the subheadings of many of those titles reveals a tendency to duplication; that is, one of the above descriptors having appeared in the main heading, a different one (sometimes even more than one) appears in the subheading. This tendency is even more frequent in the bodies of the texts. There are two possible inferences to be drawn from this employment of more than one term. One is that the terms used are to be taken as synonyms. And indeed, some works are quite explicit about this conflation. Dynel (2012: 26), for example, warns that no distinction is attempted between the various lexemes "despite any differences these terms exhibit, according to their dictionary definition". Likewise, Salmani Nodoushan (2016: 241), after extensive exemplification of the variety of labels used, professes to employ "swearword/ swearing, bad language, and foul language interchangeably". The psychologically based study of Vingerhoets et al. (2013) indicates that it uses 'swearing' and 'cursing' as synonyms; Dewaele's (2004b: 205–6) 'S-T words' are a conflation of swearwords and taboo words; Stapleton (2010) equates 'expletives' and 'swear-words', which is in keeping with Ljung's (2011: 74) observation that the former (i.e. an exclamation through the use of taboo lexis) are the prototype of the use of the latter in most people's minds.

Work of a less academic flavour is less explicit about the tendency to treat several terms as synonymous. The practical study by Millward-Hargrave (2000), commissioned by British broadcasters and designed to assess the relative acceptability of various linguistic items to TV viewers, is a prime example. The word 'expletive' is in its title but its aim, avowed in its first sentence, is to test public attitudes to 'swearing'. In the main body of the text the compound noun phrase 'swearing and offensive language' is used thirty-nine times (but 'swearing or offensive language' only four times). In addition, the compound 'swear words and terms of abuse' occurs three times, once with the phrase clearly marked as a single phenomenon and in the other two cases arguably so. Most tellingly, the questionnaire items testing the relative severity of words identified by the author as specifically 'terms of abuse' have a severity scale with 'very severe' at one pole and 'not swearing' at the other.

The deduction from these usages must be that, in this work at least, 'swearing', 'expletive', 'terms of abuse' and 'offensive language' are all effectively synonymous. In this respect, they reflect general parlance in the English language, which has numerous labels for language and/or the use of language which has the potential to cause offence. Some labels (e.g. swearing, cursing, cussing and the euphemistic effing-and-blinding or effing-and-jeffing) denote an activity. Others (e.g. swearwords, expletives, four-letter words, dirty words, rude words, terms of abuse) refer to potentially offensive lexical items. Still others (e.g. bad language, vulgar language, strong language, abusive language, offensive language, foul language, lewdness) refer to the flavour of discourse more generally. And some (e.g. blasphemy, profanity) refer to the nature (and to some extent the result) of a perceived transgression.

Not only do these different items have a number of different types of referent; they also have different emphases. Some call to mind most strongly the emotional state of the user (e.g. cursing, expletives), some the function of such language use to insult (e.g. terms of abuse, abusive language) and some its referential lexical content (e.g. dirty/rude words, obscene/strong language). Some are evaluative (bad/vulgar/foul language) and some are euphemistic (effing-and-blinding/ jeffing, strong language, four-letter words). As can be seen, when taken together these lexemes straddle several semantic domains, cover overlapping but never quite identical semantic fields and foreground divergent connotations.

A similar profusion of terms with overlapping references and varying emphases exists in many other languages. This certainly is the case for Dutch and Modern Greek.[2] Of particular interest in these cross-linguistic comparisons is the appearance of lexemes equivalent to the English 'insult' (the nearest English from the list above being 'abusive language'). It is a moot point as to whether some language use is labelled this way when it is used to perform a speech act of insulting or simply because people find it insulting to be in the presence of such language use. Perhaps it is both.

The other possible interpretation of the use of two or more terms in the same text is that they are in a relation of hyponomy. Of those studies that are explicit about or hint at such a relation, there seems to be general agreement that swearing is one aspect of something larger. For McEnery (2006: 2) it is just one type of 'bad language'; for Allan (2019b: 12) it is "the strongly emotive use of taboo terms" (i.e. just one type of taboo language use); for Ljung (2011: 7) only a "small subset" of taboo words can be used in swearing; in Yule's (2010: 260) general overview of linguistics he observes that "taboo terms … are often swearwords" (entailing that some aren't). On the other hand, many accounts of 'swearing' as an activity include types which seem not to have any hint of taboo words in them (e.g. Ljung 2011). As Goddard (2015: 192) observes, little attempt has been made to either define or differentiate the various and numerous lexemes used to denote linguistic behaviour regarded, in one sense or another, as socially unacceptable.

3.1.1 Typologies

One way to approach an understanding of what it is exactly that we are talking about is to survey the various attempts that have been made to itemize different types of it. And notwithstanding Goddard's remark above, there have been quite a number of such attempts. Jay (1992) and Ljung (2011), for instance, attempt to differentiate between swearing and cursing, while Croom (2014) and Blakemore (2014) distinguish between expletives (e.g. fuck, damn) and slurs (e.g. nigger, slut).[3] Goddard himself defines and distinguishes 'swear words' and 'curse words' (2015: 193) ethnographically in terms of the recognized negative assessment of their use and the emotional state of the speaker.

The practical attitude study by Millwood-Hargrave (2000: 12) identifies a large number of types. These are: racial abuse, abuse of minorities, directive abuse (e.g. wanker, slag), sexual references (shag, dick, pussy), adjectival, expletives (shit, fucking hell), blasphemy and even eye-catching abbreviations (e.g. f.c.u.k.) before shading off into 'Americanisms', euphemisms, slang and baby talk. However, these distinctions are not consistently maintained and it is fairly obvious that they are not mutually exclusive. Moreover, like the abovementioned distinction between expletives and slurs, they are categories of different order: some index pejorative reference or address (racial abuse, abuse of minorities), some denotation (sexual references, blasphemy), some discourse function (adjectival, expletive), some pragmatic function (directive abuse, expletive) and some language form (adjectival, abbreviation), while some index primarily an attribute of their producers (Americanisms, euphemisms, baby talk).

Mixing of categories of different kinds is in fact frequently found. Andersson & Trudgill (2007) identify four types of 'swearing', three of which (expletive, abusive, humorous) denote its function for the user and one (auxiliary) denoting grammatical function.

Pinker's (2007) five different ways of using the word 'fuck' comprise two which index user function (abusive, cathartic), two indexing semantic content (descriptive, idiomatic) and one indexing discourse function (emphatic). Ljung's (2011) functional categories of swearing include personal user functions (expletives), interpersonal function (e.g. insults, name-calling) and discourse function (e.g. emphasis). Wajnryb's (2005) elaborate classification falls into the same trap, some highlighting semantic content, some speaker function. McEnery's (2006: 32) numerous categories of 'bad language' straddle grammatical function, discourse function, user function and semantic content.

Among those typologies which confine themselves to function for the user, a useful basic distinction is drawn by Montagu ([1967] 2001) between intra-individual functions (e.g. catharsis) and inter-individual ones, which are labelled annoyance swearing and social swearing respectively. Some studies (e.g. Jay 2009a, Vingerhoets et al. 2013) focus mainly on the former, which, having nothing to do with the interactional effects, are beyond the scope of the study here. Stapleton's (2010) four motivations, however, refer to intended effects. These are: expressing emotion (including aggression); humour and verbal emphasis; constructing and displaying identity; social bonding and solidarity. (There is, of course, strong evidence for the function of swearing to enhance in-group solidarity – see Daly et al. 2004.)

3.1.2 Definitions

Along with this bewildering riot of types, there is similar lack of agreement and confusion of classes when attempts are made to circumscribe the field; that is, to define what kind of linguistic behaviour or which linguistic items qualify as swearing, expletives, taboo language (or whatever one chooses to call it – see below) and which don't.

Among those who focus on the items, Dewaele (2004b: 205–6) defines what he calls 'S-T words' (= swearwords and taboo words) functionally as "multifunctional, pragmatic units which assume, in addition to the expression of emotional attitudes, various discourse functions" and implies they are recognized by their offensiveness. For Andersson & Trudgill (2007: 195), taboo lexical items are recognized by fulfilling criteria such as pertaining to a taboo sphere, having the potential for the expression of strong emotions or attitudes, including employment as a term of abuse, and having both literal and metaphorical uses.

Among those who start from the linguistic behaviour, Ljung (2011: 4) defines 'swearing' as follows: the use of utterances containing (1) taboo words used (2) with non-literal meaning, (3) often subject to severe lexical, phrasal and syntactic constraints, suggesting formulaic language and (4) having a mainly emotive function. This definition, like those of the 'lexical' approach exemplified above, contains a mix of characteristics of different orders: it has formal criteria (1 and 3), a semantic criterion (2) and a functional one (4). Jay (2019: 97) defines swearing as "the use of offensive emotional language to vent our feelings and convey them to other people", which emphasizes criterion (4) and hints at criterion (1).

Ljung also addresses the matters of distinguishing swearing from other, related, aspects of language. He quotes the lexicographer Landau's (2001: 38) attempt to separate taboo words from slang, which refers to two qualities: one is denotative content – "most slang expressions do not deal with sexually or scatologically offensive concepts", so that by implication taboo words do; the other is the user's intention – "slang is often meant to shock the staid or discomfort the pretentious", while taboo words are "intended essentially to violate the properties of common decency". This particular attempt at distinguishing between the two raises a number of questions. (What about the many slang words which do indeed have sexual or scatological reference? What are 'sexually or scatologically offensive concepts' as opposed to inoffensive ones? What on earth are 'the properties of common decency'?) Nevertheless, the distinction between what is taboo and what is merely very informal is a matter which needs to be addressed.

Another question of delimitation concerns slurs. These are words referring to a person, usually by a socially attributed category (e.g. ethnicity, gender, sexual orientation), which are pejorative because they are loaded with negative connotations. They have received a fair degree of scholarly attention in their own right (e.g. Croom 2011, Hedger 2012, 2013, Anderson & Lepore 2013a, 2013b, Bianchi 2014, Blakemore 2014, Croom 2014, Vallée 2014, Allan 2015, Jay & Jay 2015, Allan 2016) but very little of this work has addressed their relation to (other kinds of) swearing or taboo language or even what delimits *them*. For example, while Allan (2019b: 2) refers to 'idiot' as a slur, Padilla Cruz (2019) classifies this word as a 'qualifying insult' and reserves slurs for references to social groups. Goddard (2015) also distinguishes slurs from 'swearwords'. Some of these words appear to be so heavily loaded that we must certainly see them as taboo. Millwood-Hargrave (2000: 3) notes that for younger British people, 'terms of racial abuse' are regarded as extremely offensive. More than one student of mine in recent years has asked me whether it is acceptable even to quote the word 'nigger' in their written work. As with slang, the only sensible approach is to accept that clear boundary lines are not possible. Some expressions are only very mildly taboo and could also be characterized as slang, among which we could count mildly disrespectful references to social groups.

Interestingly, much of the work on slurs has focused on their creative strategic use by their conventional targets (i.e. the people they refer to) in order to 'reclaim' them. The question of who is using such linguistic items and to whom also arises with regard to another problem of delimitation. Among Ljung's (2011) functions of swearing are 'ritual insults' and 'name-calling'. As Drange et al. (2014: 36) observe, there is disagreement about whether the first two of these should count as swearing at all. And indeed, their study of teenage talk includes examples of insults that have no hint of what would conventionally be regarded as swearwords. Likewise, Salmani Nodoushan (2016) includes in his study of 'swearing' in Persian any insulting kind of linguistic behaviour and general malediction. As with slurs, it must surely be a question of whether the derogatory terms and heavily negative descriptions are being used, on the one hand, of the addressee or someone associated with him/her or, on the other hand, of someone else. If the latter, I cannot see how they can be regarded as taboo.

Conversely, it is perfectly possible to predicate something very undesirable about one's addressee (that is, insult them) without using taboo language. At the same time, as Culpeper (2011: 136, 141–5) finds, words which are conventionally regarded as taboo are often used to intensify an insult.

3.2 A definition of taboo language

A common thread running through the above attempts at definition, delimitation and typologizing of this kind of language use is that they index the point of view of its function for its producer. Almost all mention the expression of strong emotion and/or the producer's intention. This viewpoint raises a number of problems. For one thing, a moment's thought tells us that emotiveness cannot possibly be a defining feature; potentially offensive use of language can take place in complete tranquillity and strong emotion can be expressed without the faintest hint of such language. For another, intention is an intrinsically dubious candidate for definition, both because we can never have direct evidence for it and also because, even when it can be plausibly ascribed, it can sometimes miss its mark. At a certain very young age, my youngest brother got it into his head that the word 'bucket', when uttered in isolation, was a naughty word that could be used to shock and thrill. It never did.

Most crucially, though, definitions in terms of function for the user sit very uneasily with the notion of offensiveness, which is regarded as a defining characteristic by Dewaele (2004b: 205–6) and Landau (2001: 38), and implied as such by those who cite terms of abuse (Millwood-Hargrave 2000, Andersson & Trudgill 2007), and is where I situate taboo language – as one kind of potentially offensive language. They sit uneasily because an assessment of offensiveness rests primarily not with the producer of language but its recipient. (Despite his intentions, people were amused by my brother's 'bucket', not offended by it.) It is for this reason that in this text so far I have been careful to refer to potential rather than actual offence. In this respect, Millwood-Hargrave's (2000) work has the advantage that, being an empirical study of public attitudes to the use of certain lexical items in the mass media, it is oriented to the recipient. And yet, as we have seen, this work is no more helpful than any other in defining what it is we are talking about. One characterization from the viewpoint of reception rather than production is Shakiba (2011: 240), who, from an avowed sociolinguistic viewpoint, sees 'swearing' as "a type of linguistic behaviour that society regards as disrespectful, vulgar, even offensive".

At this point, it is helpful to remind ourselves that whether offence is actually caused is, of course, radically context-specific. This fact is recognized by Goddard (2015: 199–200), who points out that the items 'Jesus!' or 'Christ!' as swear/curse words have not a hint of taboo about them when uttered in certain contexts (e.g. a Christian ceremony). It is also recognized by Valdeón (2015: 366), who writes that "Cursing, taboo words, dirty words, offensive language or swearwords are some of the terms used in connection with expressions that can cause offence to certain listeners in certain contexts." This description, in its use of potential rather than actual offence and its reference to 'certain contexts', is the best I have found so far. However, as can be seen, it avoids definition of terms.

Taking the lead from this emphasis on reception and on potential rather than actual, and in order to pin down what it is that is being received, I offer here a definition of taboo language. In his editor's introduction to the *Oxford Handbook of Taboo Words and Language*, Allan (2019b: 1) reminds us that "what is in fact tabooed is the use of those words and language in certain contexts; taboo applies to instances of language behaviour". Yes, indeed it *applies* to these instances. But a particular instance can only be assessed negatively and labelled taboo because it breaks some kind of generally perceived rule. In order for the instance to qualify as taboo, there must be reference to a context-spanning, or at least situation-spanning, norm. So, when seen as potential, a definition of taboo language must be expressed in terms of norms. The kinds of norms I have in mind here are what Culpeper (2008: 29–31) calls 'cultural norms' and 'situational norms'. From the point of view of any one individual, the former are based on "the totality of [his/her] experiences of a particular culture" and the latter on "the totality of [his/her] experiences of a particular situation in a particular culture" (Culpeper 2008: 30). Notice the embedding. The idea is that the situational norms are part of the cultural norms. Together, they amount to a person's knowledge of what is normal in certain kinds of situations in a certain culture. And the particular kinds of situation I have in mind are those in which (the individual knows) 'polite' norms apply (the inverted commas to indicate I am referring to the first-order notion of politeness – see section 2.1).

Accordingly, I define taboo language as

> any (string of) words whose production is transgressive of polite social norms.

By 'polite social norms' I mean those norms of verbal behaviour which operate between people of a certain minimal social distance (i.e. those who are not intimates or close friends, where 'politeness' has little salience) and which operate in public, non-specialist domains. Further, by 'public, non-specialist domains', I mean *all* general-public domains (i.e. broadcasting, mass-media news reporting) and those semi-public domains in which the focus of communication does not address or involve the taboo. (For example, much of the language appearing in this book is taboo, but I presume it will be found acceptable because here we are in a specialist domain, which is about this very topic.) And still further, by 'semi-public domains' I mean those which in principle are accessible to a large number of people, many of whom are not personally acquainted, and which through recording (if it is spoken) or reproduction or forwarding (if it is written) may be made available to limitless numbers but which in practice are participated in by a limited number (e.g. workplaces). An expanded definition of taboo language is therefore

> Any (string of) words whose production is transgressive of the norms which operate in interaction between people who are not intimates or close friends and in situations where the language produced is accessible, at least potentially, to limitless numbers of people.

Obviously, this approach to the notion of taboo assumes some sort of consensus in society about what particular (strings of) words are taboo. Of course, there will be some considerable variation in perception as to the severity of the taboo attached to particular (strings of) words, but taboo items are simply those recognized as widely regarded as transgressive of polite social norms, regardless of the attitude held personally to an item (or indeed to taboo items in general) by the person doing the recognizing. The claim is that it is by virtue of this transgressive power that taboo language has the potential to offend people when they encounter it. (Whether it actually does is of course situation-specific.) It is about the *possible* reactions of recipients in certain *kinds* of situation (nothing about the *actual* reactions of identified recipient(s) in an actual, *particular* situation).

3.3 Three kinds of taboo language

A further overview of the literature on taboo language reviewed above reveals that most of its focus, or more precisely its starting point, is very much language form – lexical content. Among the descriptors found in titles of works were 'swearwords, taboo words, taboo terms, taboo lexis, word taboo, obscene words, curse words, bad words, dirty words, forbidden words' and 'expletive' (denoting a kind of word or phrase). In addition, it is clear the most popular descriptor of all, 'swearing', is often taken simply to equate to the use of swearwords. However, it may also be noticed that the attempts at typologies and definitions also encompass, or at least nod towards, subject matter (e.g. references to 'offensive concepts') and/or illocution (e.g. insults) and/or intended interactional effect (e.g. social bonding, humour).

In the introduction to his book on 'swearing', Ljung (2011: viii) remarks that "It is an interesting but so far unresolved question whether taboo has more to do with form or with content". After observing that "[p]enis and *prick* denote the same theme, but only the second is offensive and hence a swear word" (2011: viii), he goes on to cite Andersson's (1985: 83) attempt to describe the relations between the words used in swearing and the things they refer to, this being that "potential swear words are words that are 'bad' both with regard to their content and their form, viz. words whose literal meaning is 'bad' and whose form is frowned upon by most speakers" (Ljung 2011: 7). This is true enough. However, the fact that these words are just as taboo when used metaphorically suggests an analytical necessity to separate form and content. Conversely, there are many situations in which the mention of the male sexual organ would be taboo whatever name is given to it. Sometimes what is taboo is the form and sometimes the content.

Accordingly, I identify two kinds of taboo language. *Taboo words* are words whose mere *animation* (see section 2.3) is taboo. Uttering them transgresses polite social norms regardless of their denotation or what they are used to refer to. For example, in modern English 'nigger' is taboo even though other words with the same denotation such as 'African American' or 'black' are not. Likewise, it doesn't matter whether the lexeme 'fuck' is used literally ("We had a fuck") or metaphorically ("It's all fucked up", "He fucked off") – it's still taboo.

Taboo reference, on the other hand, is the bringing up of topics which are taboo. In England today, it transgresses polite social norms as I have defined them above to refer, for instance, to one's defecating habits, the physical details of all sexual activity and many medical ailments or to give or ask for detailed information about a person's salary. It doesn't matter whether I refer to my practice of 'having a shit', 'taking a dump', 'having a poo', 'going to the toilet', 'evacuating' or 'losing a kilo or two' at eight o'clock every morning – it's still taboo.

In addition to these two types, there is another way in which what is said can transgress polite social norms, which does not have to contain taboo words or taboo reference to do so. I call this *taboo predication*; that is, the expressing of a proposition which is taboo because it transgresses the polite norms which apply in particular situations or simply by virtue of it starkly conflicting with existing widespread consensus. For the latter, a simple extreme example will do for now. The expressing in the public domain of the opinion that "the holocaust [i.e. the murder by the Nazis of about 6 million people, mostly Jews] never happened" is illegal in several European countries. People who do this go to prison. As to the former, there are certain settings and encounters involving specific role relationships which dictate that certain kinds of propositions should not be expressed. That is, their expression is seen as a flagrant breach of a generally understood 'rule'. (See Chapter 6 for more detail.)

As a simple example of all three aspects of taboo in action, I return once more to the example in section 1.2.1, in which an advertisement for a language school was banned because it contained the lyric (the only spoken words in the whole ad) "I wanna fuck you in the ass". What was found so offensive about it? First, it contained the strongly taboo word 'fuck' and the mildly taboo word 'ass'. Second, it referred to anal sex. Third, it predicated the speaker's desire to impose himself sexually on the hearer. The lyric, then, is taboo on all three counts because it was (intended to be) uttered in the public domain (broadcast TV). This precise instantiation of taboo language is 'over the top', deliberately chosen by the advertisers to drive home the point about the vital necessity of knowing English. But in fact, in such a public domain as broadcast TV advertisements, an instantiation in the song lyric of just one of these three aspects of taboo language (e.g. "I fucking love you", "Let's talk about anal sex" or "I want to impose myself sexually on you") might have been enough to instigate a ban, or at least censure. Of course, much taboo language use contains more than one of its three aspects. But I show in the next three chapters that they are each in principle separate analytical categories.

Taboo words

For this category of taboo language, the taboo inheres simply in the production and reception of a particular sequence of sounds or particular sequence of letters of the alphabet which together form a recognizable lexical item. The previous chapter argues that taboo words are a category of taboo language in their own right, regardless of what they are being used to refer to on any one occasion and regardless of the propositional content or illocutionary force of the utterance of which they might be part. An obvious observation in support of this argument is simply the fact that taboo words are so often used metaphorically. Some of them are used most often this way. It is telling that in McEnery's (2006: 32) 'categorisation of bad language' (in my terms taboo words), one category of the sixteen is labelled 'literal', entailing that the other fifteen are non-literal uses. Consider the following British English examples:

- What the *fuck*? [= expression of surprise]
- That was *fucking* amazing [= extremely amazing]
- By the time we got there, we were *twatted* [= drunk]
- Piece of *piss*! [= very easy]
- You *bastard*! [= nasty person]
- He's a right stupid *cunt*, he is [= person whom I dislike and for whom I have no respect]
- I suppose I could, but I can't be *arsed* [= can't be bothered]

Utterances such as these are just as taboo as when the italicized words are used with their literal meaning.

Further evidence of this autonomy can be found in Dewaele (2004b), who found that the taboo words in a language have less 'emotional force' for people who are not native speakers of that language (see also Colbeck & Bowers 2012). These people are perfectly well aware of the denotation of the words and of their common usage, but it seems the words are simply not *felt* by these people to the extent that they are viscerally felt by native speakers. This finding is reminiscent of the well-known humour to be found in strings of sounds or letters which are innocuous in one language but taboo in another. Even if the context in which the string appears is overtly and transparently connected with the language in which it is innocuous, its appearance among speakers of the language community in which it is taboo can have serious effects. I know of one case in the 1970s in which an English-language teaching coursebook whose publishers hoped would sell well in Greece was to feature a central character whose surname had the same set and order of phonemes (albeit with different primary stress) as the Modern Greek equivalent of the English 'cunt'. Upon discovering this near-homophony, the publishers had to change the name at the very last minute. (See Trudgill 1983: 31 for a similar example involving speakers of Nootka in North America.) All languages contain homophones and their users are perfectly able to put up with this to the extent that when one of a homophonous pair is used, the other member of the pair doesn't even occur to them: when native English users encounter the spoken word 'leak', for example, the onion-like vegetable does not spring to their minds. But it seems that this ability to disassociate cannot occur when a taboo form is involved.

A further indication of the reality of taboo words as a separate category of taboo language can be gleaned from a passing observation of Clark & Carlson (1982). In the course of discussing overhearer design (the phenomenon by which speakers often take into account the presence of bystanders who may be overhearers), they cite avoidance of taboo words as one reflex of this tendency and comment in a footnote that

> Strikingly, it isn't the meaning of a particular expression that is eschewed, but rather its form or sound … people will use circumlocutions like 'She's ready to go' or 'The hammer's back' just to avoid saying 'The gun's cocked'. The idea is, apparently, that an overhearer might hear only the critical word, and mistake it for an obscenity.
>
> (Clark & Carlson 1982: 346)

This reaction to homophony involving taboo is one impetus for lexical change (see section 5.4).

Taboo words seem to be the prototype of taboo language, which is one reason why they and taboo reference are often conflated in people's minds (see next chapter). Perhaps this is why it is they more than any other type of taboo language which are used for social indexing. McEnery (2006), for example, discusses and exemplifies this tendency with regard to social classes. I offer here a telling example from the film *My Fair Lady*, set in early-twentieth-century London, in which a mad professor teaches Eliza Doolittle, a girl from the London slums, to abandon her Cockney accent and adopt an upper-class one. When he takes her to a horse-racing event so that he can test his pupil by getting her to converse with his upper-class friends, she succeeds magnificently, even while employing spectacularly low-prestige grammar and lexis. While the combination of a geographically limited, and therefore not upper-class, accent with standard British English is quite common in Britain, its reverse as portrayed here (high-prestige accent with low-prestige grammar and lexis) has never been attested. This incongruity is the source of the risibility in this episode – it sounds ridiculous to British ears. However, when Eliza's excitement during a race leads her to cry "move yer blooming arse", we hear her accent mask slip and she reverts to Cockney vowels. The idea, of course, is that in this moment of intense emotional engagement, Eliza is unable to maintain her pronunciation act. But it is ironic, given that *this* combination, of high-prestige accent and taboo lexis, is by no means impossible in Britain, that here disrespectable words and disrespectable accent are assumed to somehow belong together.

As has long been documented (e.g. Mulac 1976, Cheshire 1982, Macafee 1989, Hughes 1992), taboo words are associated with the lowest socioeconomic groups. In a discussion of this association, Christie (2013: 161) draws attention (parenthetically) to the possibility that the statistical evidence of actual use – drawn from McEnery & Xiao's (2004) excavation of the British National Corpus – does not completely support it. Nevertheless, the association is ensconced in the public mind. When a British judge (i.e. a member of a very *high* socioeconomic group) retorted in court to an offender who had just called her "a bit of a cunt" that "you're a bit of a cunt yourself", it made news around the English-speaking world. Notably, when the same national newspaper which originally reported this exchange of words featured a follow-up article about the judge the next day, it referred to her as the judge who had 'told' this offender he was a bit of a cunt. That is, the co-text has been elided. It was merely her animation of the word which was newsworthy.[1]

4.1 Taboo words and the mass media

The need to avoid or, if that is not possible, apologize for the intrusion of taboo words in situations where polite social norms operate is remarkably powerful and all pervasive. Tabooness is of course scalar, but one can find instances when speakers distance themselves from the potentially offensive lexical item even when it is very much borderline with slang or figurative speech. One such example occurred in early 2017 on BBC's breakfast TV news magazine programme, when the presenters were discussing with an interviewee an online health survey that was being featured. In the course of this discussion, the (male) presenter, when uttering the word 'knackered', felt obliged to preface his animation of this word with "excuse my language". It was *not* actually 'his' language – he was quoting a word which appeared in the survey and his discourse had already made it clear this was what he was doing. He was merely its animator. Nevertheless, he was prompted (either by himself or his producer through his earpiece) to insert this metapragmatic comment as a plea for latitude.[2]

In fact, though, on broadcast media in Britain, apologies for the use of taboo lexis go further. Presenters routinely apologize for their intrusion even when it is not they who are animating them. On 26 July 2017, there was a discussion on BBC Radio 4's midday news programme between the presenter and two guests. At the end of the discussion the presenter brought up the question of whether Brexit would or should involve the UK staying in or leaving the EU's single market. The opinion of one of the guests, the boss of a plumbing firm, was that "Of course we should stay in the single market". The presenter then pointed out that this meant he didn't agree with the leader of the Labour party, Jeremy Corbyn, to which the guest responded, "Well, Jeremy Corbyn's a twat, isn't he?" The host wound up the discussion more or less immediately after this and before moving on to the next item on the programme said, "Apologies to Jeremy Corbyn for the language used".[3] The fact that this apology was issued by a presenter who did not animate the offending word and had no forewarning that it would be uttered indicates that a presenter on a broadcast programme feels that in some sense s/he is principal of everything uttered.

In the context of an interview or discussion about a serious matter such as politics, this sense of responsibility is perhaps understandable. But the same apology is also sometimes forthcoming in contexts where the animator of the taboo lexis is not addressing the camera and words are not in any case the object of attention. Such a context is coverage of a live sporting event, where viewers are bystanders with respect to any words uttered by the players (see Holt & O'Driscoll forthcoming). Thus on 5 February 2017, during a rugby match between Wales and Italy, the microphone carried by the referee and largely (though not entirely) audible to the TV audience picked up a Welsh player uttering "Fuckin' 'ell, ref" (presumably in an appeal that Italy were doing something illegal). One purpose of the microphone on the referee is to make it easier for TV viewers to understand the decisions s/he makes as s/he explains these to the players on the pitch. It is not designed to pick up and relay to the TV audience the utterances of players and these are usually at best only half audible to TV viewers. And indeed in this case, my consciousness did not register the utterance of this Welsh player until the commentator drew attention to it by then saying, "Apologies for the language you may have heard on the referee's microphone just now". So here we have a case in which someone apologizes for the occurrence of taboo lexis when s/he is not only not the animator of the word but is not understood to be responsible in any way for what takes place – the commentator, like the viewers, is a mere bystander. It would seem that so virulent is the contagious capacity of taboo words that action must always be taken to isolate them; that is, to distance participants from them.[4]

The above are all examples of 'live' spoken utterances; that is, their production and reception are simultaneous. When, on the other hand, there is a delay between production and reception, the opportunity arises for the broadcaster to take steps to prevent the potentially offensive item being heard. For instance, on British television, if the programme in which the item occurs is broadcast before the 'watershed' (nine o'clock in the evening), the item in which it occurs is usually 'bleeped out'; that is, a musical tone is inserted over it in the recording.

Visual representations of someone else's language (whether spoken or written) are, of course, never 'live'. In print mass media, the publisher has the choice to prevent the offensive item being seen. One means of such prevention is simple replacement, as in the tactic used by some English speakers on themselves when wanting to utter an expletive but wishing to avoid using a taboo word to do so; instead of 'shit!', they say 'sugar!' However, this means of taboo avoidance is never used in the British press, presumably because it would leave the publishers open to charges of misrepresentation. Instead, taboo lexical items appearing in photos are routinely blacked out and those in direct speech quotations have most of the letters with which they are conventionally spelt replaced with dashes or asterisks. In such cases, the first letter of the taboo word is left untouched, thereby ensuring that few readers would be unable to fill in the blanked letters. So it would seem that such expunging is almost ceremonial – there is little attempt to hide from readers what the expunged word actually was, but nevertheless it is not articulated in full.

An example of this kind of censorship in the representation of direct speech is the following quote of the Irish footballer Roy Keane, remonstrating with the manager of the Irish national team in 2002, as it appeared in several British newspapers at the time.

> He said: "Who the f*** do you think you are, having meetings about me? You were a c**p player, you are a c**p manager. The only reason I have any dealings with you is that somehow you are manager of my country and you're not even Irish, you English c**t. You can stick it up your b******s."

Again, it is relatively easy for readers to fill in the blanks. It is noteworthy that this censorship is self-censorship. There is no legal requirement for the British national press to expunge some of the letters of taboo words from their reports. And in fact not all publications do so. I know of at least two national publications, the *New Statesman* and *The Guardian*, which decline to do so. The decision is thus a matter of editorial policy.[5]

4.2 The Downing Street gates affair

It is because this policy of not expunging taboo words on the part of these two publications that we know of one example of re-animator censorship which is somewhat disturbing. This is from the log of a police officer following an incident at the gates of Downing Street in London in 2010. Downing Street, being the official residence and workplace of both the Prime Minister of the UK and also the Chancellor of the Exchequer (i.e. chief finance minister), is security-sensitive and there are gates to its entrance guarded by police officers. The incident involved a government minister of the time who wanted the police to open the main gates so that he could ride his bicycle out through them. But the police refused and told him to use the pedestrian (side) gate instead, to which they then escorted him. The minister got angry at this refusal. The police log of this part of the encounter reads as follows:

> There were several members of public [sic] present as is the norm opposite the pedestrian gate and as we neared it, Mr Mitchell said: 'Best you learn your f****** place ... you don't run this f****** government ... You're f****** plebs.'

The above is a faithful reproduction of the police officer's log. We know this because even the two non-censoring publications cited above represented it this way.

The first, most obvious, thing to note about this report is that, strictly speaking, it is inaccurate (the minister did not say 'ef asterisk asterisk asterisk

asterisk asterisk asterisk') or, slightly less strictly, sloppily ambiguous (flipping? festering? failing?). One might have thought that detailed accuracy was a prime criterion for the reports of police officers. But this reporter of someone else's words, claiming neither principal nor author roles of the words used, felt the need to take the editorial decision to alter them.

In fact, the reporting *is* precise in that, assuming that each asterisk represents a letter, the number of them is precisely the same as the number of letters needed to complete the word 'fucking' after the letter 'f'. This is one way in which the reader is encouraged towards the interpretation 'fucking'. The other, of course, which is prior to the first in the reader's inferencing process, is that this blatant flout of Grice's (1975) maxim of manner, which expects that meanings will be expressed as clearly as possible, generates the implicature that there must be some reason for this opaque means of expression. And since this is part of a factual report (not a crossword or a quiz), the deduction reached by the reader is that what is represented here is a taboo word. The reader is first led to the interpretation that this is a taboo word and then given help through the number of asterisks as to which taboo word it is. The degree of care needed to produce the correct number of asterisks suggest that this was the officer's intention. Nevertheless, he took it upon himself to effectively adopt an author role in the reporting of the words – and in doing so, a principal role as well in the world of the reporting.[6] He has made himself accountable for this exact representation and thus has conveyed an attitude – that taboo words have no proper place in this domain, regardless of the requirements of accurate reporting. (The issue of the accountability of the reporter of someone else's words is taken up in Chapter 11.)

The same precision with asterisks can be witnessed in the Roy Keane quote at the end of the previous section, this time with the author of the report giving us even more help by including the last letter of the taboo words as well as the first. In neither case, then, is there any attempt to conceal what word it actually is that is being represented in this opaque manner (quite the opposite). But polite social norms apparently dictate that its form be changed.

4.3 Why taboo words can cause offence

As Christie (2013: 153) observes, "scholarship in the field of politeness has shown that the interactional effects of swearwords are context-dependent". True enough, and indeed these effects are sometimes positive. Daly et al. (2004) is among the most oft-cited studies demonstrating that taboo words can have a relationship-building effect. So why is it, then, that, as the discussion above shows, pains are so often taken to avoid them, and that when they aren't, they create 'news'? Why is it that, as Jay (2009a) observes, 'swearing' can elicit negative reactions even though it causes no obvious harm to the swearer, the listener or society? This question is prompted by what linguists have long known about the near-total arbitrariness of the relation between signifiers and signified, in this field exemplified above with the reference to it as a source of cross-linguistic humour. It is further prompted by the apparent arbitrariness of the fact that in a single-language community only some of a number of words with the same denotatum are taboo and in varying degrees. For example, in British English, 'cunt' is highly taboo, 'twat' less so, 'fanny' only very mildly so (see Millwood-Hargrave 2000) and 'vagina' not at all (although of course even the last might be involved in taboo reference – see next chapter). The question is even further prompted by the fact that many of the apparently most offensive taboo words (in English anyway) are more often used metaphorically than literally, so that taboo reference is not a factor. It really is just the form which is taboo. Why?

A first answer is a fairly well-established matter of association and can be explained through Culpeper's (2011) conventionalized impoliteness formulae (see section 2.1.2). Just as these are associated with offensiveness by virtue of their preponderant use for causing offence, so taboo words can be associated with offensiveness for the same reason. Although Culpeper (2011: 134-6, 141-5) found that in his data taboo words only very rarely caused offence all by themselves, they frequently feature as essentially obligatory elements, or one of a small number of obligatory elements, of some formulae. (He compares, for example, 'shut up' and 'shut the fuck up', the latter correlating with assessments of impoliteness much more frequently than the former.)

However, this chapter has argued and illustrated that taboo words do indeed have the potential to offend all by themselves, so there must be more to it than their associations with offensive formulae. Part of the explanation may be found in other associations, such as that cited above with lower social strata. Another possible reason is association with their taboo referents, even when they are used metaphorically. And there is presumably a kind of snowball effect about all these associations which emerges in metadiscourse. Once a word acquires the *reputation* of being 'offensive', its offensiveness is reinforced.

This last observation points in the direction of a further possible reason, which has the advantage of also explaining why the uttering of taboo words can have positive interpersonal effects as well as negative ones. This concerns my conception of positive and negative faces, in which these pertain solely to the horizontal dimension of personal relationships, the poles of which are close intimacy and complete strangers (O'Driscoll 1996, 2007, 2011). Recall that the definition of taboo language used here refers to polite social norms, these being norms which start to apply only when there is a certain minimal distance on that horizontal scale. Once a consensus has been established that a word is 'offensive', its use transgresses polite social norms and in doing so implicates relative intimacy between producer and recipient, the implicature being that we don't need to pay attention to those 'polite' norms. It is doing what I call positive facework. Such facework can be received as face-enhancing or face-threatening. If recipients dislike this implicature, they will experience it as an attack on their negative face(s). A relation with the producer which they find inconsistent with their assumption of interpersonal distance has been posited. Their 'personal space' (or if you prefer, integrity) is being invaded. It is for exactly the same reason that the use of taboo words can be received as face-enhancing. The implicature of relative intimacy is interpreted as a celebration of social closeness.

This explanation for the offensive potential of taboo words – that the social consensus of taboo causes their use to be received as either threatening to negative face or enhancing of positive face – works quite well. It can explain the anxiety of those operating in very public domains such as in broadcast media to avoid their use, since it would be improper, in fact ridiculous, to claim such a relatively intimate relationship with all recipients. The explanation can also be applied to taboo reference, perhaps more obviously because certain topics are by nature more intimate than others. But regarding taboo words specifically, it is only a partial explanation. It just shifts the question backwards. Why does this social consensus of norm transgression exist in the first place? There is, after all, nothing intrinsically intimate or distancing about a particular sequence of particular sounds or letters of the alphabet. I suspect the answer to this subsequent question lies in what amounts to a fetish with mere language form, one that we have all been brought up with, and which may be the result of such upbringing or may just be a feature of the human condition. But addressing that question is beyond the scope of this work.

A final observation: the arbitrariness of which words are taboo and to what extent is further evidenced by the fact that items with the same denotation can vary greatly in this respect across language communities. To take just one example, numerous phrases in the volume *Una historia de España* by the highly respected writer Arturo Pérez-Reverte (2019) are liberally sprinkled with metaphorical usages of items which translate into English as 'cunt', 'fuck', 'testicles/bollocks/balls' and 'penis/prick'. The fact such items appear in a serious volume, intended for the interested general public and written by someone with a writer's reputation to uphold, indicates distinctly divergent attitudes to these items in the Spanish- and English-language communities.[7] Such usages do not appear in equivalent volumes in the latter language. It would seem, then, that items denoting sexual organs are far less taboo in the former than in the latter – and/or that the point on the dimension of interpersonal distance at which polite social norms start to apply, so that such items become potentially offensive, is very different in the two cultures.

Taboo reference

This chapter explores the nature of utterances which are taboo not because of the words themselves but rather because of what they refer or allude to. Most researchers simply hint at what such subject matter might be by noting the semantic fields covered by certain groups of taboo words (a further indication of these as the prototype of taboo language). One or two, however (e.g. Abrantes 2005: 87), attempt to classify taboo topics into major categories. Such an exercise is a potentially useful one because it offers us the possibility of a standard of comparison across cultures. Just as individual lexical items vary in the strength of their taboo status across language communities (see end of last chapter), and even from region to region within the same language community (see section 8.1 for an example), there is no doubt that cross-cultural variation exists as to what kind of subject matter is taboo and to what degree. A simple example can be found in two contrasting excerpts from the memoir of the British novelist Tim Parks recounting his first year living in a village in the Veneto region of northern Italy. After having been startled on more than one occasion by the intimate details shared between comparative strangers, he comments that

> While people from the Veneto are generally reserved and formal, nevertheless when they get on to the subject of their health there is simply nothing, nothing they will not tell to the most casual acquaintance, from varicose veins to mastectomy, prostatitis to mere constipation.
>
> (Parks 1992: 139)

On the other hand, he relates how before an upcoming Italian general election,

> I played a little game with my students on our last lesson of the year. I suggested they write down who they think their barber/hairdresser votes for and why. Normally responsive and fun to teach, my request left them nonplussed,

diffident, reticent. It was as if one had asked some ancient Athenian to explain the Eleusinian mysteries. A completely taboo subject.

(Parks 1992: 310)

He goes on to remark that his village voted 70 per cent for the Christian Democrats on this occasion, as apparently it always does, although having lived there several years, "I have yet to meet anyone here who will speak well of the party".

In both cases here, polite social norms apply, in the first because of the social distance involved, in the second because the interaction took place in a semi-public domain. The fact that Parks takes the trouble to record these incidents shows how, from the point of view of someone born and brought up in Britain, each is remarkable. The second anecdote is also indicative of the fact that taboo reference need not be confined to the usual suspects of death, disease, sex, excretion and body parts, as in the reputation of British people in other parts of the world that they never offer or ask for details about each other's salary.

What counts as taboo reference can also change over time. Ethnicity, or at least that part of it known as 'race', has become an increasingly taboo subject in the last fifty years in the English-speaking world. In 1968, it did not apparently transgress polite social norms for the well-known white British comic actor Peter Sellers to do a 'brownface routine' in the Hollywoood film *The Party*, in which he plays a bumbling Indian in a western environment, complete with a stereotype of English spoken with an Indian accent. In this year, the BBC regularly broadcast the *Black and White Minstrel Show*, a light entertainment programme in which white singers with blackened faces sang traditional American songs, again with cod black American accents. At the time, the show was very popular but even then there were protests. Now, it is seen as an embarrassment in the history of British television. In twenty-first-century Britain, it is taboo to mimic such accents, regardless of whether the figure thereby represented is portrayed positively or negatively.[1]

By way of emphasizing that taboo reference is a separate category, the first two examples below involve words which in the abstract are totally innocuous. That is, their mere animation would not by themselves be taboo but they become taboo in context because of what they are used to denote. To recap, we are addressing here language which transgresses polite social norms because of its referential content. It therefore has the potential to cause offence. (This does not mean that it actually *does* cause offence, though – see the second example.) However, it cannot be denied that in the general public's mind, little distinction is made between this taboo category and taboo words. The third example, while at the same time demonstrating the robustness of the category of taboo reference, illustrates this conflation. Moreover, it appears that the words most commonly used for certain kinds of taboo reference can over time become taboo in themselves. This development is discussed in the final section.

5.1 The black guy in West Building

Like all aspects of language, what is and what isn't taboo is a matter of individual perception and can change over time. This example concerns something that was *not* said because the speaker decided that it would be improper to do so. I know this because the speaker was me (hereafter Jim).

> The scene is the foyer of a university building in England. Sitting there are three schoolteachers who have brought a small party of their students to visit the university. A number of activities and tours have been arranged for these visitors. At this point in the programme, Jim has the task of escorting the visiting students from the place where one activity has finished to where the next one is to take place. But he has noticed that one of the students does not seem to be with the rest of the party. So he approaches the teachers to ask them if they know the whereabouts of this missing student.
>
> He does not know the names of any of these visitors, so in order to ask his question he needs to refer to the missing one by some visible identifier. What identifier can he use? The missing student is male, but as the gender composition of the party is about 50:50, this information is not useful. He is tall, but not noticeably taller than the others, so this is not a very good identifier either. As far as Jim can remember, he is wearing a red shirt, but he may not be the only one (Jim is not very good about noticing clothing). There is, though, a visible feature that distinguishes this missing student from all the others – he has very dark skin pigmentation (while all the others have markedly pale skin).
>
> But Jim cannot bring himself to ask the teachers if they have seen 'the black guy'. After explaining that one of their students seems to be missing, and after some false starts and hesitation, he asks the teachers if they have seen the guy in the red shirt.[2]

In this situation, in which he did not know any of his interlocutors personally, so that polite social norms applied, Jim held back from referring to someone by the colour of their skin, even though it would have been the most practical way of identifying that person in the circumstances. Clearly, Jim must have felt that it would be improper to do so. I like to think that Jim was wrong about this, that the teachers would have regarded it as perfectly OK to refer to the missing student this way. But for this speaker (Jim) at this time, a person's skin colour was taboo reference, presumably because it would have risked the interpretation that he regards 'race' as a very salient social category, perhaps bestowing on him a face with a tinge of racism in it.

The taboo in this case, as in the next example below, is purely a matter of reference. Jim did not regard the *words* 'black' and 'guy' as taboo, nor was he intending to predicate anything about the missing student (see next chapter).

5.2 Not going up one of those again

While the example above exemplifies 'race' as taboo reference during a brief face-to-face encounter at the workplace, this one illustrates taboo sexual reference during a conversation aired on broadcast television. The action takes place on the *Parkinson* chat show, probably the most popular of its genre in Britain at the turn of the last century, in which host, Michael Parkinson, chats with each of three celebrity guests in turn in front of a studio audience. The first guest remains on stage when the second guest comes on, as do both of them when the third guest appears, so that at this point all three are sitting next to each other (at a 90-degree angle to Parkinson). This format means that it is therefore possible for an earlier-appearing guest to contribute to Parkinson's conversation with a later-appearing one. And indeed, Parkinson sometimes invites them to do this.

On one particular edition of the show,[3] Parkinson has been chatting with Larry Hagman, one of the stars of the world-famous American drama-soap *Dallas*. He then introduces the British author, actor, comedian and intellectual Stephen Fry. Of particular relevance in this context is that Fry is openly gay. He is renowned as a witty conversationalist and during the 15 minutes in which the conversation has him at its centre, the audience erupts into laughter several times. Parkinson then brings on his final guest, introduced as the "singer, actress, director, fashion icon and survivor", Cher. After about 40 seconds of conversation between Parkinson and Cher, during which Fry has twice interjected humorous comments, Cher turns to Fry and tells a story about how moving she found the experience of watching the film *Wilde* (in which Fry had played the leading role of the gay late-nineteenth-century playwright Oscar Wilde). This topic allows Parkinson to bring up the fact that Cher's daughter has recently announced she is gay. His remark has a hint of accusation in it that, while Cher is known to have a positive attitude towards gay people, she has expressed some dismay that her daughter is gay. Cher responds by explaining that she first felt guilty about not being a good enough mother and then also bad because of all the publicity that her daughter will now be exposed to as the daughter of a famous person. She describes it as "such a hard life choice for her". Fry then intervenes and defends Cher, praising her honesty, contrasting this with others who might just *pretend* to be pleased in public, and arguing that most people in the gay community understand her reaction because they know that being openly gay does not make a person's life easy.

At this point, Parkinson intervenes and asks Fry:

Parkinson:	Well, well what di *your* parents did er-say when *you* told them
Fry:	I think they'd known for (with some laughter) such a long time for some reason
Parkinson:	I mean it wasn't— you didn't have to go and say oh by the way Mum and Dad—
Fry:	No, well I think, my first words as I was being born was— I looked up at my mother and said that's the last time I'm going up one of those

At this point:

- Cher immediately breaks into loud, high-pitched laughter and continues for more than 5 seconds.
- so does the audience, then commences clapping, which lasts for about 10 seconds.
- Parkinson also laughs.
- Hagman first shifts uncomfortably in his chair, alternately pursing his lips and smiling broadly, then blows out an exhalation and comments "refreshing".

  After 10 seconds, Fry continues his narrative ("No, they were absolutely terrific about it") and commences to make the serious point about the prospect of not becoming a grandparent if your only child is gay, but short bouts of laughter from Parkinson and the audience continue for some time.

In this excerpt, Fry refers to the act of heterosexual coupling in a markedly explicit way, referring not merely to the act but also to the details of its physical essentials. He first describes a situation in a manner which invites the listener into a narrative of an ongoing event; not the simple past "when I was born" but the progressive "as I was being born", thus pinning the situation down to a far more specific point in time. He then takes a first-person-narrator viewpoint ("I looked up at my mother") which, because it is not just "looked at" but rather "looked up at", is from between his mother's legs. And what he purportedly said ("the last time I'm going up one of those") can only refer, in the co-text of an account of how his parents always knew he was gay, to a penis entering a vagina.

The description is shockingly vivid. General references to heterosexual sex are only mildly taboo in British culture, and in a chat show of this kind would most likely pass without overt reaction. But the extended, uproarious reaction which follows at this point shows that this very detailed reference definitely *is* taboo.

Two points to note about this example. The first is that there is not a hint of even the mildest taboo word in Fry's sexual referencing. This is achieved entirely through pronouns ("I" denoting his own penis, "one of those" denoting a vagina) and an innocuous phrasal verb ("going up" denoting sexual penetration). This example is thus a prime illustration that taboo reference can occur without taboo words. (Nor is there any taboo predication here – to state that one has no desire for heterosexual activity attracts no mainstream censure in twenty-first-century Britain).

The second point is that Fry's narrative, while potentially offensive (i.e. taboo), causes the very opposite of offence. The uproarious reaction to it among all those present is almost entirely positive. It is one of extreme mirth. (Even Hagman's initial reactions – see above – are exaggerated. The video shows him *performing* uncomfortable shifting in his chair and lip-pursing and his comment of "*refreshing*" is obviously ironic. He wishes, presumably, to go on record as recognizing that he finds Fry's description normatively unacceptable.) There are several clues as to why this was the case. Most generally, this is an entertainment show and therefore licensed for some relaxation of polite norms. More particularly, this chat-show activity type is one which aspires to off-the-cuff, unscripted conversation of a pseudo-intimate kind, imitating a situation in which polite norms do not apply. Still more particularly, Fry is an accredited humourist, expected to say somewhat 'outrageous' things. Finally, his story is of course just a surreal comic fantasy – children can't speak that (very) early in life. But this inventive whimsicality is not enough by itself to generate the very high degree of general hilarity which ensues. Arguably, this is also caused by its unexpectedness in the co-text of a potentially serious and emotional account of coming out as gay to one's parents. (While Parkinson quizzes Fry about this matter, Cher projects a look of concerned empathy.) But mainly, the hilarity is caused precisely *because* the reference is taboo.

5.3 Sorry, I meant 'masturbation'

This example also concerns a sexual reference.

> At Leeds train station, England, in the early evening in early July 2018. The station is noticeably noisier than usual, with raised voices and a certain amount of shouting and singing in celebratory reaction to England's recent quarter-final

victory in the football World Cup. Two elderly men and an elderly woman, all strangers to each other and all trailing luggage, get into a lift. Just as the lift door begins to close, three young men rush into the lift. Like many around the station, these lads are in a boisterous mood. As the lift slowly ascends, they swap loud remarks continuously.

This situation puts the three elderly occupants of the lift in a tricky interactive position. On the one hand, the lads give no sign (e.g. direction of gaze or propositional content of their talk) that they are open to being joined in their ratified circle, so that the elderlies are in the position of overhearing bystanders. This status is, of course, one which often falls to people in public places and the normal line appropriate to it, in northern Europe at least, is what Goffman (1963: 83–8) calls 'civil inattention', whereby people give a minimal sign of recognition of others' presence but otherwise behave as though these others are not there. However, the circumstances of this particular situation make such a line impossible to sustain. It is not only that the lads' banter is loud enough for the elderlies to follow every word of what is said and who says it. Crucially, they have no means available for mounting a credible pretence that this is *not* the case: the enclosed, windowless space of the lift means that there are no other potential foci of interest to which they could overtly direct their attention; the short duration of the situation (perhaps 20 seconds before they have to take themselves and their luggage out of the lift) means that it would not be credible for them to extract a phone or book and project involvement in that; and the fact that they are all 'singles' means that the opportunity to project an ongoing involvement with each other is also unavailable. They have become a captive audience – and are seen to be captive.

For their part, the lads' continuous loud conversation means that they are not practising the minimal recognition of others which constitutes civil inattention. Their behaviour amounts to what, to develop and twist Horgan's (2019) discussion of '*un*civil attention' in public places, might be called 'uncivil *in* attention'.

> After a couple of exchanges in the lads' banter, one of them (Lad 1) proffers the information that he is really 'made up' (= energized, ready for action) and the talk proceeds as below.
>
> Lad 1   … yeah, I tell you I'm really made up
> Lad 2   (to Lad 3) Yeah, he hasn't been so made up since he saw you trying to have a wank
> Woman (with level tone) Language
> Lad 3   (but not looking at woman) Yeah, sorry, come on lads, behave yourselves

Lad 1   I'm gonna go straight down to [utterance continues …]
Lad 2   (simultaneously, with back to woman) Sorry, I meant masturbation.
At this point, the lift comes to a stop and the door opens.

The woman's single-word utterance is understood in British culture to indicate disapproval of and offence taken at what has just been said. When uttered with the intonation used in this case (neither rising nor falling), it is understood to have the illocutionary force of a rebuke to the previous speaker, a warning that s/he should be more circumspect about his/her utterances in this situation. At the same time, it is understood as mere punctuation in the discourse, not as an attempt to take the floor.

Given the overt captive-audience status of the woman, it is not surprising that the lads project no sign of shock at this interpolation from a bystander. Following Lad 3's perfunctory apology, which is issued without turning his gaze towards the woman or either of the other two overhearers, he and Lad 1 then resume conversation as if the interpolation had never occurred. It is during this resumption that Lad 2 utters the faux apology for his earlier 'language'.

Almost certainly, what exacerbates the mild social discomfort already felt by the woman and the other two elderlies as a result of the existing participation framework (see above) is the loud reference to auto-erotic activity; that is, it is the topic thereby raised which turns a feeling of awkwardness into a feeling of being offended. It is not considered proper in British culture to refer to such matters in the close presence of strangers (or indeed, that of anyone except one's more intimate associates) and we can assume the woman's rebuke indexes this reference. In the terms used here, her rebuke and the occupants' discomfort exemplify a case of taboo reference. And yet, following default practice, the rebuke itself appears to refer to lexical choice – the 'language' that Lad 2 has used rather than what he is using the language to talk about. His faux apology has the effect of calling the bluff of the woman's rebuke, pretending that it really was his choice of words rather than of subject matter that caused offence, that if only he had used the clinical 'masturbate' rather than the colloquial 'have a wank', no offence would have been caused. This is almost certainly untrue – and the fact that Lad 2 made sure he was facing away from the woman when uttering the 'apology' shows that he knew this. It was an ironic riposte for the benefit of his fellows. Indeed, it is possible that 'masturbate' would have caused greater discomfiture among the overhearers than 'have a wank', since a clinical term, being precise, sometimes has greater power to conjure up a vision of its referent than a loose, colloquial equivalent.

5.4 The taboo-ification of words used for taboo reference

The case immediately above is just one example of how popular attitudes in the realms of taboo tend to give pride of place to language form, to the words used rather than to the topic of talk. And sometimes, as this case shows, people censure the former when what has really offended them is the latter. The British comedian Ben Elton once pointed out, in reaction to some viewers' complaints about his 'swearing' during his stand-up comedy TV show of the early 1990s, that in fact he was careful never to 'swear' on the show. But these viewers, it seems, had conceptualized his numerous explicit references to aspects of sex and other bodily functions in this way.

Notwithstanding the validity, as demonstrated in the examples above, of taboo reference as a type of potential offence generator separate from taboo words, it must be recognized – and perhaps this goes some way to explaining the conflation of the two types of taboo language in many people's minds – that words used for some kinds of taboo reference, if used often enough, can over time become taboo in their own right. We are talking here about the converse of, and indeed the impetus for, euphemism. The classic example here for the English language concerns reference to the room in a house used for urination and defecation. Traugott & Dasher (2001: 59) describe the process by which the item 'toilet', at one point in its etymological career used to refer to bodily grooming in general, gradually became used as a euphemism for the place – both the room and the receptacle – used for bodily excretions. Then, the more established this latter reference became, the more its use for any other reference declined, to the point when the aforesaid receptacle and room became its only denotation. But this fixture, and the activities associated with it, being a taboo reference in 'polite' circles, the word itself has by now become somewhat taboo, being often replaced in North America by 'restroom' or 'bathroom'. A British reflex of the same development, it seems to me, is the disappearance in the workplace domain of references to a 'toilet break' – rather, it is a 'comfort break'.

This process of semantic change involving concurrent euphemisation and taboo-ification, has been dubbed by Allan & Burridge (2006) the 'X-phemism mill', by which euphemisms coined by deploying a general term for something more specific then narrow in their semantic range to become the neutral term and later, because of their taboo reference, develop into dysphemisms (i.e. taboo words). As Burridge & Benczes (2019: 189) put it, "euphemistic expressions become sullied by the disagreeable concepts they designate … undermin[ing] the euphemistic quality of the word and the next generation of speaker grows up learning the word either as the direct term (orthophemism) or as an offensive term (dysphemism)". They regard this process as potentially endless. However, for a word to work its way through to its dysphemistic conclusion, a referent has to retain its taboo status. One feels, for example that the originally euphemistic and now orthophemistic 'gay' is unlikely to complete the journey to dysphemism any time soon because homosexuality, and therefore reference to it, is far less tabooed than it used to be.

Still, there are a number of indications that words used for topics the reference to which has become more taboo in the last few decades are, for this reason, possible candidates for taboo-word status. Ethnic categories based wholly or mainly on skin colour are one such case. Regarding Jim's perhaps oversensitive desire to avoid referring to "the black guy" in section 5.1 above, I asserted that Jim had no qualms about using the actual *word* 'black'. However, there are indications that the association of colour words with ethnic difference has caused some nervousness about the use of such words. Presumably this is the reason why the ethnic category 'black American' has now been largely replaced with 'African American' as the polite norm in the United States, and why the variety of English formerly described by sociolinguists as 'Black English Vernacular' now goes by the name of 'African-American Vernacular English' in sociolinguistic circles. Cameron (2012: 116–18) cites some absurd and/or apocryphal examples concerning attempts to avoid use of the word 'black' which have nothing to do with ethnic identity. By way of balance, one may add the furore which took place in 2019 concerning the word 'white' as used on the 'Little White Town' welcome signs on roads entering the town of Bideford in Devon, England. The word here refers to the colour of the buildings and streets and the phrase is a quote from a description of the town in a famous nineteenth-century novel. But fears that this could lead to charges of racism initiated a proposal to change the signs. After much heated debate and publicity, the proposal was rejected.[4] While there is no serious possibility that the words 'black' and 'white' could become fully fledged taboo words (i.e. taboo regardless of what they are used to refer to), there are, it seems, indications of increasing circumspection about their use in any context which might possibly be interpreted as alluding to ethnic identity. Part of this development, I predict, is a decrease in their metaphorical use for phrases which have strongly positive connotations (e.g. white magic, white lie, whiter than white) or negative connotations (e.g. the black arts, black looks, blackleg, blacklist, black mark).

There is at least one other way in which a word can aspire to taboo status. One of these is phonetic identity or similarity with a word which is used for taboo reference or is itself already taboo. The former phenomenon is well known as the cause of various X-phemism and even word replacement diachronic processes. It is why in North America a male chicken is no longer referred to as a 'cock' but rather as a 'rooster' because the former word is also a slang term for 'penis'. Burridge & Benczes (2019: 186–7) note the advice given on Mumsnet (an online parenting forum) to avoid naming a daughter 'Regina' (Latin for 'queen') because its English pronunciation is different from that of 'vagina' only in its first segment.

What looks like a rather stark example occurred in 2019 at the University of York in England, when students made a complaint about the repeated animation of the word 'negro' by a lecturer while quoting aloud from works by well-known black writers. The complaint elicited a written apology from the head of department concerned.[5] As the lecture in which the quotes occurred was part of a module on race, it cannot have been the reference which caused offence but the word itself. One can only assume that the offence taken at the animation of 'negro' was its similarity to the word 'nigger'. While the former word has moved taboo-wards in the United States since around 1970, its precise status is still a matter of debate there – it is regarded as a slur by many, but others prefer it to the alternatives 'black' or 'African-American'.[6] The latter word, on the other hand, has been taboo in North America for more than a century and is now extremely taboo throughout the English-speaking world.

Taboo predication

This chapter is about strings of words which are taboo not because of the words themselves or because of what they refer to but rather because of their propositional content. More than the other two categories of taboo language, this one hinges on contextual specifics; that is, the same predication may be taboo in one context but not in another. Remarks such as "Lucky you didn't find the bomb" or "Careful with that bag, it's got a bomb in it" are, I feel, in pretty poor taste in any gatekeeping situation. But if made when going through an airport security check, they become taboo (and are explicitly illegal in many countries[1]).

Partly as a result of this situational dependence, whether a string of words constitutes taboo reference or taboo predication – or neither – may sometimes be hard to determine. The issue of the 'little white town' welcome signs discussed at the end of the previous chapter can serve as an example. First of all, as we have seen, whether it is taboo at all depends on whether the word 'white' is being interpreted as a reference to people's skin colour. The fact that the town council decided not to change the signs means that they dismissed this interpretation as invalid, or at least too marginal an interpretation to make it worth spending the money on changing all the signs. But let *us* interpret it this way for now, so that we can ask the question: does this taboo reference also amount to taboo predication in this context? We can ask it because any such sign which contains more than a word of welcome and the name of the town must be predicating *something* about the town. If the sign had been interpretable as a statement such as 'This town is for whites only' and therefore as an indirect speech act of instruction for people with non-white skin to keep out (as in many public signs in South Africa during the apartheid era or those in the United States when the 'colour bar' was in operation), it certainly would qualify as a taboo, indeed illegal, predication. But as modern Britain does not practise institutionalized apartheid, the sign cannot realistically be interpreted this way. The political context disqualifies this interpretation. However, a welcome sign is understood to have a kind of promotional function – one will not find any examples of 'the ugly town' or 'the boring town' on such signs anywhere – so that it being a town full of white people can be interpreted as claiming that this is a positive feature. And while a statement characterizing a town as predominantly white cannot in itself be taboo (it would merely be a factual observation which could be made of many towns and villages in Britain), the appearance of this sense on a welcome sign would make it taboo.

In this case, reactions to the proposal that the signs needed to be changed suggest that it was the inferable reference rather than any inferred predication that caused the furore. The poor councillor who made the proposal because he had received some complaints that the signs could be interpreted as a racist slur was then accused of being a racist himself for proposing it – presumably because it was felt to be somehow indecent of him to entertain this interpretation.

The distinction, then, between taboo reference and taboo predication has a fuzzy boundary and in some cases it may be hard determine whether an instance of taboo language qualifies as one or the other or both. This is inevitable if only because, just as what is and isn't assessed as taboo language varies subjectively, so does what is and isn't assessed as taboo reference and/or taboo predication. For some, that sign may have been objectionable because it indexed the taboo subject of race; for others, the objection may have been that it additionally predicated the ethnic identity of the town inhabitants as a 'good thing'.

However, the existence of fuzzy boundaries between categories does not itself invalidate them. It is perfectly possible to point to examples of predications which are manifestly taboo but have no hint of taboo reference (or taboo words) in them. The most obvious are those which are illegal, and the starkest example of all these is the act of apostasy (understood here as formally renouncing one's religious faith). At various times in European history, this act, when it involved renouncing the prescribed faith, resulted in execution. Even today, it is illegal in many countries and carries the death penalty in some of them.[2]

6.1 Factual taboo

Fortunately, there are few other examples in the twenty-first century where the mere saying of something can get you judicially killed. But many examples of severe legal consequences for the predicator can be found. For example, in several European countries, holocaust denial is a crime; that is, it is illegal to assert that the murder of around 6 million people, mostly Jews, by the Nazis never actually happened. This is a particularly stark case of taboo predication because it concerns a matter of historical fact, in which a proposition is not simply regarded as wrong (in this case absurdly wrong) because it is contrary to all the evidence; rather it is wrong to *say* it. Other propositions of fact have incurred similar reactions on the part of the authorities in European history, for instance that the earth revolves around the sun (instead of the other way around). That the holocaust-denial proposition is false while the heliocentric proposition turned out to be true is not at issue here. The truth of the latter was contested for some time after it had been made. But what caused the authorities to confine one of its proponents, Galileo, to house arrest for most of the rest of his life was not their belief that his position was factually wrong – it was that it was heretical. As with holocaust denial, what provoked the legal sanction was the belief that its dissemination would lead to sociopolitical unrest.

This, then, is the essence of taboo predications of fact – a proposition which gets condemned regardless of its truth or falsity. Indeed, its truth value is often not considered at all. What matters is simply that it has been articulated. As a result, negative consequences often follow for those who have predicated it. The examples above involve legal(ized) punishment. Another negative consequence is the loss of one's position. The British politician Ken Livingstone was suspended from membership of the Labour Party after a radio interview in which he said

> When Hitler won his election in 1932 his policy then was that Jews should be moved to Israel. He was supporting Zionism before he went mad and ended up killing 6 million Jews.

The truth or falsity of this historical claim was not part of the widespread negative reaction that followed. There were particular background-contextual circumstances which caused it to be condemned.[3] The very idea of Hitler as a supporter of Zionism was regarded as simply indecent.

The following example led to the predicator being dismissed from his job. In 2017, a Google software engineer circulated a long internal memo arguing that many of the company's efforts to correct its gender disparity, especially at senior levels, were misguided.[4] It further asserted that "Google's left bias has created a politically correct monoculture that maintains its hold by shaming dissenters into silence". The part of the memo that caused the greatest outrage was the claim that the under-representation of women in the tech industry had a largely biological explanation, that:

> the distribution of preferences and abilities of men and women differ in part due to biological causes and that these differences may explain why we don't see equal representation of women in tech and leadership.

Reactions to the memo came quickly from senior figures in the company. One vice-president emailed that its

> incorrect assumptions about gender [are] not a viewpoint that I or this company endorses, promotes or encourages.

Another sent an internal memo describing the view that

> most women, or men, feel or act a certain way is stereotyping, and it is harmful.

The CEO also wrote to employees as follows:

> First, let me say that we strongly support the right of Googlers to express themselves, and much of what was in that memo is fair to debate, regardless of whether a vast majority of Googlers disagree with it. Portions of the memo violate our Code of Conduct and cross the line by advancing harmful gender stereotypes in our workplace ... To suggest a group of our colleagues have traits that make them less biologically suited to [Google's] work is offensive and not OK. It is contrary to our basic values.

Note that none of these comments attempt to refute the biological claim itself. The only hint in that direction is the adjective 'incorrect', which is presupposed rather than predicated. Instead, the comments focus on the fact that the claim was made, condemning it for being contrary to company values, offensive stereotyping and harmful. Despite the CEO's lip service to freedom of expression and his lukewarm assent to the possibility of 'debate', the writer of the memo still got fired. It is this tenor of reaction which shows that, in this context, the claim can be classed as taboo.

This case can be used to suggest one way in which predications of fact become taboo: when they are intermixed with other positions and are used to, or have been used to, excuse and/or encourage various undesirable practices. The co-text of criticism of company diversity policy and general human atmosphere within which the biological claim appeared means that there was more than its truth value at stake. The claim is said to 'explain' the glaring gender disparity. Whether or not this is a feasible explanation, the trouble with 'explain' is that it can get interpreted as 'excuse' and even 'justify' – in this case that the disparity is only natural and therefore somehow inevitable. And this 'natural' view can serve as encouragement, especially if held by those with power and influence in an organization, to other undesirable practices such as sexual harassment. The offending memo encouraged such an interpretation by framing itself in terms of the left–right political spectrum, which is of course not a domain pertaining to truth but one pertaining to desirability.

This incident is one of many recounted by the cultural commentator Christopher Booker as an example of the madness "of Groupthink, the phenomenon by which a group of people become so fixated on some view or belief of the world ... which [to them] is so self-evidently right that no sensible person could disagree with it" (Booker 2020: xi), the belief in this case being that differences between men and women are an entirely social construct. To the extent that reactions to the memo did not engage with its biological claim but rather simply stated or implicated that it was a terrible thing to *say*, Booker is right. However, it is misleading to present it as an example of group*think* (my italics). What according to the CEO was "contrary to our basic values" was not the propositional content itself but the illocutionary act of "suggest[ing]" it. It must be admitted, though, as both the data above and Booker's interpretation of it illustrate, that in practice there is a thin line between metapragmatic assessments of uttered propositions (that was the right/wrong thing to say) and metalinguistic ones (that's right, that's wrong) and it is easily crossed. If people find themselves repeatedly disadvantaged for *saying* that a rose is just a rose, and we all witness this repetition, it is simply practical for us to adopt the belief that a rose *isn't* just a rose. Presumably, the taboo-ness of certain predications gets strengthened this way.

6.2 Interpersonal taboo

To predicate a negative trait about someone *to* that someone is not necessarily taboo. It is unpleasant of me, assuming I am not joking, to predicate to your face that you are stupid, boring, ugly, cruel or possess some other negative trait. (For an impressively long list, see Allan & Burridge 2006: 79.) It is likely you will feel offended, assess my utterance as nasty, insulting or cruel and perhaps take it as evidence that I am a nasty person. Such a predication runs contrary to our expectations regarding mutually supportive facework. We may say that it transgresses the norms of conviviality. But it does not *by itself* transgress polite social norms in the sense that I am using that phrase, which pertains to a restricted set of contexts (see section 3.2). I sometimes feel the most stinging accusation you can level at a British person is to tell them they have no sense of humour. But there is no maxim, even implicit, in British culture that this is something you are never supposed to say to a person. Insults such as these certainly run contrary to the expectations of friendly interpersonal interaction and reciprocal face maintenance, and some of them appear in Culpeper's (2011: 135–6) inventory of conventionalized impoliteness formulae. But there may be no shock or intake of breath among those present that a 'rule' has been broken, that the norms of polite social interaction have been transgressed. Whether this is the case is radically situationally and culturally dependent.

Take as an example political insults. These, because they pertain to a public semantic field, are susceptible to taboo status. According to my own political outlook, I could attempt to insult you severely by calling you a communist, fascist, wishy-washy liberal, peasant, pleb or elitist swine. The degree of offence caused will depend partly on how much it hits home. Back in 1975, in the course of a disagreement over pay, my wife's employer in Greece said to her: "You, you are a … Communist!" Her delivery of this ascription plus the co-text (which was not about political views or affiliations) indicated she intended this ascription as a terrible, damning insult. In a country which had at the time only recently emerged from a dictatorship (when membership of the Communist Party was illegal) and which less than thirty years previously had suffered a vicious civil war (with communists on the losing side), such an accusation was in the employer's mind beyond the pale of respectable talk, and she was making it to indicate the strength of her feelings. But to my British wife, from a country which had not undergone such tragedies for centuries and where political affiliation was a relatively small part of a person's identity (and who in any case was generally well disposed to leftist ideas), it was no insult at all. She just laughed.

In fact, it *is* possible in Britain for political insults of this type to have taboo status. But this is not because its target is insulted but rather because of what it reveals about the attitude of its utterer. Returning to the incident discussed in section 4.2, you may remember that the government minister, angered at the police's refusal to let him ride his bicycle through the main gates of Downing Street, is reported to have said to the officers:

> Best you learn your fucking place … you don't run this fucking government …
> You're fucking plebs.

The reporting of this case had huge, long-running publicity and eventually the minister concerned was forced to resign his ministerial post. The reason he was forced to do so, however, was not his use of taboo words. Rather it was that he ascribed the status of 'plebs' to the police. This word (singular 'pleb') is derived from the ancient Roman status of plebeian, the lower-class of Roman society as opposed the upper-class patricians. In twenty-first-century Britain, defining someone according to hierarchical social class distinctions is frowned upon. And, although people are still acutely aware of such divisions, the absolute, institutionalized distinction that existed in ancient Roman society is inapplicable. It is doubtful, therefore, that the police officers who were targeted by the minister's ascription or the public who heard about it afterwards felt genuinely offended; several of them probably found it risible, as my wife did in the case above. But what *was* widely inferred was that here was someone in a government post whose view of society was outdated and unacceptably elitist. It was this perception which caused him to lose his job.

The argument here is that predicating something clearly negative about one's addressee is not in itself taboo, but that aspects of context can make it so. A further example from the world of politics can be found in the strictures on discourse in the British parliament. These are made explicit in *Rules of Behaviour and Courtesies in the House of Commons*,[5] which stipulate, among other things, that

> Any abusive or insulting language used in debate will be required to be withdrawn immediately. Accusations of deliberate falsehood ... may only be made on a substantive motion after writing privately to the Speaker to obtain permission ... No such accusations should be made in the course of other proceedings

In other words, while in the parliamentary chamber, no Member of Parliament is allowed to insult another Member of Parliament, and especially not allowed to call him/her, even indirectly, a liar. In that very specific setting, such an ascription is taboo.

Negative personal ascriptions may also become taboo as a result of specific role relationships. As argued above, the predication of someone's stupidity is not necessarily taboo. However, there are certain situations in which it would become so. For example, given the norms which apply in recent times, it would be taboo for a teacher to tell a child's parents that "s/he is stupid" or state that in his/her report.[6] It is even possible for propositions whose content is quite innocuous and even impersonal to become taboo if predicated to the 'wrong' addressee. Brown (2011: 80) claims that the maxim of age deference in Korea means that disagreeing with or contradicting elders is usually 'taboo', so that in that culture, a predication by a younger to an elder such as "that's wrong" would be taboo. In this case, then, what is taboo is not the propositional content but the illocutionary force of the predication in context.

All this is not to deny that there are certain formulaic maledictions in many cultures which are taboo under any circumstances (when polite social norms apply) because they are known to have the canonical illocutionary force of a curse. I am told, for example, that the Hong Kong Cantonese predication "Go die!" is treated this way. A non-verbal example from Greek culture would be an extended arm with the palm of the hand facing the target. Once again, there may always be cases when these are used ironically or jokingly but their pragmatic force depends on their recognition as normatively unacceptable.

The only personal ascriptions in modern Britain which, I suggest, would be taboo almost regardless of context would be to accuse someone of being a paedophile or a Nazi, but even here specific aspects of context can strengthen the taboo. The incident recounted and discussed below is an example. In February 2005, the left-wing mayor of London, Ken Livingstone (yes, him again), attended an LGBT reception in City Hall. The acronym stands for lesbian, gay, bisexual and transgender. In other words, it was an event to support people of non-mainstream sexual and gender orientation. As he and others were leaving the function, Livingstone evinced some irritation at photographers from the *Evening Standard* newspaper "harassing" the guests. He was then approached by an *Evening Standard* journalist, who introduced himself as working for this newspaper, and the following dialogue (audio-taped by the journalist) took place.[7] (OF = the journalist, Oliver Finegold; KL = Ken Livingstone.)

1	OF:	Mr Livingstone, *Evening Standard*. How did it …
2	KL:	Oh, how awful for you.
3	OF:	How did tonight go?
4	KL:	Have you thought of having treatment?
5	OF:	How did tonight go?
6	KL:	Have you thought of having treatment?
7	OF:	Was it a good party? What does it mean for you?
8	KL:	What did you do before? Were you a German war criminal?
9	OF:	No, I'm Jewish. I wasn't a German war criminal.
10	KL:	Ah … right.
11	OF:	I'm actually quite offended by that. So, how did tonight go?
12	KL:	Well you might be, but actually you are just like a concentration camp guard. You're just doing it 'cause you're paid to, aren't you?
13	OF:	Great. I've got you on record for that. So how did tonight go?

14 KL: It's nothing to do with you because your paper is a load of scumbags.

15 OF: How did tonight go?

16 KL: It's reactionary bigots ...

17 OF: I'm a journalist. I'm doing my job.

18 KL: ... and who supported fascism.

19 OF: I'm only asking for a simple comment. I'm only asking for a comment.

20 KL: Well, work for a paper that isn't ...

21 OF: I'm only asking for a comment.

22 KL: ... that had a record of supporting fascism.

When details of this encounter became public, there were widespread calls (including from the prime minister at the time) for Livingstone to apologize. He refused to do so but a tribunal later found him guilty of 'bringing his office into disrepute' and suspended him from office for a month. (This decision was later overturned by the High Court, on the grounds that an unelected board does not have the power to suspend an elected official.)

As can be seen, the line taken by KL in this encounter is antagonistic from the outset. He treats OF's affiliation as if it were a medical condition and projects solicitous concern (lines 2, 4). His repetition of this apparent concern (line 6), in pointedly failing to orient to OF's repeated question, dispels any possible interpretation that his concern for OF's 'condition' is genuine. When OF changes tack and phrases his innocuous questions another way (line 7), KL continues not to respond to it and instead asks a question (line 8) about OF which, in its spectacular irrelevance to the situation, has to be interpreted as a possibility that has entered KL's mind. Curiously, although this speculation about OF's previous occupation cannot possibly be true (OF wouldn't have been alive at the time of German war criminals), OF responds to it relevantly and even provides a reason why it could not be true (that he is Jewish). KL's response (line 10) suggests that he recognizes that he may have strayed beyond the bounds of politic behaviour, a fact confirmed by OF's comment about being offended (line 11). But OF is clearly a professional and having registered his offence, returns to his original question. Once again KL ignores this question and picks up on his registering of the offence (you might be) and then accuses OF of being exactly the same as a particular *kind* of German war criminal (line 12). OF's response (line 13) functions as a warning to KL that he is in trouble ("on record"), perhaps hoping that following this KL might actually answer his original question, which he then repeats. But again, KL declines to do so. His next comment (line 14) is ambiguous: "it's nothing to do with you" (if 'it' is understood to refer to the reception) could be interpreted as an explicit refusal to answer the question because OF has no right to ask it, or as a rider to the accusation he has just made (if 'it' is understood to refer to that remark), that the accusation is not personal but should be taken as indicative of his negative attitude to the newspaper for which OF works.

OF makes one more attempt to get his quote by repeating his question but KL once more declines. It is only then that OF changes tack (lines 17, 19, 21) and explains himself, pleading for KL to start playing the journalist–politician game. These final exchanges and OF's brief responses to KL's Nazi accusations are the only times in the whole encounter in which a response shows any relevant orientation to the preceding turn. KL is consistently conversationally uncooperative, at first sarcastic (line 2, 4, 6), then personally aggressive (lines, 6, 8, 12) and thereafter haranguing. But it is not this behaviour which got him into trouble. Public figures are known, and to some extent expected, to be uncooperative when accosted without warning by journalists. (Many simply refuse to engage at all. But Livingstone, apparently angered by the attention from employees of a newspaper which he disliked and, we might speculate, having had a drink or two or three, chose to engage in a hostile manner instead.) The offending utterances here, the ones which according to the tribunal brought the mayorial office into disrepute and led to KL's suspension, were his asking whether Finegold was a German war criminal (line 8) and his likening of Finegold to a concentration camp guard (line 12). We have no way of knowing whether these predications would have had the same outcome if the journalist had not been Jewish. But their taboo status was certainly amplified by this fact.

6.3 The taboo-ification of words used in insults?

It was suggested in the previous chapter that words commonly used for taboo reference could themselves become taboo (i.e. become taboo words). The same can perhaps happen with words commonly used in insults. This is through association with a word's prototypical use if its denotation is highly pejorative. In this case – if often used as vocative address or as something predicated of the addressee (as in "You are an X") – the word calls to mind a gross insult and for that reason is often rated as highly offensive by respondents to surveys. Jay (1992) even lists lexical items such as 'idiot' and 'stupid' as mildly taboo in his surveys, while some of Hagen's (2013) respondents rated 'Jew' and 'whore' as very severe swearwords, presumably for this reason. And this must also be why Dewaele's (2016b) large-scale survey of the degrees of offensiveness of negatively valenced English words found that after 'cunt', the word which his respondents judged to be the next most offensive was 'slut'. This latter item denotes a sexually promiscuous female and connotes a very negative attitude on the part of the speaker to this characteristic and the person so identified. One can easily imagine respondents imagining a scenario in which a person accuses someone of being a slut ("you slut"). Clearly, unless interpreted as banter, this utterance will be received as highly offensive, and given the required context qualifies as a taboo predication. But to qualify as a taboo word as I define it, it has to be equally taboo when predicated of a third person not present or simply animated for some other purpose. I am not convinced it is. As has been noted (e.g. Spender 1980: 15), terms used to denote sexually promiscuous females are both numerous and invariably pejorative (unlike those used for males of the same disposition) and as such can always be received as offensive when predicated of the addressee. But to refer to someone not present as a 'round heels', a 'slapper' or a 'tart' (just three of the numerous terms), while it might be interpreted by those present as deeply unpleasant, and offensive for that reason, and/or taboo reference, would not qualify as taboo *word* in the sense that I am using this term. It is possible, though, that I am out of date in this respect.

This issue points up the limitations of using questionnaire data for the purpose of gauging degrees of offensiveness. Respondents are asked to introspect (always imperfect) and make judgements about … what? Acceptability? Offensiveness? Rudeness? Their own attitude or their perception of the dominant attitude in their community? The problem is that in order to make the judgement requested, respondents naturally imagine a certain situation in which they have experienced the item in question being used. Thus, although the item they are being asked about is nothing but form, their judgements are based on their experience of its typical use.

Part Three

Actual offence: Case studies

Some more theoretical considerations

My approach to offensive language rests on the assumption that Terkourafi (2008) is correct in insisting that, while whether an utterance is *actually* offensive is situation-specific and depends on its uptake by its target, some forms are conventionalized as offensive "in virtue of occurring most frequently in situations calling for face-threat" (2008: 67). That is, these expressions can be and are recognized as conventionally offensive (i.e. associated with offence) by interactants as such and this knowledge contributes to their inferencing process when they encounter them. I have presented taboo language as their prototype. Culpeper's conventionalized impoliteness formulae (see section 2.1.2) rest on the same assumption.

This knowledge does not, however, determine the outcome of the inferencing process – the evaluation of the utterance and its felt effects (including those on face) – because various aspects of context (see section 2.3), in particular the relationships holding between participants and also more general language attitudes, carry greater weight in it. The chapters following this one examine a series of cases where offence has been attested – what I call offending utterances. The fact that only a few of them contain taboo language is testament to this primacy of context. And indeed, when the conventionally offensive *is* involved, it is often found that too much attention to this aspect of the offence can mask its underlying cause.

Most of the reactions to the offending utterances involve the exercise of power. This is, in fact, how we know about them. Because the offended parties are in a position of power over the offender, or if not have made appeals to those who are, they have not been shy about following up their offended reaction with an overt response. These frequently involve some sort of institutionally approved punishment of the offender. We thus have the opportunity to analyse not just the offending utterances but also these responses, and in doing so not only to get a greater insight into what exactly in the offending utterance was found offensive by the powerful but also to evaluate the responses. As Haugh (2015b: 37) has noted, this registering of offence by the offended is itself a social action just as morally accountable, and so subject to evaluation, as the cause of the offence.

Before commencing these analyses, this chapter introduces and discusses three other themes which are serially relevant. They are a somewhat motley collection but are best discussed here in order to avoid repetition.

7.1 Speech act theory and developments

Many of the cases analysed in the succeeding chapters involve some judicially imposed sanction on the perpetrator of the offending utterance. In order for such a sanction to be imposed, a definitive assessment of the utterance has to be reached. This assessment is of what the utterance does – in other words, an assessment of its illocutionary force and possible consequent effects on those who hear or read it (Austin's perlocutions). Therefore, the use of speech act theory suggests itself. In speech act terms, then, the question becomes: what act does the utterance perform?

Scholars have identified numerous shortcomings of speech act theory. For a discussion of these, see Levinson (1981), Culpeper & Haugh (2014: 155–96) and below. They are difficulties which have led research in (im)politeness studies, despite the fact that the most enduringly influential work in this field (Brown & Levinson [1978] 1987) uses it as a basic theoretical building block, to more or less abandon it (see section 2.1). And even studies focusing on particular speech acts have found it more useful to define their purview in some way other than by means of the felicity conditions which speech act theory uses. A notable example is compliment and compliment responses. (e.g. Wierzbicka 1987: 201, Holmes 1988: 446, Herbert 1997, Mursy & Wilson 2001: 151).

The most basic and obvious shortcoming of classical speech act theory is its near-total abstraction from language in actual use. It assumes face-to-face communication via the spoken mode, involving solely S (= speaker) and H (= a single hearer), the latter always in the role of addressee. Moreover, it definitely assumes what Goffman (e.g. 1981: 129) calls an inaccessible encounter; that is, a situation in which nobody other than those who are ratified participants is privy to what is said. There are no bystanders. In order to overcome this limitation, Blanco Salgueiro (2010: 225–6) argues that speech act theory should take on board the existence of third parties, or what he calls 'illocutionary spectators'. However, such an accommodation only partly overcomes the theory's ignoring of the inevitable situatedness of all produced language. As Mey (2010: 2882) reminds us, "speech acts as such do not exist, unless they are situated" and there is of course a lot more to this situatedness than the possible presence of overhearers. He observes that speech acts

> both rely on, and actively create, the situation in which they are realized … speech as centered on an institutionalized social activity of a certain kind, such as teaching, visiting a doctor's office, participating in a tea-ceremony, and so on. In all such activities, speech is, in a way, prescribed: only certain utterances can be expected and will thus be acceptable; conversely, the participants in the situation, by their acceptance of their own and others' utterances, establish and reaffirm the social situation in which the utterances are uttered and in which they find themselves as utterers.
>
> (Mey 2001: 219)

As can be seen, Mey emphasizes the importance of activity type and its 'allowable contributions' (see section 2.3.1). His alternative theory of pragmatic acts (2001, 2006, 2010)

> does not explain human language use starting from the words uttered by a single, idealized speaker. Instead, it focuses on the interactional situation in which both speakers and hearers realize their aims. The explanatory movement is from the outside in, one could say, rather than from the inside out: instead of starting with what is said, and looking for what the words could mean, the situation where the words fit is invoked to explain what can be (and is actually being) said.
>
> (Mey 2001: 221)

This accords with the approach I take throughout the analyses in this book by starting these with a description of (all possible relevant aspects of) context (see section 2.3). An advantage of Mey's approach for analyses in this book is that it is not tied to single predications but can rather be less or more than these in scale. Support for this scalar perspective can be found from Norrick (2015), who shows how narratives can have the illocutionary force of expressives, the suggestion by Tsiplakou & Floros (2013) that texts have overall force akin to the illocutionary force of speech acts, and Al-Owaidi's (2018) successful use of the concept of different levels of speech act. In real situations, what has caused offence is more often than not a series of predications. With this perspective, having gone some way to accommodating both footing and activity type in a speech/pragmatic-act framework (as above), we can also accommodate the last of the three crucial aspects of context which I identified in section 2.3 – co-text.

Mey is doubtful about the possibility or value of an itemization of specific pragmatic acts because they can be identified only in their situations of use and every single situation is intrinsically unique. Typologizing is only possible with what he calls the 'pragmeme', these being 'generalised situational (pragmatic) acts' which function as part of our stored knowledge (in other words, rather like Terkourafi's version of 'frame'). In his approach

> the emphasis is not so much on ... felicity conditions for individual acts of speaking, but on general situational prototypes of acts that are capable of being executed in a particular situation or cluster of situations. Such a generalized pragmatic act is called a 'pragmeme' ... Common pragmemes include such pragmatic acting as found in invitations, bribes, co-optations, incitements, and so on – all depending on the situation through which they are defined.
>
> (Mey 2010: 2884)

However, if there is one situation for which speech act theory's notion of felicity conditions seems tailor-made, it is the kind examined in some of the cases in the succeeding chapters here. The determination of whether an utterance can be unequivocally identified as act X is exactly the same yes/no question which a court or tribunal has to address: does the utterance under examination have X illocutionary force, and not some other illocutionary force, as charged? In legal cases, one would assume, merely prototypical or characterizing definitions do not suffice – it is necessary to employ a heuristic of definition which is precise and discriminates one act from another. I therefore retain this notion in the analyses which follow, but couch it within context. And in the attempted definitions below here, I give H a rather more central role than in the Searlean account from which I start. Three kinds of act are relevant to the case studies in section 8.4 and Chapter 9 – threats, menaces and incitements.

7.1.1 Threats

There is a further coincidental convenience which recommends the use of speech act theory's felicity conditions to examine many of the cases in the succeeding chapters. These are acts which have offended because they have been interpreted as threatening some harm to their target. And it so happens that the paradigm example used by Searle (1969) in his original exposition of speech acts and their felicity conditions is the act of promising, which Blanco Salgueiro (2010) argues, Haigh et al. (2011) assume and Searle himself (1969: 58, 65) implies is closely related to that of issuing a threat. In both Searle's (1975) and Austin's ([1962] 1975) earlier typology, they are both commissives. A summary of Searle's conditions (1969: 57–61) for the "act of promising to have been successfully and non-defectively performed" (1969: 54)[1] can be rendered as follows:

- Propositional content condition: U predicates future act A of S
- Preparatory conditions: S and H regard A as good for H

                                           S and H believe S is not going to do A anyway
- Sincerity condition: S intends to do A
- Essential condition: U counts as S undertaking an obligation to do A (because S intends that it puts him/her under an obligation and that H recognizes this commitment)

– where U stands for utterance, S stands for the producer of that utterance and H stands for its recipient(s).

To derive from this set the felicity conditions for the act of threatening, all we obviously need do is change 'good' to 'bad' in the first preparatory condition. Perhaps that is all that is absolutely necessary. However, it has been shown that promises presuppose a greater degree of obligation than threats (Searle & Vanderveken 1985), one reason being that while the former entail the use of words, the latter do not – threatening can also be performed through physical gesture. Note also that, as Haigh et al. (2011: 423) observe, a threat which has just been issued can be strengthened in English by saying "That's not a threat, it's a promise", but one cannot conversely strengthen a promise by describing it as a threat. So it seems wise to alter the essential condition slightly, from S 'undertaking an obligation' to S 'making a commitment'. This alteration is intended to capture the fact that, whereas committing oneself to doing something good for H results in a sense of obligation which is external to S, the predication of doing something bad to H creates a sense of obligation which resides in S alone, since H would not want to hold S to what is predicated. As Peetz (1977: 580–1) points out, whereas a promise can be accepted or rejected, "it does not make sense to talk about rejecting or not rejecting a threat". And in fact, as Limberg (2009: 1378) demonstrates in a study of threats as a product of situation rather than of S performing a speech act, "it is important for a successful threat to make the addressee believe that the threatener intends to cause harm". In keeping with the greater emphasis on H, then, the essential condition can be phrased in terms of H's perception.

Sidelining the sincerity condition

Searle (1969: 62) avows that "insincere promises are promises nonetheless" as they still "involve[s] an expression of intention" and in doing so the speaker "take[s] responsibility for intending to do A". If that is true of promises, it is certainly true for threats, where a weaker sense of obligation obtains (see above). It is intuitively reasonable to hold with the claim that a promise or threat is indeed a promise or threat, whether sincere or not. One kind of support for this view can come from how the lexemes 'promise' and 'threat' are used in the English language. To remonstrate with someone for not following through with something which I understood them to have promised, I am likely to remind them they promised, perhaps even accuse them of never intending to do A, but I won't accuse them of lying, of only pretending to promise but not really promising at all. And, conversely, if I say "But I thought you promised", I raise the possibility that perhaps what they said was not really a promise at all, not that they promised insincerely. Likewise with threats: if I realize now that you never intended to carry out the horrible thing you said you were going to do to me, I will not revise my perception of what you said as not a threat at all; rather, I will assess your threat as that particular *kind* of threat which we call a 'bluff'. And the matter of bluffing, brings up another kind of support for this view of promises/threats as real regardless of the S's sincerity. A threat/promise does not have to *be* sincere to be successful; it only has to be *received as* sincere at the time (see Limberg 2009: 1378).

Searle's response to the matter of insincere promises is to revise his sincerity condition to read "S intends that the utterance will make him responsible for intending to do A". As with some others of Searle's concepts (see Thomas 1995: 98–9), there is a suspicion of circularity about this circumlocution. Moreover, it is not clear that it adds anything which is not already present in the essential condition. If one assumes that S becoming 'responsible for intending' refers to the perceptions of H, then it is simply another way of stating that, to be a threat, it needs to be received as making a commitment.

In the light of these observations, I suggest that for the successful performance of commissives (at least), a sincerity condition is not necessary.[2] The intentionality and the recognition of that intentionality which are basic to Searle's framework are still present in the essential condition, whereby a commissive act counts as some sort of commitment because S intends that it is received that way by H. A powerful argument in favour of this view can be extrapolated from Sanders'

(2013) convincing claim that, in addition to a speaker's personal communicative intention, there is also

> the communicative intention anyone from the speaker's and hearer's community would have in producing that utterance in that context, not just that speaker in particular … [which] rests on knowledge of discursive means to ends shared among members of a community that warrants (as opposed to causes) any such speaker as this one to produce that utterance to that hearer just then with the communicative intention that the utterance will have a certain speaker meaning.
>
> (Sanders 2013: 112–13)

It seems to me that this shared knowledge is exactly what is entailed in Searle's essential condition whereby an utterance "counts" as this or that speech act.

Accordingly, we can derive the felicity conditions which I will be applying to threats to read as follows:

- Propositional content condition: U predicates future act A of S
- Preparatory conditions: S and H regard A as bad for H
  S and H believe S is not going to do A anyway
- Essential condition: H recognizes U as S making a commitment to do A

7.1.2 Menacing espousals

In many of the cases in the succeeding chapters, however, the offending utterance is charged not with being a straight threat but rather with being 'menacing'. At first glance, it is difficult to see how such an utterance can be defined in terms of felicity conditions, as it is hard to construe it as having an illocutionary point. While, like threatening, it can be understood as the predication of something bad to happen to H, it is vaguer in two ways. First, while threats (unlike promises) can also be non-verbal, they at least connote speech, so that it is possible to issue a threat. But one cannot, in the English language anyway, issue 'a menace'. The second vagueness follows on from the first: one can threaten A but not menace A, only H. Menacing describes a type of behaviour which is vague in what it predicates. In addition, it foregrounds perlocution rather than illocution. Just as one could not delineate a speech act of convincing, but rather a speech act of asserting or advising or whatever which may lead to the result of H being convinced, so it would seem more logical to posit a speech act of asserting or threatening or advising or whatever which led to H feeling menaced.

Nevertheless, this – a message 'of a menacing character' – is the legal issue in several of the upcoming cases, so the legal presumption is that such an act can be identified with reference to some kind of norm rather than the emotional state of a particular target on a particular occasion. Help can come from Austin's original typology of speech acts, in which he includes under commissives "declarations or announcements of intentions which are not promises, and also rather vague things which we may call espousal" (Austin [1962] 1975: 152 – examples being 'intend', 'declare my intention' and 'espouse'). It might seem odd to categorize such acts as commissive because they do not seem to entail S committing him/herself to do anything. Rather, s/he expresses him/herself in such a way as to be interpreted as predictive of him/her performing, or implying the wish to perform, some future act. But at least such an act commits S to the prediction or the wish. I work, then, with the speech act of espousal of the menacing kind and below try to specify the felicity conditions for an act of 'menacing espousal'.

Propositional content condition

Words which may have a menacing effect can take just about any propositional form. As an example, here is Bob Dylan's irreverent retelling of a well-known biblical story (first stanza of 'Highway 61 Revisited'), which goes like this:[3]

1. Oh God said to Abraham, "Kill me a son"
2. Abe says, "Man, you must be puttin' me on"
3. God say, "No." Abe say, "What?"
4. God say, "You can do what you want Abe, but
5. The next time you see me comin' you better run"
6. Well Abe says, "Where do you want this killin' done?"
7. God says, "Out on Highway 61."

This propositional content of God's utterance in line 5 is simply 'when you see me, you run'; that is, a future act not of S but of H. On the surface, the illocutionary force is one of advice, and indeed on this surface it conforms to all Searle's (1969: 67) conditions for the successful performance of that speech act. However, in its co-text it is actually an indirect speech act whose true illocutionary force can be derived from Grice's (1975) maxims. The giving of advice in this context is a flout of the maxim of relation: God has issued a directive (line 1) and Abe has questioned his sincerity in issuing it (line 2), thereby indicating he does not intend to comply with it; why would God then, instead of saying something relevant to Abe's query, such as insisting on the sincerity of the directive or simply repeating it in a more emphatic manner, proceed to give Abe advice about what to do the next time they encounter each other? To make this act of advising relevant to their dialogue, we have to draw the inference that it is given in the light of Abe's refusal to comply with the directive. Then, the content of the advice – to run – affords a further inference. The most likely reason for breaking into a run when you encounter someone is to avoid that person; that is, running here equals running away. And the only logical reason for taking such immediate and drastic action to avoid that person is to avoid harm of some kind. Through these means, we can infer that God intends to do Abe harm. (Given the stark power asymmetry obtaining in this relationship, it is not surprising that Abe promptly indicates compliance in line 6.)

What we have in this proposition is an implicated, rather than stated, future act of S, which is not specified. It is exactly this kind of vague presentiment of harm to befall H at the hands of S which I think can be understood as menacing. In the example, it was performed through the speech act of advising, as in English it often can be (e.g. "You'd better watch your back"). But in the appropriate context it can just as well be performed through a prediction ("You're gonna get what's coming to you"), an explanation for an expressive ("I hope there's a hospital nearby, 'cos you're going to need one"), an expressive itself ("Nice business you got here. Shame if something were to happen to it"[4]) or even a straightforward assertion ("I know where you live"). Both the indirectness and the vagueness of the propositional content are necessary: if one is missing, it becomes a threat (provided, of course, that the other conditions for a threat are met).

Preparatory conditions

The same preconditions hold as for a threat: S and H must believe that the implicated act, albeit of unspecified nature, is bad for H and that it is not going to happen in the normal course of events. But here we have to make an addition. In her presentation of Searle's conditions for a successful promise, Thomas (1995: 94) specifies as a preparatory condition the belief of S in his/her ability to do A. Clearly, this belief is necessary for a proper promise. Searle, however, regards it as subsumed under the sincerity condition because "the proposition that he intends to do it entails that he thinks it is possible to do it". Above, I have followed Searle, and when I got rid of the sincerity condition, I transferred this belief in S's ability to the essential condition which specified that H receive U as S committing himself to A. But the essential condition this time contains no such commitment (see below), so we need a precondition here that there is a belief that S is at least possibly capable of doing that kind of act A. However, for H to feel menaced, it matters little whether S believes he can do that (kind of) act. But it *does* matter that H believes that A is at least feasible. We therefore arrive at the additional condition: *H believes S might be able to do A.*[5]

Essential condition

No commitment is involved in what S says. As suggested above, the essence of this kind of utterance is a vague presentiment of harm to befall H. And for it to be successful it is merely necessary that H recognize it as such; that is, as indicating that S may have the wish to do A and therefore suggestive of a threat (because it is a recognizable trope) so that, the other conditions being fulfilled, s/he feels menaced.

Sincerity condition as optional extra

From the point of view of effects, if someone has driven dangerously, what transparently matters is not whether they intended to do so but the possible harmful effects of doing so. Their driving may be described as menacing. Just so with language; what matters is not whether S intends to menace H but whether the effect of their words is to do so. However, one possible aspect of the feeling of being menaced is the inference that S intends to menace, or at least have some effect on, H. Stalking is a paradigm example. All stalking has a menacing effect and the intention is not required in order to have this effect. Some stalkers may intend to menace their victims and some may not. But the stalkee who perceives or even suspects such an intention feels that much *more* menaced. From the point of view of intended perlocution then, this condition must be seen as an optional extra.

I arrive in the light of the above discussion at the following conditions for the performance of a menacing espousal:

Propositional content condition:	U implicates future type of act (A) by S
Preparatory conditions:	S and H believe A is bad for H (same as above)
	A is not going to happen anyway (same as above)
	H believes S might be able to do A
Essential condition:	H recognizes U as suggestive of a threat and so feels frightened
Optional booster (sincerity):	H perceives S as intending to menace H

7.1.3 Incitements

An incitement has a minimum of three participants: someone to do the inciting (S), someone to be incited (H) and a target (who may or may not be privy to the act and therefore a different H – see below). This act is of course a kind of directive. It attempts to get H to do something. But it is not simply a request because it is a very specific kind of something – to a third party. So its propositional content condition has to include all three. Two of the preparatory conditions, the negative outcome for the victim and the absence of inevitability, are identical to those for threats and menacing espousals. The third, that of ability, is slightly different in that participants' belief is not a factor. It only matters that, relatively objectively, H can feasibly perform the proposed act. (Unless you are a very particular person, it is not felicitous for me to direct you to explode a nuclear device over England.) The intention of S is unimportant for incitements. As we will see in the cases in the following chapters, people often hammer out relatively unconsidered (and certainly, it turns out, ill-considered) words on their various technical devices. What matters, especially for incitement, is how they are interpreted. The act can count as incitement whenever H perceives it as encouragement to perform the proposed act, regardless of H's perception of S's intention. However, incitement can also be relatively vague. Like the menacing espousal, the proposed act may be interpreted non-literally as standing for a type of act represented by the specific propositional content. Accordingly, I arrive at the following conditions:

Propositional content condition:	U predicates future act A of H on a target (T)
Preparatory conditions:	S and H believe A is bad for T
	H is not going to do A anyway
	H is able to do A
Essential condition:	H perceives U as encouragement to do A or something similar

7.1.4 The trouble with H

The above definitions have done little to overcome the woeful underspecification of this character known as H in classical speech act theory. As we know (see section 2.3.2), there can be many different kinds of H. It is not enough to admit that 'H' could designate a plurality of recipients of the utterance. The cases examined in the subsequent chapters run into two problems in this respect. The first problem is that they feature participants who have a number of different roles relative to the offending utterance, not just addressed participants but also others who are easily able to 'hear'. These participants sometimes seem clearly ratified and at other times less clearly so. Some are obviously in a bystander role, sometimes in an overhearer position, but others appear to be eavesdroppers. It is sometimes not even easy to determine who is participant and who is not. Presumably, the individual target of incitement does not feel menaced if s/he doesn't 'hear' the offending utterance. Can we deem an utterance menacing if its target doesn't feel menaced?

The various Hs have different reactions to the utterance under scrutiny, both of degree and kind. Some may feel very menaced indeed, others only diffusely so or not at all, perhaps even evincing a positive response to the purportedly offending utterance. This is the second problem: whose interpretation is to count and be accorded the greater weight? I have been unable to find a solution to these problems at an abstract level, attesting to the limitations of speech act theory and/or my own. Instead, in the following chapters, I attempt ad hoc solutions case by case.

7.2 Technology-mediated communication[6]

Almost all of the cases analysed in the following chapters involve utterances which have been either animated through some kind of technological mediation (hereafter TMC) or, if not, made publicly accessible that way. Whether this fact points to the nature of such communication as more vulnerable to the causing of offence than embodied face-to-face interaction is a moot point. Certainly, quite a large body of scholarship in (specifically) digital communication has pointed that way. It is by now almost a truism that a marked amount of acrimony is to be found in such media. This phenomenon has been investigated empirically (e.g. Avgerinakou 2003, Nishimura 2010) and explanatory features have been suggested (e.g. Graham 2007, 2008, O'Driscoll 2013), the most common among which are lack of prosody or paralinguistic cues, indeterminate participation structure and relative anonymity. The apparent novelty of digital media – their obvious differences from more conventional media – has led to attempts to itemize some of their conditions of communication (e.g. Herring 2007). On the other hand, there are observations that actually communication by these means is not really all that special and that its distinctiveness may have been overemphasized (see Graham 2019: 311–13 for a discussion). It is possible that the preponderance of TMC cases in the following chapters is more a reflection of their accessibility than anything else.

There is, however, no doubt that the problems around participation framework identified in the previous subsection are exacerbated in such media and many attempts have been made to address them. (See Chovanec & Dynel 2015 for an excellent review.) They surface in several of the cases examined. A crucial indeterminacy in this respect is whether bystanders are involved. On the one hand, the ability of the sender in some forms of TMC, most obviously email (see sections 8.1, 8.2, 10.2 and 11.2), to restrict who has immediate access to his/her message, and their resemblance to their close historical forerunner of canonically private written correspondence, suggests they are essentially private. On the other hand, the possibility of subsequent widespread dissemination and their resemblance to other, obviously accessible forms of TMC suggest they are public.

This tension brings up three resulting features which are particularly relevant for this study. One relates to the feature which Herring (2007) calls 'persistence' and Graham & Hardaker (2017: 789–90) call 'longevity'. There is often a record of offensive acts that can be revisited by the offended party. A Twitter user, for example, can look at a comment that offended them over and over again at the push of a button. Prior to the advent of digital communication, most offending utterances were spoken and embodied, so that this possibility for them to repeat and thereby to 'stick' in the mind of the offended person was not available. The second such feature (which also involves persistence) is what I have called (O'Driscoll 2013: 372) 'ease of expedition'. With rapid, widespread forwarding, retweeting and the like, many more people can be offended than the original addressee, and offence can be taken by others on the original, or even an imaginary, target's behalf.[7] Persistence is also involved here. A sender may delete a message once they realize it has caused offence, but by the time they do so, the chances are that it has been disseminated beyond the original intended participatory group. The third such feature relates to the similarities of TMC to spoken interaction – its comparative ease of delivery, in small chunks, thereby imitating a 'conversation'. This feature encourages participants to forget that the clues of face-to-face interaction are absent. They can fall into the trap of composing their discourse as if this were the case, taking less care than they would have done with traditional written correspondence.

A final feature which I suggest may have indirect relevance to the apparent ease with which cases of offence online can be found is identified by Graham & Hardaker (2017: 790–1). They note that

> Many (perhaps most?) digital media show a host of tools to declare feelings towards others' behaviour – it is encoded into the media themselves via spam filters, Terms of Service, blocks, and 'report abuse' buttons, etc. There are also ways to indicate positive reactions such as 'Like', 'Favourite' and 'Share' buttons. This establishes a sub-text that (im)politeness is something that can (and perhaps should) be constantly not just evaluated, but also *declared* in digital interaction. While notions of (im)politeness are certainly ever-present in f-t-f [face-to-face] interactions, when interacting f-t-f we are not staring at buttons asking us to explicitly share our evaluation of that (im)politeness during each interaction.

My definition of offensive language (see section 2.1.1) has been careful to distinguish between the taking of offence at an utterance and the negative attitude towards it which constitutes Culpeper's definition of impoliteness, with the former being just one part of the latter. And I have conceptualized the expression of this negative attitude as a post-facto rationalization of the offended reaction. However, the above quote points to the possibility that the conditions of digital communication encourage the conflation of the felt experience of offence and the rationalization of this experience through an assessment. Users are encouraged to jump straight to the latter, so that the taking of offence and the taking *up* of offence (i.e. an expressed negative evaluation) become the same thing. I have no evidence from my data that these evaluative features of the structure of digital media were ever a factor, or even that they existed in the particular media from which I drew the data. But it is nevertheless possible that some cases involved habitual users of a wide variety of digital media who have thus become habituated to this taking up of offence. I suggest the cases examined in sections 10.2.1 and 11.2 as candidates.

7.3 Non-seriousness

Many of the offending utterances examined in the following chapters have claims to non-seriousness. That is, a defence of the offender was, may have been or could have been that the propositional content of the utterance was not 'meant' literally, and that therefore the offended person or organization has misinterpreted it. But there are many kinds of non-seriousness. For instance, some cases (those examined in Chapter 9) can claim to be non-serious in that they are exaggerations or metaphors employed to express emotion or attitude. (See also the politician–journalist encounter in section 6.2.) The offending remark examined in section 8.3 and the test item examined in 10.2.2 can claim to be part of a practice known as 'banter' by their practitioners; that is, the practice of repeated teasing. Banter in its classical sense is simply mock insulting for the purpose of showing solidarity (see Leech 1983: 144) and/or more general socialization within a group (see Culpeper et al. 2017c: 329). There is an example of the former in section 8.1. But this word seems to be the most popular in general parlance in modern Britain to denote, by its practitioners to excuse, almost all kinds of non-seriousness. It is even used by a judge to describe the outpouring of emotion in the purportedly offending tweet examined in section 9.2. An example of a tease, on the other hand, can be found in the colleagues' conversation in section 10.2.2. Teasing might also be used to describe the offending utterance in section 8.4, one possible explanation for which is that the offender was trying to flirt, which is a kind of mock challenging. In the analyses which follow, I use the word teasing in its everyday sense to denote an attempt at playful (i.e. non-serious) provocation, banter in the classical sense as above and 'banter' (i.e. with quote marks) to denote the practice of repeated teasing.

What these instances have in common is that they are not simply falsehoods. That is, they are not simply the opposite of serious. They cannot be read as intending the opposite of, or negating, what is made explicit. (Only the clearly mock insult in section 8.1 could be interpreted this way, and even here there is evidence that the mock outrage of which it is part is not entirely non-serious.) They are what Culpeper et al. (2017c), in the context of the interpersonal significance of such utterances, call mixed messages. They are, in other words, not just contradictory nonsense but rather have been uttered to achieve something. Culpeper et al. (2017c: 342–4) identify three non-mutually exclusive functions of non-seriousness: expressive, instrumental and interpersonal. One way of approaching an understanding of the offensiveness of many of the cases is to see each as a question of whether it is merely expressive and/or interpersonal or whether there is also an instrumental element, this last being the offending element. For instance, are the apparent invitations to violence examined in section 9.1 merely a letting off of steam and/or an attempt to bond with like-minded people, or do they also intend to have an effect on their targets? Is the remark made by the football manager in section 8.4 just a clumsy attempt at bonding or does it instead or also have a substantive effect on future behaviour? The significance for offensiveness of non-seriousness is also that it can be used as a mask for genuine hostility, especially in a community or society which places a high value on people having a 'sense of humour'. This kind of double bluff can be witnessed as a factor in many of the cases examined in the following chapters.

Offences against the person

The offending utterances and fallout from them examined in this chapter are cases of personal disparagement. They can be placed in increasing order of substantive consequence. The first caused its addressee to take personal offence and led to a temporary hiccough in the relationship between producer and addressee. But it was no more than that; an apology from the producer smoothed things over. The second caused a participant who was its producer's workplace superior to take offence, partly on behalf of another participant and partly on behalf of the organization of which he was leader. The superior issued an informal reprimand to its producer. Again, an apology sufficed to 'settle' the matter. The third caused severe distress to its addressee and was a factor in its producer eventually being dismissed from his post. The fourth, while causing no distress to its addressee, may have caused some uneasiness among thousands of people and led to its producer being fined £30,000. The offending utterances also increase in opacity. The trigger for offence in the first is transparent, that in the second slightly ambiguous, those in the third and fourth require a deal of excavation.

8.1 Bastard

The surface cause of offence being taken in this case is simple. In an email, someone called someone else a bastard and the someone else didn't like it. The interest is in the fact that the producer of this offending utterance did not intend it to be offensive. The focus of analysis here, then, is on the cause of the misunderstanding.

8.1.1 Background situation

At the time of the email thread between Bill and Robin shown below, they had known each other for about six months as working colleagues in a university department. During this time, though they had not worked on any projects together, they had partaken of numerous face-to-face encounters of an unstructured kind. Three or four times a day there were brief 1:1 encounters just outside the faculty building when they went for a cigarette. Occasionally, there were longer sessions in a pub. Their conversation was typically free-ranging, with research and other work interests as the most frequent topics. Its style had a tendency to indexical masculinity, a somewhat 'bloke-ish' camaraderie as the only smokers in the department. Bill had recently finished his temporary role in the department but was still in contact with several of its members.

8.1.2 The data

In the thread presented below, words inside square brackets are summary glosses of what was said.

Message 1: Bill to Robin
How are things?
[request for references to published work »> chat]
Note also my failure to address you in this message. It's cos I found myself hesitating
– Robin or Rob? Not sure why – I don't remember hesitating face-to-face. Maybe it's the different medium. Anyway, please put me right – and apologies for any wrong appellations in the past (names are important).
Best
Bill

Message 2: Robin to Bill
Hi Billy
Rob or Robin I don't mind. Actually, I tend to refer to myself as Rob when I'm a musician
and Robin when I'm a writer but what's in a name? Loads actually!
[chat »> promise to send references soon]
Hope you're well in Sussex and that you're missing us terribly
Rob...(insert preference)

Message 3: Bill to Robin

In which Bill responded by interspersing comments inside Robin's message in a different coloured font (spelling errors have not been corrected).

Hi Billy

I hope that's a joke. If not, you've solved the problem for me. I'll just call you Bastard!

I'm from London, not the fucking Gorbals (the only place where Billy sounds OK).

Rob or Robin I don't mind. Actually, I tend to refer to myself as Rob when I'm a musician and Robin when I'm a writer but what's in a name? Loads actually!

Interesttingly, I have a similar affectation to yours – I'm Bill in academic articles but have been William in books for EFL students. Anyway, thanks, I'll just wait and see what comes out of my mouth next time we meet

[chat »> promise to send references soon]

Hope you're well in Sussex and that you're missing us terribly

Rob...[insert preference]

[assent that he is missing them »> short narrative about a recent domestic mishap]

See you at Harriet's conference?

Bill [non negotiable]

Message 4: Robin to Bill

Sorry Bill, I have to be honest with you – I'm not sure how to take your response below. I feel it's a little over the top, even if intended humorously.

[list of the requested references provided]

Hope this is of use to you.

Robin

8.1.3 Analysis

Message 4 begins with a conventionalized formula ("have to be honest with you") for warning that a negative appraisal of something connected with the recipient is to follow. It then explicitly registers interpersonal disquiet ("not sure how to take") and criticism ("over the top") which Robin 'feels'. These predications, together with the total absence of the chat which has been a feature of the previous messages, make it clear that offence has been taken.

Although it is not explicitly identified (there is just a reference to "your response"), it is clear that the offending utterance here is "I'll just call you Bastard". Note that this is not *exactly* an instance of a 'personalized negative vocative', one of Culpeper's (2011: 133–7) insult type of conventionalized impoliteness formulae for the English language. Rather, it is a *threat* to employ such a vocative ("If not ... I shall"). Bill must have assumed that this conditional use of the insult, plus the fairly lengthy chat in message 3 which followed his outraged and retaliatory reaction to being addressed as "Billy", plus the implied wish that they meet again soon (at that conference), was enough to make it clear that it was *mock* outrage and *mock* retaliation. He was probably encouraged in this fantasy by their interactional history (see above), which constituted his frame for their spates of interaction, and the features of email which mimic face-to-face interaction (see section 7.2). But it turned out *not* to be enough. After all, had he not asserted in message 1 that names were important?

The offending utterance in this case, as with several to be examined in this and following chapters, was issued through TMC. In section 7.2, I have picked out a few of the factors which seem to be involved across most of these. Operating in this case are a number of particular factors which make this medium more vulnerable to sociopragmatic failure, and therefore more likely to engender offence than embodied, face-to-face interaction. (1) The disembodied nature of communication means that the recipient has no access to prosodic and visual clues about the producer's intentions and footings. (2) The asynchronous delivery by one-way transmission means that the producer cannot react to the recipient's *ongoing* reception and so cannot be reined in by back-channel cues. Bill gets no sign of Robin's immediate reaction to encountering "I'll just call you Bastard" and feels free to embellish extravagantly ("… not the fucking Gorbals"). (3) The 'plan-ability' (Merrison et al. 2012: 1081) of this mode of transmission encourages Bill to imagine himself in a different situation (e.g. having a ciggie on the balcony at work), where features (1) and (2) would not apply. (4) So too does the feature of email which allows the inserting of responses into a received message, aping conversational turn-taking, of which he avails himself in message 3. All these facilitate a false sense of interpretative security.

If this exchange had taken place face to face (on the balcony at work as Bill seems to have imagined), it is likely that no offence would have been taken – or at least that if it had, Bill could have dispelled it in a second. There, essentially the same words uttered in reaction to Robin's "Hi Billy" greeting, being uttered in concert with all the non-verbal forms of communication possible (see Chapter 7), would have conveyed that (1) Bill prefers not to be called Billy but that (2) he places only a limited importance on this preference and in any case is confident of Robin's goodwill so that (3) he is not really offended by Robin's use of this address form now and that therefore (4) his stated intention to address him henceforth as "Bastard" is a blatant flout of the maxim of quality and should be interpreted as an instance of banter, so (5) Robin should not feel insulted by this insulting appellation and indeed (6) can read his use of it, and the taboo adjective in a succeeding phrase, as an indication of their comradeship. After all, it is generally understood, and has long been recognized in scholarship (e.g. Daly et al. 2004, Mills 2003: 140–1), that such crudeness and rudeness are "indices of … intimate interaction" (Jefferson et al. 1987: 160). But without the immediate auditory and visual clues, these intentions and footings could not be conveyed – Robin found himself looking at an almost-bald insult. The modalities of email, together with their interpersonal history, seem to have encouraged Bill to overlook this fact. And offence was, one might judge understandably, taken. (Bill later sent an apologetic explanation in which he confessed to "a tendency to adopt this rather Australian kind of dig-in-the-ribs joshery" and describing his 'Bastard' as "a clumsy attempt at matiness". The apology was accepted.)

Of course, the blame for this case of offence cannot be laid entirely at the door of email and the failure of Bill to adapt to its features. (Perhaps it would have been possible to have accompanied the same words with emojis and thereby avoid giving offence.) It appears that he also misconstrued the nature of his relationship with Robin and/or Robin's general stance. After all, Robin's response in message 4 recognizes that Billy's 'Bastard' might have been "intended humorously" but still registers the taking of offence. There is also a possibility of a cross-cultural mismatch contributing to the offence taken. Millwood-Hargrave's survey of offensive words (see Chapter 3) found that 'bastard' was rated as significantly more offensive by people in the north of England than by people in the south of England (2000: 11). Robin is from the north of England, Bill from the south. If this is indeed a factor in the offence taken, it is an additional aspect of Bill being led into a false sense of interpretative security. In their interpersonal history, they had communicated freely and fluently, leading Bill to assume a perfect match of linguistic understandings. As such, this mismatch would serve as a micro-example of the point made by Garcia & Otheguy (1989: 2) that the spread of English around the world "has created a false sense of mutual intelligibility" among people from different cultures. These additional possible explanations for the offence taken only emphasize the general messiness of communication, due in large part to its imperfect communicators (highlighted by Kecskés 2010). And they serve as a first example of the fact that actual cases of offence being caused are radically situational.

8.2 Crap

The incident recounted below illustrates once again the remarkable offensive power of mere form – especially remarkable here as in this case the use of a mildly taboo word is apparently rated more offensive than a pejorative dismissal of another participant's view. This case also involves an email thread. This time the institutional statuses of the offender and offendee are not the same, so that the issue of institutionally supported power is in play.

8.2.1 Background context

The thread below took place between members of staff of a British university. It concerns the progress of postgraduate research students. Study at this level consists essentially of working towards a single end product – a master's dissertation or a doctoral thesis – under the guidance of a designated supervisor. There are no taught courses to pass. However, it is understood that there should be audits along the way, to ensure that there is a realistic possibility of the student producing a satisfactory end product within the envisaged time-frame. Recently, in response to increasing numbers of postgraduate research students, the university's central authorities have been taking a more active role in these auditing procedures, and in monitoring and regulating these students' progress generally.

8.2.2 Immediate context

The university's research office has sent an email message to all postgraduate research students telling them that if they are late in 'completing an assessment' or 'active research', they have to fill in a special form and submit this to 'your School Research Office' within a specified period of time. This message has now been forwarded by the research administrator of one School to all research supervisors in that School.

   On the same day, a series of messages are sent by various supervisors in that School to the same set of recipients. All comment negatively on this newly instituted procedure, which is seen as "quite undergrad-ish", as wasting students' time, diverting their attention from their main focus (their research), and as undermining the authority of supervisors and their relationship with their research students. Suggestions are made that the matter be taken up at a high level within the university. The next day, Pete, a supervisor who has so far not contributed to the discussion, writes to all recipients to add his opinion on the matter (message 1 below). Four hours later, the Dean (= Head) of the School sends message 2 addressed to Pete alone which takes issue with the manner of Pete's contribution. A further exchange between Pete and the Dean ensues (messages 3 and 4).

8.2.3 The data

Message 1: Pete to all participants in the discussion

I wholeheartedly agree with you all. My students spend an inordinate amount of time and head space stressing over this sort of crap – instead of actually getting on with their research!

Message 2: Dean to Pete (uniquely)

Dear Pete,

Use of the word 'crap' in this context is entirely unnecessary and inappropriate. Please can you make sure in contributing to work discussions you do so in ways which show the basics of courtesy to those whose decisions you take issue with.

Message 3: Pete to Dean (uniquely)

So sorry about this, [first name of Dean],

I did not mean to be rude to anyone. I confess I was not aware that those who made this decision were party to this email thread. This lack of awareness was very careless of me. I will be more careful in the future and do all I can to show basic courtesy.

I do apologise.

Message 4: Dean to Pete (uniquely)

Thanks for the apology, Pete,

I wouldn't agree that just because someone isn't themselves directly party to an email exchange, that would give carte blanche to broadcast this sort of comment across half of the academic staff of the School.

But as you'll have gathered, always worth remembering that [full name of a senior university manager] is a member of several of the [name of School] lists because

of his work in [name of subject areas], including this one.

I appreciate the promise to be careful in future.

8.2.4 Analysis

The Dean's first sentence in message 2 is a metapragmatic comment asserting that the form 'crap' could have ("unnecessary") and should have ("inappropriate") been avoided. In the context of this criticism, the directive in the second sentence that Pete contribute "in ways which show the basics of courtesy" generates the implicature that Pete, in employing this word, has failed to do so.

Pete's response in message 3 indicates that he interpreted this criticism together with the polite-but-direct formulation of the directive as also a reprimand from a workplace superior. Accordingly, he thought it prudent to respond with message 3. The opening apology here, when taken with the following sentence, shows recognition of the Dean's imputation of his discourtesy. In mitigation, it pleads lack of intention and previous ignorance that the victims of his discourtesy were participants in the discussion, a role which has been implied by the Dean's enjoining him to show "courtesy *to*" (my italics) people with whom he disagrees. That is, it assumes that the infraction which the apology addresses arose because the person or people about whose decisions Pete's earlier message has been dismissive ("this sort of crap") are participants in the email discussion. So, while leaving open the question of whether he intended to be rude *about* someone, this earlier message disavows the intention to be rude *to* anyone.

The Dean's response in message 4 accepts both the apology and the promise from Pete. However, it takes issue with the relevance of Pete's excuse that he had been ignorant of the participation, as a copied-in recipient of the email thread, of anyone responsible for the decision. Although the second sentence of message 4 appears to recognize that the participation status of the target of disparagement is a factor, it argues that "this sort of comment", in the context of this large number of participants, many of whom may know the identity of this person, is unsuitable even when that person is not a participant.

The discourtesy, then, is "this sort of comment" itself. What is 'this sort'? Like the other contributions to the email thread, message 1 is vehemently negative about the new procedure. None of these others provoked a reprimand, so it cannot be simply the taking of this stance. Pete's contribution is different, though; while the other contributions explicitly predicated their opposition to the procedure, Pete's only refers to it, his opposition being presupposed within a noun phrase ("this sort of crap"). It is possible that this dismissiveness incurred the displeasure of the Dean: perhaps communications from the top should be taken more seriously. But the main reason is clearly the manner of the dismissiveness – the use of the word 'crap'. That is what the Dean singles out in his original reprimand.

We cannot know whether a reprimand would have been elicited if Pete had instead referred to "this sort of rubbish/nonsense/idiocy", a speculation which is indicative of the problems of pinning down exactly what it is that is found offensive on particular occasions. It is in the nature of taboo speech that the precise feature (form? reference? predication?) is rarely identified, and still more rarely articulated, by those who take offence. It's taboo, so it must be cast aside immediately, without examination. What we do know is that Pete's "this sort of crap" was deemed unseemly in the context of a discussion among fifteen or so professionals in a workplace environment. As the leader of this section of a particular workplace (a university), the Dean chose to take offence at a disparaging reference (which included a mildly taboo word) to a procedure devised by a central figure in the workplace as a whole. In the sense that, as message 4 asserts, it was the language used for the reference, rather than the (possible) personal affront to the procedure's deviser, which was the main infraction, this is not a case of personal affront at all. However, as figurehead of this section of the workplace as a whole, the Dean took offence on behalf of this section – it was a personal affront to the figurehead. To do nothing, therefore, would have in his view amounted to damage to his reputation as a person able to fulfil that role and would have made his professional face vulnerable in future interaction. We see here an example of how a person in this kind of role feels entitled to police discourse.

The Dean's description of the opinion being 'broadcast' in his last message is significant. It illustrates a different feature of email communication from those identified in the 'bastard' case above which makes this medium vulnerable to the causing of offence: its frequently indeterminate participation framework. (In fact, Pete had not known who was responsible for the instituting of this new procedure when he wrote message 1. He only learns this when message 4 provides a name.) It is not just that in practice a participant making a contribution to a thread does not always take account of the identity of all the other participants (so that sometimes a disparaging comment about a person can be mistakenly sent to that person); it is also that whatever is sent can be so easily forwarded in toto to new recipients. It is this feature which the Dean must have had in mind when describing Pete's comment as being 'broadcast'; he chose to interpret this encounter (this email thread) as an accessible one. This issue of breadth of and different understandings of participation is raised more than once in the cases examined in succeeding chapters.

8.3 Ebola

In the 'crap' case above, offence was taken at a disparaging reference which could be interpreted as attaching to an individual, but in particular because the reference contained a taboo word. This next case is one which exemplifies the fact that, just as taboo language use may not cause offence, an utterance can be very offensive even when it contains neither taboo language nor any explicit negative attribution of its addressee.

8.3.1 Context

The data below is an extract from a transcript of an interview with Eni Aluko, who until recently had been a regular member of the women's England football team. It was published in a national British newspaper in August 2017.[1] Aluko is talking in the context of complaints which she had made a year earlier to the English Football Association about bullying and discrimination from the team manager, Mark Sampson. The encounter she describes here is just one of many incidents involving Sampson. (Sampson was dismissed from his post a month after this interview. At first, the FA insisted that his dismissal did not concern the claims made by Aluko. However, a month later, it apologized to her.)

8.3.2 The data

We were in the hotel before the Germany game [in November 2014]. Everybody was excited. It was a big game. On the wall there was a list of the family and friends who were coming to watch us and I just happened to be next to Mark. He asked me if I had anyone who would be there and I said I had family coming over from Nigeria. 'Oh,' he said. 'Nigeria? Make sure they don't bring Ebola with them.'

I remember laughing but in a very nervous way. I went back to my room and I was really upset. It might have been easier to take if it was about me alone. Lots of things had been said about me over those two years but this was about my family.

8.3.3 Analysis

Clearly, Sampson's remark was experienced as very personally offensive. Aluko was "really upset". Why? The mere fact of linking her family's country of domicile with a terrible disease may in itself have been felt as only mildly offensive – some countries are known to be vulnerable to certain infectious diseases. The high degree of offence caused was that he chose to articulate this association of 'Nigeria' and 'Ebola' as a response *in this context*.

Two aspects to the offensiveness may be detected. One is interactive. The mood of the gathering is positive. The participants are all "excited" and the list of family and friends on display allows an orientation to the personal. Sampson's enquiry to Aluko, in which he takes a line of personal interest, is perfectly in keeping with this context. Accordingly, she responds with the relevant information.

Given this trajectory of talk, the default expectation would be that Sampson's next turn will sustain his line of personal interest. This could have been sustained, for example, by exclaiming what a long way her relatives were travelling, which would have enhanced the occupational aspect of Aluko's face by foregrounding the fact that there are people who are prepared to go to a lot of effort to watch her play. Alternatively, he could have displayed interest in her relatives' circumstances – how they were getting to Germany, how long they were staying, where they were staying. Or, if he did not wish to continue with this topic of conversation, or even the encounter itself, he could at least have suggested, either to Aluko herself or more generally to the other players present, that Aluko's visitors be added to the list on the wall.

His Ebola remark, however, effectively forecloses any of these possibilities. Indeed, it makes any kind of continuation difficult. Sampson has abandoned the line he was taking. He has played an interactive trick on Aluko. She was presumably happy that she was able to respond to his enquiry in the affirmative, thereby supporting her positive face in two respects, presenting herself both as someone in the same position as other members of the team who have people coming to watch them play and also more generally as someone who is not alone in the world. But Sampson's remark undermines these face claims. In Goffman's terms ([1955] 1967a: 8), she has been wrong-faced, displayed as interactively incompetent.

The second aspect of the offensiveness in Sampson's remark is directly personal. Sampson associates people connected to Aluko (her relatives) with something deeply unpleasant – and thus associates Aluko herself with this unpleasantness. This attack on her face is exacerbated by three features of the utterance which have a positive-face-affronting effect by implying a general lack of interest in and/or knowledge of Aluko and her world. Firstly, ignorance of her personal background is suggested by the exclamation and question intonation in "Oh, Nigeria?", as if he is surprised she has relatives there. Secondly, his remark betrays ignorance of a part of the world with which Aluko is associated. The Ebola outbreak at that time was mainly confined to three countries some one thousand miles to the west of Nigeria.[2] Thirdly, there is the marked lack of interest in Aluko's relatives as people. He is not interested in them but only in the dangers he imagines they could pose. All these features of his attitude are displayed in an encounter accessible to Aluko's teammates, thus positioning her as a relative outsider and thus significantly damaging her positive face.

It may be objected at this point that Sampson's remark was not 'serious'. After all, he cannot really have been instructing Aluko to conduct a health check on the visiting members of her family. It could be interpreted as 'banter', a practice that is known to be widespread in some British sporting milieu, as witnessed by numerous websites explicitly dedicated to it. The established style of interaction in some sporting communities involves playful insults and 'put-downs' among teammates as the norm. It is apparently particularly entrenched in football and is often regarded as an essential part of team cohesion,[3] presumably on the grounds of a 'tall-poppy' discourse – for a team to function well, no single member must get above themselves, so they must be cut down to size by this means. Indeed, the value of 'banter' for this purpose is mentioned by Aluko herself elsewhere in the interview. If such a style was the norm in *this* community of practice, it may be argued that the solicitous or supportive responses suggested as alternatives above would simply not have been politic, and that the wrong-facing of Aluko was just an expected part of the general cut-and-thrust of interaction. Her laughter in response to Sampson's remark suggests she was familiar with the practice of 'banter'. At such a juncture, it was socially appropriate and maintains her own face to some degree by indicating that she can 'live' with this style of interaction. In this view, the fact that Aluko was so 'upset' by Sampson's remark indicates a failure to bond.

However, this argument does not hold water. For one thing, there is the aspect of power here. For the competitive, aggressive style of interaction to function as a social lubricant, its practitioners need to be of equal status. The manager of a football team, the person in charge who decides whether a player will be picked to play or not and who instructs players how to play, is of starkly higher status than all the players. For him or her to adopt this aggressive style was, in the rosiest possible interpretation, a misguided attempt to be 'one of the gang'. Secondly, if just plain 'banter' had been Sampson's aim, there are plenty of teasing, less face-attacking alternatives available: for example, mock warning about the responsibility laid on her shoulders by her relatives' presence ("You'd better score a hat-trick to make it worth their while coming all this way") or mock competitive complaint ("Nobody's ever travelled that far for me"), even goading ("Ooh, you *are* an important person, aren't you?"). But Sampson goes for a far more socially excluding remark. In any case – and this is the third reason why the banter argument doesn't work here – there is no evidence that such a style was the norm in this particular group in this particular kind of situation. 'Banter' is especially associated with male sporting teams and the general excitement mentioned by Aluko and the list of family and friends on the wall testify to a straightforwardly positive and supportive tenor of the situation.

Of course, the degree of offence which people take at a particular utterance cannot be explained entirely by features of the utterance itself, which is often merely the trigger. It is a repeated theme of the analyses in this book that both immediate and background context need to be taken into account. In this case, Aluko's upset was presumably the greater because she experienced it as just one in a series of offending incidents which she felt amounted to "discrimination, victimisation and bullying".

The citing of discrimination brings to light another facet of this case which must be mentioned. In the interview, Aluko frames the incident examined here as an example of things which Sampson said to her "because of race". The news article published the same day as the interview is headlined "Eni Aluko accuses England manager Mark Sampson of 'racist' Ebola remark" and a letter from the Professional Footballers' Association to the FA described the remark as a "racist joke". To characterize Sampson's remark this way is to claim a particular motivation for it and his behaviour towards Aluko more generally. Perhaps it is an accurate insight, we cannot know. But to label the remark this way risks missing the point and getting lost in arguments about what is or isn't to be deemed racist, diverting attention from the observable, analysable fact that the remark was deeply, deeply nasty. Racist language is taboo language and, as in the 'crap' case above, this tends to mean it doesn't get examined.

A final observation on this case and the 'crap' case above: the offence was demonstrably the greater in the Ebola case, and yet, while the offence taken at the latter was expressed immediately, the victim of the greater offence did not register her being offended until some considerable time after the event. At the time, she tried to hide it. The reason, of course, is that the power relationship between offender and offendee is the other way around from the 'crap' case. This differential is crucial in many of the cases examined in the next three chapters, in which institutional power is involved.

8.4 Slap

This case, also from the domain of football, involves an apparent threat of physical violence. It was never considered that the person who issued the threat to 'slap' his addressee might actually carry it out. Nevertheless, this person eventually found himself £30,000 the poorer (a fine imposed by the relevant professional body) as a result of his words. Clearly, then, these were deemed offensive to a wider group than its target.

8.4.1 Context

The BBC's football programme *Match of the Day* (*MOTD*) is watched by several million viewers on Saturday nights. It presents recorded highlights of a series of matches. After each match has been shown, it is the invariant practice for the programme to show interviews with the managers of the two opposing teams. These typically last no more than a minute or two (or at least only a minute or two is shown to viewers). Below is a transcript of the last few seconds of the interview which took place in April 2017 with the Sunderland manager, David Moyes, conducted by the interviewer Vicki Sparks, plus remarks made by the manager after both participants understood the interview to have concluded. The TV camera had stopped running but a colleague recorded what happened next on his phone.[4]

8.4.2 The data

Interviewer:	And the owner Ellis Short was here today, does it put any extra pressure on you as the manager when you know the owner's in the stand watching on?
Manager:	No, not at all
Interviewer:	That's brilliant, thank you very much
Manager:	(nods acceptance of thanks)
	(smiling slightly) Just getting a wee bit naughty
Interviewer:	(begins to laugh, loudly at first)
Manager:	at the end there so … just watch yourself you might get a—
Interviewer:	(laughing stops)
Manager:	you still might get a slap even though you're a woman
Interviewer:	(short, quiet burst of laughter while walking away)
Manager:	Careful the next time you come in

8.4.3 Analysis

The target of the manager's remarks accepted a later apology from him and did not issue a complaint. But offence was widely taken and registered as soon as the footage emerged. The presenter of *MOTD* called his behaviour "inexcusable"; Britain's shadow sports minister referred to "sexist threats"; the director of a local group supporting female victims of domestic violence found it "absolutely appalling" and, like the shadow minister, called on the FA to discipline Moyes; the professional group Women in Football were "deeply disappointed and concerned by the threatening language". What was it about Moyes' remarks that were so widely found to be offensive? And what motivated them?

First, we consider what motivated Moyes to make them. It is clear that Moyes regards the interviewer's question as in some way improper: 'naughty' is one of the words you can use of a person who you consider to have broken a rule. In the sense that the question conflicts with his expectations and/or beliefs about acceptable behaviour in this situation, this metapragmatic comment registers an assessment of the question as impolite (Culpeper 2011: 23). Presumably, his expectation/belief is that the interviewer's questions in a post-match interview should be confined to his reactions to what happened on the pitch and to his players, any decisions which he had made during the match (e.g. substitutions) and the result.

There is every indication that Sparks is aware that her question was somewhat transgressive. First, notice that she chooses this as her very last question and then swiftly closes the interview after only the briefest of answers to it. Her manner of closing expresses appreciation ("That's brilliant") and formulaic gratitude ("Thanks very much"), suggesting that she never really expected anything other than this terse denial. Second, there is her jovial laughter when Moyes begins to upbraid her. She *knows* she was 'pulling a fast one' by sneaking that question in at the end of the interview.

Given this agreement in assessment of the propriety of the question, the offence which Moyes causes is not that he expresses criticism of it. If he had stopped after "bit naughty at the end there", it is very unlikely that widespread offence would have been taken. Unfortunately, Moyes does *not* stop there. Why not? There are two possible, non-mutually exclusive, reasons. First, it is possible that his objection to Sparks' question was not merely his belief that it was not within the set of allowable contributions to this activity type (Levinson [1992] 1979). It may also have been the precise content of the question, which has an aspect of face-threat about it. He is being interviewed as the 'boss' of the team, the person who is thereby entitled both to make judgements about its performance and that of individual players and also to represent it to the TV audience. He expects that the questions he is asked will allow him to sustain this line (and presumably, so far they have). Suddenly, this new question shifts Sparks' footing from elicitor-of-expert's-opinions to solicitor-of-potentially-vulnerable-individual's-feelings. It draws attention to the fact that Moyes is not actually the ultimate boss. Moreover, it asks him not about his judgements but about his feelings. While questions about his feelings related to performance may be seen as permissible, this is a question about his feelings concerning his own position as manager and suggests that these might be affected by his desire to please his paymaster. As such, it is a threat to his professional face. We may say that he is offended by it.

At the same time, his characterization of the question as "a wee bit naughty" (rather than, say, 'outrageous', 'off-limits' or simply 'wrong') suggests he is not *very* offended by it and regards it as only slightly transgressive, as does the laughter of the person who asked it when it is remarked on. After all, it is generally accepted that interviewees in powerful positions must expect 'difficult' questions from journalists. Moyes made no complaint to the BBC about it. Indeed, in that he makes his remarks after broadcasting of the encounter has ceased and therefore (he mistakenly believes) no longer accessible to a wide audience, his remarks can be interpreted, simply by being remarks of any kind, as a kind of positive facework (see section 2.2) with Sparks. He is indexing the two of them as fellow performers who have just left frontstage, sharing a joke about her performance.

It is in this context, of a professional performer registering with another in a somewhat non-serious manner that he is mildly offended, that he warns her to "just watch yourself" because she "might get a slap". Despite the widespread use of the lexeme 'threat' in condemnation of his remarks, it was never entertained as a genuine threat to perform the specified act and would fail to meet the criteria for such an act if we applied the felicity conditions of speech act theory (see section 7.1.1). The advice to "just watch yourself" and to be "careful the next time you come" would get closer to meeting the conditions for what I call (section 7.1.2) a 'menacing espousal' but even then not actually 'pass'. Rather, Sparks is being warned that she now has her 'card marked' as a tricky interviewer, but neither she nor anybody who watched the encounter can have felt menaced by Moyes himself.

In what, then, does the rather serious offence lie? The answer is in his precise choice of lexis combined with his reference to his interlocutor's gender. To take the latter first, there is an irony that his bringing up the gender of the interviewer ("even though you're a woman") on the one hand seems to avow that gender is not an issue with him but on the other hand simultaneously makes gender terribly salient; the "still" before "might get" and "even though" both generate a conventional implicature that men and women normally get treated differently. And in this light the words 'naughty' and 'slap' take on a new significance. The former is prototypically predicated of children, an association which is foregrounded here by the diminutive premodifier "a wee bit". For this reason, when predicated of a person *to* that person, it enacts power. And in the context of the reference to the female gender, a likeness is thus suggested of women and children, both less powerful than men. And indeed, it seems far, far more unlikely that a football manager would ever characterize a male interviewer's performance with this word. As for 'slap', it has two prototypical scenarios: one is punishment meted out to children, the other the physical reaction of a woman to being insulted. So again a connection between these two groups is suggested. The word denotes a comparatively mild and spontaneous type of physical violence, the kind rather casually perpetrated on social inferiors and/or people who would not be expected to retaliate. Again, it would be very hard to imagine a football manager even mock-threatening a slap to a male interviewer. (This consideration is why Moyes' apparent disavowal of any relevance to gender doesn't hold water.) Thus a picture emerges of slapping a woman being a rather quotidian thing to do. It is this that caused offence to be taken far beyond the actual target of the 'threat'.

It has been suggested to me (Billy Clark, personal communication) – and this is the additional possible motivation for him not stopping after the mild criticism of Sparks' question – that Moyes' remarks to the interviewer constitute his version of flirting. This seems to me quite plausible. Why otherwise bring up the fact of her being a woman at all? Note also that another connotation of 'naughty' is sexual. This view might also explain his final remark ("Careful the next time you come in"), which is superfluous both propositionally, as he has already enjoined her to "watch yourself", and interactively, because by this time the video shows that Sparks is leaving, or possibly has already left, the scene of the encounter. A flirting motivation allows us to interpret the remark as an attempt, albeit a failed one, to prolong this encounter and set up a relational history for their next one. If accurate, though, this view does not get Moyes off the hook but rather hangs him more securely on it. It means his version of flirting includes allusions to violence. A whole unsavoury world of one man's approach to male–female relationships leaks out. And while Sparks herself may not have felt directly menaced, the wide dissemination of this incident caused a whole group of people of whom Sparks has been identified as a representative (women) to feel obscurely, indirectly menaced, all the more so because of the casual manner in which the remarks are made, thereby assisting in normalizing their propositional content. Predications of violence are the subject of the next chapter.

Offences against 'the peace' – and social control

The cases examined in this chapter all involve predications of physical harm. Their interest lies in the fact that they are not entirely 'serious'; that is, there is doubt (of varying degree) about the extent to which the predications of violence can be interpreted literally (as in, for example, a declaration of war, a judicial sentence of death or an impassioned speech inciting a large crowd to riot), so that the threat felt is not simply to life or physical wellbeing but also to a more diffuse sense of security and psychological comfort. Four of the five cases cited here led to a criminal conviction. In the two cases discussed in section 9.1, analysis suggests that the judicial authorities arrived at the 'right' decision. But in the cases discussed in the remainder of this chapter, they very obviously arrived at the wrong decision.

9.1 Invitations to violence

Although the two cases examined here cite a single individual as their target, such predications are regarded as a matter for society at large. Public bodies play a role in deciding what reaction to take to the offence. One encouragement for this involvement is that both of these 'threats' were issued in public or semi-public domains and thus widely disseminated. In fact, they were not (unlike the 'slap' case in the last chapter) even addressed to their target. There is a feeling that if a perpetrator of a personal threat in these circumstances is seen to 'get away with it', this will encourage him/her and perhaps others to behave in the same way in dealings with other individuals and that, knowing this, these other individuals who suspect they could be potential future targets will also feel some disquiet (i.e. they will be offended too).

9.1.1 Stone her to death

Context and data[1]

At the time the tweet was posted in November, the journalist and social commentator Yasmin Alibhai-Brown was a regular contributor to a British national newspaper. She had just featured on a discussion on human rights abuses on a national radio station during which, according to the poster of the tweet, Gareth Compton, she had expressed the opinion that "no politician [presumably British] had the right to comment on human rights abuses, even the stoning of women in Iran". This had apparently irritated Compton enough for him to tweet the following:

> Can someone please stone Yasmin Alibhai-Brown to death? I shan't tell Amnesty if you don't. It would be a blessing, really.

On the same day, one of the readers of the tweet alerted the police and Compton, a local government councillor representing the Conservative Party, was arrested on suspicion of "sending an offensive or indecent message". He was questioned and then released "pending further inquiries". He was not eventually charged with this (or any other) crime, apparently because neither the person who alerted the police nor Alibhai-Brown, despite her declared intention at the time to do so, came forward to make official statements to the police. He was, however, temporarily suspended from the Conservative Party and did not stand for re-election in the local elections the following year.

The first predication in this tweet is a request for 'someone' to kill Alibhai-Brown. It was not, however, interpreted by anybody as a genuine request. One reason was presumably that it could not be imagined that a public figure, with a position to lose, would – publicly – call for such an act to be performed. If it had been interpreted this way, he would have been arrested on suspicion of conspiracy to murder. Nevertheless, it was interpreted as highly offensive. Alibhai-Brown said at the time that she was "really scared", reading it as "incitement".

Analysis

The fact that the tweet was not read as a genuine attempt to have Alibhai-Brown killed is understandable if we examine it in terms of the proposed felicity conditions for an act of incitement (see section 7.1.3). First, there is the exotic absurdity of the specific means by which it is proposed she be killed. It is impossible to imagine that, in twenty-first-century British society, any H or group of Hs would have the ability to carry out the specific mooted act, thus failing a preparatory condition. In addition, genuine attempts to get something done normally entail arranging it with a specified person or group of people, not just "someone". It is also hard to imagine that someone in this public position who really wanted the deed done would broadcast it in this manner. Both these features call into question the success of the essential condition for this act.

It is, however, a markedly vicious way of expressing antagonism, so it is still possible to interpret this predication as expressive of a wish that something nasty happen to Alibhai-Brown. To find the extent to which the tweet can be read as genuine encouragement for someone to *do* harm to her, we need to look at the tweet as a whole. We can appeal here to the concept of sequencing as used in conversation analysis. It has been shown (e.g. Holt 2013: 69–89) that there is a type of conversational contribution which orients to non-seriousness. An invitation which is not to be construed as a real invitation, for instance, will have something in the manner of its issue which indicates this. There are several such indications in what follows this first predication in the tweet. In order to encourage the interpretation that an expressed wish that some act A be carried out is genuine, there are a number of possible continuations. There could be (a) some detail about how A is to be carried out and/or (b) a reason why A would be desirable and/or (c) some encouragement that carrying out A is feasible. There is nothing whatsoever forthcoming with respect to (a), and we have already seen that the impractically exotic nature of A causes its status as the expression of a genuine desire to be called into question. There *is* some evidence of (b) in the final predication of the tweet but it is unconvincingly vague.

What most clearly points to the non-seriousness of the tweet is the incongruence of the sentence in-between. On the face of it, it can be read as (c) above. It appears to say 'don't worry, I'll make sure you don't get caught'. But appearing in a tweet addressed to a large number of people ("someone"), its prospect of secrecy is self-contradictory nonsense, all the more so because the proposed method of killing is not one that could be carried out surreptitiously. Moreover, the reference to Amnesty International is inapposite, as this organization is not responsible for and plays no role in the apprehension of wrongdoers. (It has, though, mounted campaigns on behalf of those condemned to die that way, which is presumably why it occurred to Compton.) This second predication, then, allows a reinterpretation of the first as a type of what Haugh (2016) calls 'jocular pretence'. True, it contains no explicit claim to non-serious intent as there is in Haugh's examples (though Compton issued such a claim afterwards), but its promise not to 'tell on' any perpetrator to the authorities has the effect of representing the propositional content of the first predication not as something horrifically violent but rather as something merely 'naughty' (see the 'slap' case in section 8.4), which once again is absurd.

However, notwithstanding these indications of non-seriousness, the inference to be drawn from the prosecuting authority's statement announcing that Compton would not be charged, which referred to the 'refusals' of the person who originally alerted the police to provide a statement and of Alibhai-Brown to make an official complaint, is that if such statements from these two *had* been forthcoming, he *would* have been prosecuted for the tweet. It was, in other words, rated as highly offensive. No doubt a major cause of this rating was simply the chilling propositional content in the wish itself ("stone to death"), its exoticness contributing to its impression of viciousness. An additional cause is provided by the wider context, which, as in the 'slap' case in Chapter 8, concerns one socially ascribed attribute of the target being foregrounded. In the 'slap' case it was Sparks' status as a woman; in this case it is the status of Alibhai-Brown as a Muslim. Because in modern times stoning a person to death has legal status (and is very occasionally utilized) only in Muslim-majority countries, it has a reputation as an Islamic practice and thus can be used as an index of the Islamic religion. In this context – of reaction to her comments on that radio discussion – it draws attention to her religious affiliation, an association strengthened by the use of a word from the semantic field of religion ("blessing") in the final predication of the tweet.

This case displays an example of the subjectivity of context, especially likely on a medium such as Twitter which imposes a maximum text length. For Compton, by his own post-facto account, there was a prior context for his reference to stoning – it was mentioned by Alibhai-Brown on the radio programme which he heard. From his perspective, then, this was not a method of harming Alibhai-Brown which he himself picked out but rather a reference made by her which he was just repeating. But it is not obvious that readers of the tweet would have known this. The tweet, then, is highly offensive from either perspective. For readers not aware of this context, the propositional content in its first predication is startlingly vicious. For readers aware of this context on the other hand, it has the effect of 'othering' Alibhai-Brown as someone who, as a Muslim, has no right to voice her opinions on a national broadcast – as well as the foregrounding of her minority religious affiliation, notice the appeal to the majority in requesting "someone" to perform the act. (A person who asks an indefinite one member of a group he is addressing to do something is a person confident of his place among that majority.) For the target herself, it is both – frightening *and* alienating. As we saw, Alibhai-Brown did not pursue the case by making an official complaint.

Perhaps this is because, if she had, the clear indications of non-seriousness in the tweet would have emerged in a court case – and she would have found herself informally 'accused' of the terrible 'crime' in British culture of having 'no sense of humour'.

9.1.2 Run her over

Context and data[2]

The referendum in Britain in 2016 resulted in a very narrow majority in favour of leaving the European Union. Partly because of the narrowness of the majority (52 per cent), partly because of accusations of lying during the referendum campaign, and partly because there then commenced a very protracted process of negotiation before the country actually exited the EU, the issue proved to be the most divisive in British society for a very long time.

Following the referendum result in June of that year, the businesswoman Gina Miller mounted a legal challenge that the British government should consult Parliament before formally beginning the Brexit process. This angered many 'leavers' because they saw it as a tactic to delay Brexit, or possibly even avoid it entirely. Miller's action caused her to receive a large amount of abuse on social media, including death threats. When, in November of the same year, the High Court ruled in her favour (the government was indeed required to consult Parliament first), the quantity of this abuse escalated.

Not long after the decision, Rhodri Colwyn Philipps, a minor aristocrat, posted a message on Facebook, part of which read:

> £5000 for the first person to 'accidentally' run over this bloody troublesome first generation immigrant. This fucking boat jumper come to country [sic], then believes she knows better than the people of our country, what is best for us. If this is what we should expect from immigrants, send them back to their stinking jungles.

As a result of this post, Philipps was later found guilty of sending a 'menacing and racially aggravating' electronic message and was sentenced to twelve weeks in prison.

Analysis

At a superficial level, there is a lot of similarity between this Facebook post and the tweet analysed above. It is, like the tweet, issued to the poster's followers in general and calls for a volunteer to do serious physical harm to the target. And like the tweet, it cannot be read as evidence of a genuine plan to cause the target harm, for the same reasons as outlined above.

But there are a number of differences. This time, the means of causing harm ('run her over') is at least feasible. Moreover, there is some encouragement which is also feasible ("accidentally") and two kinds of reasons for the desirability of the mooted act are given. One is the reward offered. The other, rather than being the vague appeal to the general good (the "blessing") in the tweet, is the implication that the attributes cited of Miller mean that she somehow deserves this fate. These attributes hinge on her immigrant history. This time, the othering of the target is not implied but made explicit, with a clear construction of opposites (Jeffries 2010), in which Miller is first opposed to "the people of our country" and "us" and then "we" is opposed to "immigrants". Given these characteristics, the essential condition for an act of incitement as I have defined it (section 7.1.3) is fulfilled. The post is entirely devoid of the whimsicality of the tweet above, but instead contains the highly pejorative attribution "fucking boat jumper" (which, by the way, is not true – Miller was not a refugee who was rescued from the sea; rather, she came to Britain as a 10-year-old to attend school).

Like the tweet above, this case also reveals the subjectivity of context. Philipps' Facebook post was sent in reply to a post asking for "naughty suggestions, dirty ideas and anything that will give me an orgasm". His reply began, "Mine includes, torturing Tony Blair, Hilary Clinton, Isis, Dave (PM) the forgettable, Murdoch … Oh and that hideous jumped up immigrant Gina Miller". His post then continued with the data quoted above. In his mind, his offending post was situated in this shallow, non-serious co-text. Unfortunately for him, as so often happens with online communication, this post was forwarded, the attention of Gina Miller was drawn to it, so that it no longer remained in this context.

9.2 The Twitter joke trial

This is the (rather uninformative) name by which one particular case of the conviction, and eventual acquittal, of a private individual for sending a menacing tweet has become widely known. The case attained a degree of celebrity, reflected in the fact that it has not passed without a certain amount of scholarly attention. It has been used, for example, as the material for a series of different readings which illustrate different approaches to the concept of 'internet governance' (Ziewitz & Pentzold 2014) and for a discussion of what it can tell us about the nature of power relationships in a world of social media (Kelsey & Bennett 2014).

My immediate interest, as with all the cases examined in this book, is more directly focused and more straightforward: what exactly was found offensive about the tweet. (However, some of the issues raised in such studies are taken up in the final section.)

9.2.1 Context and data[3]

In the early days of January 2010, bad weather caused Robin Hood airport in South Yorkshire, England to cancel all flights. In reaction to this situation, on 6 January, one intending passenger, Paul Chambers, who had booked a 15 January flight to visit a girlfriend, sent a tweet to his 600 followers which read

> Crap! Robin Hood airport is closed. You've got a week and a bit to
> get your shit together, otherwise I'm blowing the airport sky-high!!

Five days later, an airport manager, while searching for mentions of the airport on Twitter, came across this tweet. He passed it to the manager responsible for assessing the credibility of any perceived threats to the airport. This person assessed the 'threat' as 'non-credible' but following standard practice passed it on to the airport police. They passed it on to South Yorkshire police, who, on 13 January, arrested Chambers on suspicion of involvement in a bomb hoax, as a result of which he lost his job. They also searched Chambers' house and impounded his phone, laptop and hard drive.

Four weeks of investigation later, the log of one of the investigating officers recorded there was "no evidence at this stage to suggest that there is anything other than a foolish comment posted on 'Twitter' as a joke for only his close friends to see". However, on the advice of the Crown Prosecution Service (CPS), Chambers was subsequently charged with "sending a public electronic message that was grossly offensive or of an indecent, obscene or menacing character contrary to the Communications Act 2003". On 10 May that year, he was convicted of this crime, fined £385 and ordered to pay £600 legal costs (in addition to his own legal costs). A widespread outcry at this conviction, principally conducted on Twitter itself, ensued. Nevertheless, Chambers' first two appeals against the conviction were unsuccessful. It was only at the third attempt in July 2012 (some two years later) that the conviction was finally quashed.

9.2.2 Analysis

The rest of this section puts Chambers' tweet and the judgments of the courts to the test. What is the most accurate interpretation of the tweet? The analysis is conducted at a level of minute detail which risks irritating the reader. After all, in retrospect, or simply from the point of view of common sense, it might seem obvious that Chambers' tweet was neither indicative of a substantive plot nor in itself genuinely threatening or menacing, that he was just, rather crassly, letting off steam. It may be objected, therefore, that the detailed analysis which follows is unnecessary, that it is using a pragmatic sledgehammer to crack a textual nut. However, as the story shows, it took several years for common sense to win out. Before it did, a great deal of public time and money was spent, one person (Chambers) had his life ruined unfairly and at least one other person (his girlfriend) had theirs disrupted, also unfairly. Moreover, this absence of the common-sense interpretation is not an isolated case (see section 9.3 below), raising concerns around the principle of free speech. Given these substantive outcomes and this substantive import, there is a need to interrogate that common-sense assessment, to spell out the perceptions and inferences on which it is based.

As explained in section 7.1, in the context of a legal case, this needs to be done through a somewhat expanded version of speech act theory. In terms of the theory, this question becomes: what act(s) did Chambers' tweet perform? What follows, then, is that a series of possible acts are chosen and each is tested against the felicity conditions for that act. It can be seen from the narrative of this case above that three levels of offence were mooted. In decreasing order of substantive seriousness, they are that Chambers' tweet was:

- evidence of a genuine threat to blow up the airport (the reason it was forwarded to the security manager);
- a non-credible threat to blow up the airport (the bomb hoax on suspicion of which Chambers was arrested);
- menacing in a more diffuse sense (cf. Chambers' conviction).

Accordingly, we can start at the top 'threat level' and work downwards until (if ever) we get a 'yes' answer. In the colour-coding currently fashionable, I label these levels red, orange and yellow respectively.

Red level: genuine threat?

Having put this apparatus in place, however, we can immediately dismiss this red-level possibility without further ado. At this level, the issue is whether the tweet can be taken as evidence of an actual plot to blow up the airport. Police investigation found no material, 'extra-tweet', evidence that Chambers had even the faintest intention to do so, let alone the ability (which Searle 1969: 60 regards as entailed in a genuine intention). The 'intra-tweet' evidence that he gave his name away in the tweet (using the handle @pauljchambers), so that it would have been relatively easy for the police to forestall any such plan, leads to the same conclusion. Chambers' tweet was not a genuine threat.

Orange level: insincere threat?

At this level, substantive linguistic import obtains because the tweet is no longer potential evidence of a crime but is itself the purported crime. Did the tweet constitute a threat which, although not 'meant', was a threat nonetheless. (See section 7.1 for argument that this is not an oxymoron.) To assess whether Chambers' tweet was indeed a threat, albeit of the bluffing variety, I proceed to test it against the felicity conditions set out in section 7.1.1. As a reminder, these are:

1. Propositional content:		U predicates future act A of S
2. Preparatory:	2a	S and H regard A as bad for H
	2b	S and H believe S is not going to do A anyway
3. Essential:		H recognizes U as S making a commitment to do A

1. Does the tweet predicate a future act by Chambers? Clearly, yes. An act ("blowing the airport sky-high") is predicated of Chambers himself ("I'm blowing ... "). And in the context of this act being conditional ("otherwise") on a future circumstance "a week and a bit" from the time of posting the tweet (and given that a present progressive construction is one way in English to indicate future time), it is clearly a future act. What is the particular circumstance on which this act is conditional? Drawing the inference from the opening of his tweet ("Crap!") that Chambers is angry, or at least disgruntled, and the further inference that the reason for his anger, because it is stated immediately afterwards, is that "Robin Hood airport is closed", we can infer that "get[ting] your shit together" refers to the airport authorities reopening the airport. This act on their part and his mooted act of "blowing the airport sky-high" are presented as mutually exclusive alternatives ("otherwise") – if they reopen the airport, he will not blow it up; if they don't, he will. This speech act is therefore what Blanco Salgueiro (2010) calls a directive-commissive (You do X or I will do Y).

This much we can tell from the content of the tweet alone. Using what we know of the personal circumstances of Chambers, we can add more detail to its directive element. The reason he is angry at the airport being closed is because he has a flight booked from there for nine days later. (As his flight is to visit a romantic connection, we can presume he is particularly keen that this should go ahead as planned.) With this knowledge, we can deduce that "a week and a bit" means nine days and that "get your shit together" includes not only reopening the airport but arranging for flights to run normally – so that *his* flight will take off as scheduled.

We have no way of knowing whether this knowledge was available to all the readers of the tweet. It will certainly have been available to @crazycolours (the girlfriend) and those of his followers who were apprised of his upcoming travel plans. It is unlikely that all of his 600 followers were in this position, and extremely unlikely that any other readers (such as the airport managers and police) were. But even these people probably interpreted "get your shit together" as meaning something along the lines of 'fix things so that flights to/from the airport are not disrupted' because by far the most likely reason for someone to be angry at the closure of an airport is that they have a stake in an upcoming flight (either as passenger or as host to an arriving passenger). Such readers, having made this inference, may well have also inferred that "a week and a bit" is a reference to the date of the flight in which he has a stake.

2. We can take it for granted that Chambers is not going to blow the airport up anyway. Not only is blowing up airports not something that anybody does in the normal course of events; in this case, the commissive being of the directive type, the predicated act is conditional on circumstances. The question to be answered here is: Do Chambers and his reader(s) regard blowing up the airport as bad for them? In the most general and diffuse sense, the answer is yes. Searle's original formulation of this condition (1969: 58), when reversed to produce a threat rather than a promise, is "H would prefer S's not doing A to his doing A, and S believes [this]". This atrocious kind of act, typically given the label 'terrorism', is in a sense an attack on society. And assuming that his readers, whatever else they are, are ordinary members of society, we can assume they would prefer that it did not happen.

However, to be accorded the label of 'threat' within speech act theory, something more personal and directed is required, something which is more than the doing of a generally recognized 'bad thing'. Searle distinguishes a threat from a promise by describing it as "a pledge to do something *to you*, not for you" (my italics). Without this targeted personal aspect, the predication of the unwanted deed is no more than the announcement of malign intent (and would thereby fall short of meeting the essential condition of making a commitment – see below). An unspecified member of society reading this tweet would not regard the predicated act as something to be done *to him/her*. S/he would not feel personally threatened. This preparatory condition states that H specifically – not just anybody – would prefer A not to be done.

The question we therefore need to ask is: Do both Chambers and his reader(s) regard blowing up the airport as bad for *them in particular*? Chambers had been in Twitter conversation with crazycolours earlier that day, concerning the possibility of the airport closing due to bad weather. It was two hours later that he sent the tweet at issue, which may therefore be seen as a continuation of the conversation with crazycolours and in that sense is addressed to her. However, he posted the tweet on the public timeline, which meant that his 600 followers were able to see it should they choose. In participation framework terms (see section 2.3.2), we can regard all his followers as ratified participants and, in the context of the recent conversation, we may regard crazycolours as the addressed participant and all the others as unaddressed – but ratified nonetheless (he knows they are able to see his tweet and that they can easily join in the conversation if they want). For now, we can regard H as comprising this set of people.

Would blowing up Robin Hood airport be bad for any of these people? For it to cause them direct harm, they would have to be on the premises at the time, which is unlikely because a major condition for going ahead with the act is that the airport remains closed. One could, though, posit a situation in which the airport has reopened but flights are still disrupted – that is, the airport authorities have not got their 'shit' fully 'together' – so that the condition has not been fully met. And even if none of his followers were on the premises at the time, the destruction of the airport would at least be inconvenient for those of them in the habit of using the airport. To this extent, then, we can say that the predicated act would be against the interest of this section of his readership, and to the extent that Chambers is aware of any such followers, we can say that he believes it would be against their interest.

However, we cannot know whether any followers of Chambers are in this position. In fact, the only two participants who it would definitely inconvenience would be the addressed participant (Chambers' girlfriend) and Chambers himself, since it appears to be a link they use to meet up with each other. To the very limited extent that this preparatory condition has been met at all, then, one has to extend it to include the issuer of the 'threat'. In other words, this is a cut-off-nose-to-spite-face kind of threat (the extreme example of which would presumably be a threat to conduct a suicide bombing).

The crucial obstacle to the fulfilment of this preparatory condition, though, arises from the fact that this is a directive-commissive (see above). These participants are not the people who have the power to avert the blowing-up of the airport by complying with the directive to "get your shit together". From this perspective, it might make more sense to categorize Chambers' predication of the (possibly, slightly) bad thing which is going to happen to his readers not as a speech act of threatening but rather as one of warning. And for this particular, directive kind of commissive, it seems necessary to add an additional preparatory condition – that "H has the ability to forestall A".

The considerations above lead to the conclusion that this preparatory condition is met in only a trivial sense. However, in the sense in that, tweets being potentially accessible to anyone with an internet connection, one could argue that anyone can qualify as the H of this condition. In Goffmanian terms, these others are bystanders: the duty manager who 'came across' the tweet while looking for something else may be described as an overhearer; the people to whom he then passed it on – his manager and the police – would be eavesdroppers. It is known that producers of language often design their utterances to take account of bystanders (Goffman 1981: 85–98). Is there any evidence that Chambers did so?

Newspaper reports quote Chambers as claiming it never occurred to him that his tweet would be seen by airport managers. However, his use of "you … your shit" does indeed index them as, clearly, theirs is the 'shit' referred to, thus raising the possibility that he was 'trailing his coat', with the thought that these people might 'overhear' (half) in mind. After all, doesn't everybody these days realize that these kinds of electronic messages are universally accessible?

The evidence in the co-text indicates that this possibility is only a weak one. Just before the directive-commissive part of the tweet we read that "Robin Hood airport is closed". This information is not presented in a subordinate clause (e.g. "As Robin Hood airport is closed") but rather as a main clause and, therefore, as 'new' information (Quirk & Greenbaum 1973: 408–9). Such information would not, of course, be new to airport managers. However, it *would* be new to his followers, who (we can be sure) are not at the airport at the time (because it is closed). This suggests it is only them that he has in mind.

How, then, do we explain Chambers' use of 'you/your' in this co-text? A clue can be found in Searle's original exposition of the conditions for a successful speech act of promising, in which he identifies a first, preliminary condition for the performance of any speech act that "normal input and output conditions obtain". It never appears in summaries of his set of conditions (e.g. see above), presumably because it is assumed to be self-evident. However, his 'normal' excludes not only system impediments to communication (e.g. S and H not sharing a language, deafness, aphasia) but also "parasitic forms of communication such as telling jokes or acting in a play" (Searle 1969: 57). It can plausibly be argued that this is what Chambers is doing at this point in the tweet: acting out for his followers an imagined scene in which he confronts the airport authorities and berates them for their inefficiency. Such 'embedding' of one participation framework within another is actually quite common (Goffman 1981: 153–5). Bearing in mind the tweet's information sequence noted in the previous paragraph plus Chambers' avowed unawareness of these other readers, this play-acting seems the most likely explanation of Chambers' motivation to write 'you/your'. (See O'Driscoll 2013 for a case of a similar imagining on the part of an email sender.)

Of course, to the extent that the airport managers have 'become' H by overhearing/eavesdropping, the predicated act is certainly and particularly bad for them. The airport provides their livelihood and, moreover, they might reasonably be expected to be on the premises even when it is closed, opening the possibility of them suffering direct and extreme physical harm if Chambers carries out his proposed act. However, in summary, the evidence for the fulfilment of this preparatory condition is both partial and dubious: partial because the predicated act is bad for his obvious readers only in an attenuated sense; dubious because the act is only obviously bad for people who are readers only in a very attenuated sense.

3. Do Chambers' readers recognize his tweet as the making of a commitment, unless his directive is complied with, to blow up the airport? Several pieces of evidence from the text point against such an interpretation. Firstly, we may note again his use of the present progressive ("I'm blowing"). In British English, this verb construction is typically used to describe plans which have already been *arranged*; future *intentions*, on the other hand, are indicated either by the use of 'going to [do]', indicating the intention was formed before the time of the utterance, or by '(I think) I'll [do]', indicating the intention is being formed at the time (Leech 2004: 55–63). If Chambers had used one of these two constructions – "I'm going to blow/I'll blow" – it might be possible to interpret his proposition as stating some sort of intention, but the use of present progressive here only highlights the yawning gap between the proposition (blowing up the airport) and the reality on the ground (the lack of any other evidence of this plan).

Other evidence from the text also suggests a lack of intention to be committed to the act. The use of taboo words ("crap ... shit"), the colloquial phrasing ("get your shit together ... sky high"), the vagueness of "a week and a bit" (and even the possibly intended irony in the idea of causing a place whose activity involves *sending* things into the sky to be *blown* into the sky) all suggest a non-serious intent in the composition of the tweet. They also conform to the expected register of language among Twitter users, whose 140-character limit partly dictates and partly has led by convention to forms which index off-the-cuff remarks and informal style (see Scott 2015). This is not a *considered* piece of prose. Indeed, its very first word is a bare expletive, a blurted imprecation which very much fixes the utterance in the time of production and presages an outpouring of present emotion rather than possible futures, indexing a person who is not so much speaking his mind as 'speaking his feelings'. In this co-text, the predication of the act itself might just as well be read as an expressive type of speech act rather than as a commissive one. He has just expressed his anger and the reason for it. The directive-commissive which follows, it has been suggested above, is a dramatic representation of his feelings at this point. Note also that the language used in this embedded play-act indexes a face-to-face confrontation. Threats when issued through remote, text-based media typically state more precise and unambiguous conditions (e.g. reopen the airport and see that flights are taking off at the scheduled time) than "get your shit together", in a more precise time-frame (e.g. 'nine days and four hours') than "a week and a bit" and also eschew exaggerations such as 'sky-high'. This precision and parsimony function as a means of conveying their credibility. Rather than threatening, what this tweet also does is refer disparagingly to the activities of the airport managers as shit.

When people feel angry they want to lash out – at the first people they can think of to hold to account. The intention in predicating the act is to express that anger, not to assert the veracity of any propositions. If there was any thought for the effect on readers in the composition of the tweet, I suggest it was to make his addressed participant (his girlfriend) feel flattered at the implication, by this exaggerated reaction, of how desperately he wants their planned assignation to go ahead. Notice the double exclamation marks at the end of the tweet. As Vandergriff (2013) demonstrates, the repeated exclamation marks are multifunctional and their meanings "only emerge in the context of co-occurring emotive markers" (2013: 7). The only other emotive marker in the tweet is the exclamation mark after 'crap', again suggesting that this predication about blowing up the airport is an expression of emotion.

There is also extratextual evidence for the fact that readers of this tweet did not receive it as a commitment to blow up the airport. As the High Court judgment pointed out, not one of his followers thought it necessary to alert anybody to this horrendous predicated future act, suggesting they did not take the 'threat' seriously. Neither did the security manager at the airport when it was shown to him. We know this because if he had, his duty would have been to alert the Ministry of Defence, which he did not do. In summary we may list the 'performance' of the tweet against the felicity conditions for a threat as follows:

1. future act A of S?   YES (but exact timing perhaps unclear to bystanders)
2a bad for H?   YES for a few particular bystanders
                               NOT REALLY for all others (= yes only very weakly)
2b not doing A anyway? YES
3. recognized as commitment to do A?   NO

Speech act theory requires that all the conditions for a successfully performed act be met, so Chambers' tweet was not a threat.

Yellow level: menacing?

As a reminder (see section 7.1.2), here are the felicity conditions for a menacing espousal.

1. Propositional content: U implicates future type of act (A) by S
2. Preparatory: 2a   S and H believe A is bad for H
                       2c   H believes S might be able to do A
3. Essential: H recognizes U as suggestive of a threat and so is frightened
   Optional booster: H perceives S as intending to menace H

The reader may be relieved to learn there is no need to go through all the same detail as above. As above, condition 2b is met and the same severe doubts as above apply with regard to the fulfilment of condition 2a. As for condition 2c, we must say it is met, if only because act A is this time non-specific. But in fact, these conditions fail more often than those stipulated above for a threat. In the case of condition 1 here, blowing up the airport need not be taken literally (and as we have seen, it can't be). Rather, it can be taken as simply an example of the class of acts which involves Chambers running amok in some way, doing something grossly violent which is dangerous to a large number of people's physical wellbeing. However, the tweet is just too specific (bombing) and explicit ("I am blowing", rather than, for example, 'shame if something were to happen to the airport') to meet this condition. As for condition 3, the same analysis as above can show that, just as the tweet is clearly not a commitment, it is not suggestive of one either, again because it is just too specific. Finally, as more than one condition has not been met or only very partially met, the 'booster' condition cannot apply. Chambers' tweet is not menacing. As the High Court judgment says, no reader should feel, or indeed appeared to feel, 'menaced' by it. Even if taken semi-seriously (not as just 'a joke'), the mooted act in the circumstances smacks of childishness rather than menace (if I can't fly, then nobody is going to!).

9.3 Reactions to 'terrorist' threats

Before trying to understand the trajectory of the Twitter joke case above and discussing its significance, it is worth noting that it is by no means unique. In 2013, Caleb Jamaal Clemmons, a 20-year-old student in the United States, was arrested within three hours of sending the following message on Tumblr:

> Hello. my name is irenigg and I plan on shooting up georgia southern. pass this around to see the affect it has. to see if I get arrested.

Any fool can see that this post could not possibly be interpreted as evidence of a plan to perpetrate a mass shooting – and indeed no other evidence of such a plan was found. As with the airport tweet, the language is not evidence of criminality – rather it *is* the criminality. Clemmons was convicted of 'making a terroristic threat' and spent six months in jail.[4] And yet, it would not pass the tests above for either a threat or a menacing espousal. (Try it out, if you want.) In a more extreme but similar vein, below is a text message intended as an ironic comment on the difficulty of finding a decent job in Cameroon without qualifications which read

> Boko Haram recruits young people from 14 years old and above. Conditions for recruitment: 4 subjects at GCE, including religion.

When in 2014, Fomusoh Ivo Feh received the message, he forwarded it to a friend who forwarded it to another friend. Then all three were arrested and later convicted of 'non-denunciation of terrorism related information' and sentenced to ten years in prison.[5]

What was it that caused Chambers and these others to fall foul of the authorities? In Chambers' case, why was it thought proper, first by the police and then by the CPS, to pursue this matter and bring a prosecution? How was such a silly – and costly, and negatively impacting on one citizen's life – mistake made? What is at issue here is the *reception* of the tweet. Just as Marsilli-Vargas (2014: 42) argues persuasively for a study of 'listening genres' as "a framework of relevance that surfaces at the moment of reception and orients the apprehension of sound", so one way to understand the reaction of authorities here is to entertain a parallel concept of reading genres. Bluntly, (1) Chambers' followers, (2) the airport manager who originally found his tweet and (3) the authorities (airport, police, courts) were all reading for different purposes and thus in different ways. As a result, their apprehensions of the encoded meanings are different. The first group are looking for conversation and entertainment. For the latter two groups, a central issue is the discharge of their responsibilities (and therefore the safeguarding of their jobs), among which ensuring the security of such a public place is paramount. As a result, they scan, or have programs which scan, messages for anything 'suspicious'. It is quite possible that "blow the airport sky-high" was a flagged phrase.[6] If this was the case, it means that such a phrase qualifies as what I have called a taboo predication.

It is for this reason that the airport manager, despite his assessment of a non-credible threat, passed it to the police – his instructions obliged him to do so. And the police are looking for security risks. To put this another way, these different readers had different footings. And indeed the participation framework changed each time the message was passed on. Once the originally overhearing airport manager had passed the tweet to the police, he became an animator in its production. And the police and prosecuting authorities, eavesdroppers from Chambers' viewpoint, became addressed ratified participants. We have seen a similar variability in writer and reader footings in the cases in section 9.1 above.

From the point of view of those managers and that of the police, if there appears to be any risk whatsoever, however slight, of a person committing such an atrocity, they have to investigate. These personnel work with the constant anxiety that one day they might dismiss a possible indication of mass violence … and then the atrocity takes place. Accordingly, they feel obliged to pursue any clue, however flimsy. And having pursued it and – as in this case – found it to be leading nowhere, it is perhaps understandable they would wish to see the person who has, from their viewpoint, put them to all this needless trouble punished. Their job becomes that much harder if every Tom, Dick & Harry is tweeting about blowing airports up in the same offhand manner. So they need to teach this person a lesson. The tweet was transparently not menacing to individuals.

But they chose to construe it as menacing to society, as contributing to a sense of unease.

The decisions of the courts in this case are also of interest. When Chambers was first convicted, the judgment was that the tweet was "of a menacing nature in the context of the times in which we live". Thus the decision of 'menacing' was justified by an appeal to one aspect of the wider context: the very broad-view aspect of a general societal awareness of the present-day danger of 'terrorism'. The judgment in the first of his two unsuccessful appeals described the tweet as "menacing in its content and obviously so … Any ordinary person reading this would see it in that way and be alarmed". In this judgment, then, justification of the 'menacing' tag was given by appealing to the likely evaluation and reaction of readers of the tweet. The judgment thus recognized, at least by implication, that whether a piece of language can be deemed menacing is not an entirely objective matter of its form and propositional content but rather of its reception. What it did not consider, however, was participation framework: who the actual readers of this tweet might be – just 'any ordinary person' (whoever that might be). Only when his conviction was finally quashed did the judges (of the High Court in London) refer to likely readers of the tweet: "If the person or persons who receive or read it [the message], or may reasonably be expected to receive, or read it, would brush it aside as a silly joke, or a joke in bad taste, or empty bombastic or ridiculous banter, then it would be a contradiction in terms to describe it as a message of a menacing character". This judgment is in accord with Chambers' own understanding of the participation framework for his tweet, as expressed in the first appeal: "It did not cross my mind that Robin Hood would ever look at Twitter or take it seriously". From Chambers' viewpoint, airport staff (and therefore the police) were eavesdroppers rather than overhearers; his message did not take their presence into account.

There is, then, an aspect of social struggle in such cases: whose participation framework is to be rated as the 'real' one? This case exemplified such a struggle. In protest at his conviction, thousands of people, including many celebrity comedians, retweeted Chambers' original message with the hashtag #iamspartacus (an allusion to the 1960 film in which Spartacus' fellow gladiators show their solidarity with him by each proclaiming "I am Spartacus"). Note that in adding this hashtag, they adopted not only an animator role but that of principal as well. But of course they could not all be prosecuted. In their investigation of this case as an example of the power relations on the internet, Kelsey & Bennett (2014: 42) opine that "If Chambers had lost his appeal then the implications for freedom of expression online could have been catastrophic". They position their study against Foucault's concept of the panopticon, by which the powerful 'few' can observe and control the powerless 'many', and "propose the concept of synoptic resistance, which mobilizes oppositional power against authoritative surveillance" (2014: 37). They see Chambers' eventual acquittal in this case as an exemplar of such resistance, one in which the few were watched by the many and eventually defeated. This rather optimistic view does not take account of the fact that observers of the powerful kind cannot usually be personally identified by the observed, whereas those of the relatively powerless kind can.

Threats to social harmony – and social control

This chapter explores utterances considered offensive on the grounds that they constitute a threat to social harmony. A common theme running through the analyses is that labelling an utterance as offensive without examining why it is deemed this way can constitute a threat to social wellbeing just as significant as the purportedly offending utterance itself.

10.1 (Dis)harmony in society: Rivers of Blood

This example examines a piece of data which is widely believed to have been deleterious to social harmony and thereby caused offence. The fact that it occurred half a century ago allows us a special perspective on it.

10.1.1 Background context

During the 1950s and 1960s, more than a million people from parts of 'the Commonwealth' (i.e. the disbanding British empire) came to settle in Britain. The vast majority of them came from the Caribbean or the Indian subcontinent. By 1968, they constituted slightly less than 4 per cent of the country's population, but their black or brown skins, contrasting with the pale skins of nearly everybody else in the country, meant that they were instantly identifiable on sight, and thus a more noticeable phenomenon than this tiny proportion might suggest. 'Foreign' clothing and adornment sometimes intensified this visible otherness and 'immigration' had become a major political issue. People easy to pick out are easy to pick *on* and so, for those who felt the need to find somebody to blame for their ills, these immigrants were the targets of choice.

Early in 1968, in response to several attested incidents of discrimination and more general antagonism, the British government, run by the Labour Party, was attempting to pass a new law (in which it was eventually successful) making it illegal to discriminate against a person (e.g. refuse them a job, promotion or housing) on the basis of their race. During this time, the country's Conservative Party formed the official parliamentary opposition to the government. It had tabled several amendments in Parliament to the proposed law designed to weaken its provisions. One of the party's most prominent members was the MP for Wolverhampton South-West Enoch Powell, who held the position of Shadow Secretary of Defence (i.e. the opposition counterpart to the government minister responsible for defence).

10.1.2 Immediate context

On 20 April 1968, Powell gave an address to the General Meeting of the West Midlands Area Conservative Political Centre. This gathering, then, was potentially an inaccessible encounter in that only accredited members of this association were attending. However, Powell, knowing that what he was about to say would make the headlines, had posted advance copies of his speech to the national broadcast and local newspapers, so that cameras were there to see and record him giving it. It is notable also that Powell is very clearly reading aloud a written speech, slowly, at neither a high enough (declamatory) nor low enough volume to prioritize those physically present as his addresses. The timing of the speech, just a few days before the proposed new law was due to be debated in Parliament, is also significant. This was clearly a speech 'for the record', intended to reach out far beyond the gathering (which it did – see analysis below).[1]

10.1.3 The data

In the speech, Powell argued against the proposed new law on the grounds that it interfered with the right of citizens to conduct their "own affairs" as they saw fit and would effectively put "the immigrant and his descendent (*sic*)" in a privileged position in British society. But this argument came towards the end of his speech. Before that, he advocated the immediate near-total halt of further immigration from the Commonwealth and financial support to be given to existing Commonwealth immigrants to encourage their re-emigration. He advocated these measures on the basis of (1) a prediction that, unless they were implemented, immigrants and "the immigrant-descended population" (a phrase he used three times in his speech) would constitute at least 10 per cent of the population by the year 2000 and would in some areas constitute a majority, and (2) observations that the indigenous (white) people in some parts of the country were already suffering discrimination, abuse and threats of violence from these immigrants, some of whom had plans for their "domination and deprivation". He finished his speech by professing himself "filled with foreboding" and, like the Roman poet Virgil, he foresaw "the River Tiber foaming with much blood". In other words, he predicted widespread intercommunal violence amounting to civil war. It is because of this quote that the speech has become universally known as the 'Rivers of Blood Speech'.[2]

10.1.4 Analysis

Reaction to Powell's speech was various. Opinion polls at the time showed a majority in sympathy with his views. However, the most respected national newspapers condemned the speech as 'evil' in its 'appeal to racial hatred' and he was dismissed from his post in the shadow government role the next day by the leader of the Conservative Party. Slightly longer-term effects were likewise various. Despite his dismissal, it is widely believed that his speech contributed to the surprise victory of the Conservative Party in the general election two years later. It is also widely believed to have encouraged the increase in expressed antagonism, including physical assaults, towards people with black or brown skins which took place over the following decade. And certainly, these people suddenly found themselves scared. (This fostering of social disharmony was presumably the reason for his dismissal.)

Half a century on, opinion about the speech is still divided. Some see it as prescient in its concerns about unrestricted immigration, which is almost certainly the most important single motivation for half of the British electorate voting to leave the European Union in 2016. And in fact, his prediction of 10 per cent of the British population being non-white has turned out to be a slight underestimation. On the other hand, others point out that his prediction of non-whites being able to dominate whites has not come true, still less true that of widespread, interracial violence amounting to civil war. (Indeed, the cause of what comparatively little intercommunal violence there *has* been is in large measure the result of the first part of this prediction being diametrically the wrong way around.)

However, neither the accuracy or otherwise of his predictions nor the wisdom or otherwise of his proposals to reverse immigration is the issue here. What is not in doubt is that it caused some people to feel afraid and many others to feel disturbed. What is it about the speech that caused this offence? To investigate this, we can analyse one statement made near the start of the speech, which is the extract from it most often quoted and played back, indicative of the fact that it encapsulates many of his views. Indeed, it was presented as the justification for much of what he proceeded to say in the speech. Powell is recounting a conversation with one of his constituents, a middle-aged working man, a few weeks earlier, who told him he would emigrate if he could afford it and wouldn't feel satisfied until all of his three children had "settled overseas". The man finished, according to Powell, by saying to him:

> In this country in 15 or 20 years' time the black man will have the whip hand over the white man.

Powell claimed that hundreds of thousands of others were thinking what this man had said. In the light of this co-text, we can assume that, although he was only animating the prediction, he was at this point identifying himself with the proposition it contained; that is, he was making himself a principal, accountable for the prediction.

At one level, this predication is simply a prediction that black people will be in charge of, or at least the dominant force in, public affairs and everyday life. The prediction is in itself no more offensive than any other prediction that one group of people will have more influence and power than another group of people, such as older people having more power than younger people, or trade unions more than employers, or Republicans more than Democrats. However, given Powell's position of influence, the co-text of his speech (see above) and its wide broadcast capacity, when issued from his mouth the prediction takes on the illocutionary force of a warning.

The first, most obvious thing to note is that the referential content is about what is known as race – it makes a person's skin colour salient. Two groups of people in society are identified within this conceptual field and presented in a relation to each other, which in lexical semantics is known as complementary opposition. As Jeffries (2010: 19–20) notes, two characteristics of this kind of opposition are mutual exclusivity and exhaustiveness. Applied here, these mean, respectively, that if you're black, you can't be white (and vice versa) and if you're not black, you must be white. (The whole conceptual field is covered by these two entities – there are no other categories within it.) While the first of these characteristics might seem obvious, note how the context of Powell's speech implicates the feature of exhaustiveness. He is a national politician and the co-text of his speech is about his fears for the 'country' as a whole, encouraging the listener to assume that black and white comprise the totality of the population – in Britain in 1968, everybody is either black or white.

In predicating this kind of opposition between black and white and its high salience to society, Powell is simply reinforcing what was very much a socially accepted one at the time. It is worth pausing here to reflect on the oddity of these assumptions. We can do this by comparing skin colour with another social category – gender. Both are very immediately visible in individuals, which is presumably one reason why both tend to have high salience. However, the latter dimension has far less fuzzy boundaries. There will be many more cases of doubt on the part of observers as to whether a person can be identified as of this or that 'race' on the basis of their appearance alone than whether they can be identified as male or female. The colouring of people's complexion is infinitely variable. The same is true from the point of view how people tend to identify themselves. The vast majority see themselves as either male or female, while how people identify themselves ethnically varies greatly (and by no means always correlates with skin colour).

Note, then, that the utterance we are examining reinforces the notion of a binary distinction where none actually exists. This presupposition is all the stranger because, while colour of skin may be perceptually salient, it is genetically trivial. It is in this reification of, and primary importance given to, race as indicated by skin colour and its reduction into two mutually exclusive groups that this utterance and Powell's use of it may be deemed racist.

However, simply to label the utterance racist is to capture only half of its unpleasantness. What makes it truly nasty and dangerous is that the relation between the two groups is presented as one of power and the nature of that power. As to the former, there is a transitive relation which is mutually exclusive. That is, if A has power over B, then B cannot have power over A (as opposed to, say, 'A loves B', which does not preclude B also loving A, or 'A kissed B', which can be interpreted as B also kissing A, or 'A married B' which actually entails B also married A). The two groups are not just opposed but assumed to be engaged in a struggle for power. As to the nature of the power, the expression "have the whip hand over" connotes the capacity for the powerful group to exert violence on the other. Note also how a sense of the physical immediacy of this capacity for violent dominance is suggested by referring to the two groups as typified entities – not 'black people' and 'white people' but "the black man" and "the white man".[3] And this "black man", we are told, "will have" this capacity, while the lack of this capacity in "the white man" is emphasized by the fact that he appears in a non-obligatory part of the clause structure. More particularly, in the context of historical relations between black and white, a further possible inference derived from the word "whip" is that the former will enslave the latter.[4]

And in the context of the speech as dire warning, it would imply that the reverse situation – the 'white man' having power over the 'black man' – would be the right-and-proper situation. It is a brutish view of society. It is this view which deeply offended, by terrifying, all those in the country who could not plausibly put themselves in the 'white' pigeonhole. The view also offended, by disturbing, those 'whites' who could discern its incitement to (what we might call) proactive retaliation.

10.2 (Dis)harmony in the workplace

The data from which the analyses begin in this section are in one sense imaginary. That is, they are test items involving fictional scenarios, although it is possible these are derived from attested cases. However, the fact that people took these test items *is* attested and the thrust of analysis is a critique of the real-life ramifications of their 'correct' answers.

Soon after taking up my post at an English university, I was required to take an online training module entitled *Diversity in the Workplace*. Some ten years later, I was required to take it again. The email message informing me of this fact read, "all [research active] staff … are required to undertake and pass the e-learning *Diversity in the Workplace* module". Passing the module involved reading through the material and then achieving at least 80 per cent correct answers to a battery of test questions.

10.2.1 A potentially offensive joke

On both occasions when I took the module, one of the test items was as follows:

> It is more appropriate to e-mail a joke than to say it aloud in the office in case others who hear are offended by its content.
> ○ true
> ○ false

A brief analysis of this test item appears in O'Driscoll (2013: 281–2), as an example of the increasing tendency for 'public-ization' of communication. Here, I want to examine the item as an example of social control more generally.

What, dear reader, would your answer to this item be? I am not especially proud to tell you that I chose 'false' because I had surmised, correctly, that this was the answer which those who devised this module wanted – even though I disagree. The rest of this section is an investigation of the foundations and implications of the 'correct' answer.

I first present my case for the 'wrong' answer. The fact that the choices are labelled 'true' and 'false' encourages us to examine the propositional content of the statement. It concerns the telling of a joke whose content apparently has the potential to cause some people offence ("in case others … are offended"). And it asserts that, *given this potential* ("in case"), emailing it is better than delivering it in the spoken mode "in the office". Its semantic structure is a comparative statement of the form: A1 [email] is better than A2 [spoken] because X [A2 risks causing offence], which logically entails A2 is worse than A1 because X. As X (causing offence) is a result that presumably most people would regard as undesirable, and certainly any sensible person wishing to pass a test called *Diversity in the Workplace* would know is supposed to be undesirable, it is a natural interpretation that the issue here is: which course of action is less likely to cause offence?

The reason given in the test item for preferring email is the desire to avoid the risk of any unratified participants becoming overhearers during the spoken encounter in which the joke is told. The idea is that email communication carries fewer risks of overhearing bystanders than the physical office setting. This assumes different participation frameworks for the two modes of delivery. And indeed they *are* different. An email message is a canonically closed encounter, in that participants comprise only the sender and those to whom s/he sends it by typing their email addresses into the 'To' and/or 'Cc' boxes. The possibility of the presence of immediate 'overhearers' is extremely small. (All I can think of is someone who happens to be looking over a recipient's shoulder at that person's screen at the precise moment s/he opens the message and thereafter examines its content – an 'overlooker'.) The environment evoked by "the office" (note: not 'your office'), on the other hand, is a space shared by many, with relatively unfettered minute-to-minute entry. It thus suggests an open encounter in which possibly unnoticed others of relatively unpredictable identity may be within or move into earshot – in other words, bystanders who become overhearers, all the more so as the choice offered is to deliver the joke "aloud" (i.e. no attempt at hushed exclusion of some participants).

Given these different participation frameworks for its two possible modes of delivery, the potentially offensive joke is indeed much less likely to cause actual offence if sent by email than if broadcast around a multi-person, open-access gathering. And given that the motivation for the decision to deliver the joke by email is to avoid accidentally offending anyone, it can be presumed the sender would take care not to send it to anyone they believe it might offend (and therefore that the possibility of offending ratified participants is not at issue). The statement is therefore a perfectly reasonable one.

However, this is not how a final-year undergraduate class of mine saw it. When first presented with the test item, they unanimously deemed the statement 'false'. In the discussion which then ensued, the most persuasive reason given for their choice was that the joke would be circulated by email to all except anyone who the sender suspected might be offended by it, who may then, when they eventually came to hear of the joke (as, it was argued, they inevitably would) be doubly offended; that is, as well as perhaps being offended by the joke itself, they would certainly be offended, and suffer significant damage to face, by the realization that they had been 'left out' of the sociable circle.[5]

This outlook imagines a very different kind of participation framework to the one I have put forward above. It imagines that the list of potential recipients of the joke is largely confined to a fairly well-defined network of individuals in 'the office' and that the joke, if it is to be told at all and through whatever medium, is to be told there and then. Under these circumstances, it is indeed very likely that anyone excluded will become aware of their exclusion fairly easily. The participation frameworks imagined in this case is one in which ratified participants can already be identified, these being the regular occupants of 'the office', so that the sending of an email which excludes one or more of them would be a fairly blatant, and almost certainly offensive, act of excollusion (Goffman 1981: 134).

What these divergent scenarios show, of course, is that communicative acts presented prototypically as items for consideration (not only in online test items like this but also by pragmatics tutors in seminars!) can never be specified fully enough to avoid a variety of interpretations. More interestingly, in the filling-in of the gaps by different groups of people we get a glimpse of their divergent outlooks on the conduct of social life. My group of 20-something undergraduate students and I have very different world views. Two aspects of this divergence are relevant here. Firstly, being at the start of their working careers, they are more inclined than me to conceptualize the 'workplace' of this online module's title and 'the office' of this test item as an open-plan space, with colleagues in 9-to-5 co-presence, so that picking and choosing which of these should receive an emailed joke would feel to them like an act of exclusion. My notion of 'workplace', on the other hand, since I work as much at home as I do on campus (where I work not only in an office shared with just one colleague but also in seminar rooms and lecture halls), is much more diffuse. When I send an email message, I only rarely have a sense of having excluded someone to whom I have chosen not to send it.

Secondly, my students, unlike me, grew up in the age of the internet. They live in a world in which e-communication feels as normal as embodied communication and the default participation frameworks for which is open access. Their prototype is more likely to be SMS, in which potentially innumerable people can access a post or tweet, rather than email, in which access is, in the first instance, confined to those who have been selected by the sender. From this viewpoint, it is inevitable that everybody in 'the office' would soon find out about the joke and the manner of its dissemination.

But of course the test item specifies none of these aspects of contexts. Because of these lacunae, then, we cannot hope to arrive at a context-spanning 'right' answer to it. In my world 'true' is the right answer while in my students' world their 'false' answer is right, for exactly the same reason – the concern to avoid giving offence to anyone. However, by now examining the reasons given by the test producers for 'false' being *their* correct answer, we can deduce *their* assumed participation framework for this test item, and also enquire into the possible effect of this institutional prescription. Here it is:

> E-mailing a joke that could cause offence is just as inappropriate as speaking it aloud. An e-mail is a legal document that can serve as evidence in an employment tribunal or disciplinary procedure.

Notice that the explanation given is not that the opposite of the original proposition is true (i.e. not that spoken delivery is more appropriate than email). Rather, the two modes are claimed to be equal ("just as") in their level of appropriateness. This assertion diverges from *both* the arguments above: my argument was that email delivery of the joke would be *less* likely to cause offence; my students' argument was that email would be *more* likely to cause offence (because of the excollusion). The assertion here is that they are equally likely. The comparative element of the original statement ("more appropriate") has been elided. What was presented as a gradable phenomenon in the test item has been presented in the reason given for the 'correct' answer as one of mutual exclusivity instead – if it's not appropriate, it must be inappropriate. Jeffries (2010: 19–22) exemplifies how, depending on syntactic frame, an opposition which would conventionally be regarded as gradable (here, appropriate/

inappropriate) can be interpreted as one which "admits no intervening values between its extremes" (2010: 19). This is certainly a likely interpretation in this case. Because it is potentially offensive, telling that joke is simply *in*appropriate, in any mode of delivery. In this respect, the test item is a trick question; test-takers, it turns out, were not being asked to decide which course of action is more appropriate – *neither* course of action is.

Additional explanation is provided in the second sentence of the reason given for the 'correct' answer. By implication, it imagines the possibility of the original message being subsequently forwarded to others – others who by virtue of this re-animation become overhearers and who, like those imagined in the original statement if the joke were delivered in spoken mode, are offended. This possibility, that one of the original recipients of the joke-by-mail should later retell it, is of course no different from what is possible if the joke were originally delivered in the spoken mode – one of the original addressees could do the same thing. It is presumably on these grounds that the telling of a potentially offensive joke is deemed inappropriate by any means – the original teller may be concerned not to give offence but recipients/addressees may not be so sensitive. However, by alluding to the possibility of the email being subsequently used in (quasi-) legal proceedings, the explanation imagines not only overhearers but also eavesdroppers, people who become privy to the emailed joke by design rather than by accident, some of whom have power over the original teller. The effect is to nuance the participation framework of email as outlined above. It draws attention to the persistence feature (Herring 2007) of TMC messages. In doing so, the reason given in the test item for taking or not taking a course of action becomes, in the explanation, transformed from concern for others ("in case others who hear are offended") into concern for self ("evidence in an employment tribunal or disciplinary procedure") – the joke-teller (and maybe the institution for whom s/he works) might find themselves in hot water!

It is, of course, perfectly understandable that the university should not want its employees to spend their time telling jokes that offend some of them. And no doubt the correct answer in this case is not merely driven by a corporate desire to avoid time-consuming and interpersonally unpleasant (quasi-) legal proceedings and/or negative publicity but also a genuine desire for general harmony among its employees. But the fact that the ability of its employees to abide by this desire was tested in this particular manner means that a subtext is produced: if telling a potentially offensive joke is not acceptable in any medium, even when the teller takes care not to give offence, then the implied message is simply ... don't tell jokes.

Two other features of the wording of this test item and the reasons given for the 'correct' answer have the effect of strengthening this proscription by encouraging test-takers to take it on board as a general, context-spanning one. First, note that the choice for test-taker was not 'agree' or 'disagree'. By offering instead 'true' or 'false', the test presents the item statement as one subject to truth conditions. Of course it is not – the item addresses a matter of desirable behaviour, which is a matter of opinion, not one of objective truth, which isn't. But this presentation of the choice of answers connotes objectivity.

Second, the use of the lexeme '(in)appropriate' is significant. Words such as 'acceptable' or 'permissible' would entail that the joke-telling is accepted or not accepted, permitted or not permitted, *by the employer*, being part of the employer's required standards of behaviour. But '(in)appropriate' carries no such agency. Moreover, note that although a reason for the assertion of inappropriateness can be inferred from the sequencing of the two sentences in the explanation (first "inappropriate", then "employment tribunal or disciplinary procedure"), this is not made explicit – there is no 'because' in there. The telling of this joke is inappropriate per se. Thus the 'correct' answer is presented as a matter of everyday personal interactive conduct, the right way to behave in a more general sense. No doubt numerous other organizations are equally anxious to preserve harmony among their workforce and avoid the hassle of offended people making complaints. Through this means we can see how institutional prescription can trickle down into more general mores. My students, for example, were not employed by the university and didn't have to pass this module; yet they genuinely thought that not sending this joke by email was the right way to behave.

10.2.2 Ageist harassment

Another way in which institutional prescription can affect everyday behaviour is through 'ism-condemnation'. If behaviour can be labelled sexist, racist, ageist or indicative of some other 'ism', it can be context-spanningly condemned. Here is another item from the same test, with the 'correct' answers included.

> Barry, a lecturer, is older than many of his co-workers, who often make jokes about him being 'past it' and 'clapped out'. His approach so far has been to 'grin and bear it', but for his 50th birthday, he gets a card from his colleagues addressed to 'An old fart'. Barry decides he's had enough, and makes a complaint. What's your opinion of the situation?

A   Barry's colleagues are harassing him
B   Barry is taking this too seriously
C   Barry's colleagues are being ageist
D   The situation is unfortunate, but acceptable

Select the two options you think are correct and then click on the submit button.

That's right. The correct answers are A and C.

Barry's colleagues' comment could be defined as harassment if Barry finds them offensive or humiliating, and his colleagues are certainly being ageist.

For the purposes of throwing light on the 'correct' answers, I briefly analyse now a remark made to me by a colleague of mine. We were chatting informally in the corridor outside our offices about our upcoming work-related plans. At one point in the conversation, I confided that I had an additional instrumental reason for my plans. This was that given my relatively advanced age, I felt the need to achieve something notable in order to "avoid being somehow placed in the 'old codger' category" (i.e. a more fondly viewed version of 'clapped out' and 'past it'). As an interpolated contribution, my colleague at once retorted "too late for that". I made a brief facial expression indicating outrage at an insult and the conversation immediately returned to the details of our working plans.

Was I offended by that remark? Yes, but only in the most trivial sense and the feeling was outweighed by one of interpersonal warmth. First, the offensive aspect. By confessing to this very personal aspect of my motivation for my working ambitions, I was changing the topic from working plans to myself and my anxieties, thereby shifting my footing from fellow-professional to vulnerable-individual. There are various ways that my colleague could have oriented to this shift. S/he could have interpreted it as an invitation to shift her own footing to that of reassuring-confidante and proceeded to reassure me that my fears were groundless (e.g. "I don't think you need to worry about that"). Alternatively, s/he could have interpreted it as not a shift of significance for the trajectory of the discourse but rather as a temporarily embedded footing, so that s/he could orient to the 'confession' as a non-serious aside, in which case her response would be a brief laugh. I think I would have found either of these reactions satisfactory from a face-maintenance point of view. But by responding with a remark which asserted that my aspirations concerning my workplace image were pointless and thus implicated that I already had the image I professed to be trying to avoid, neither of those possible lines resulting from my 'confession' could be sustained: the non-serious, whimsical line was confounded by my image-fear being addressed as if serious; the vulnerable-individual line was attacked by not getting the reassurance it appeared to be fishing for. My colleague had shifted to a teasing footing and I was momentarily wrong-faced (Goffman [1955] 1967a: 8).

But only wrong-faced, not face-damaged, and only momentarily. Both the immediate co-text and the wider background context allowed me to interpret the remark as supportive teasing. The former was a mutually supportive discussion both before and after the remark. Both my confession and the remark itself were treated by each of us as an embedded, light-hearted digression. As to the latter, I had had years of experience of my colleague's tendency to insert teasing remarks, so this one did not come out of the blue, and beyond that I had always been confident of my colleague's support at work and goodwill towards me more generally. With this context, the remark was experienced by me as an affirmation of our relative intimacy and my colleague's desire that our relationship retain that status. It did, in fact, support the non-serious orientation to my 'confession' more effectively than a laugh would have done (which could have been interpreted as indicative of a wish to 'politely' avoid addressing my fear because actually it was well founded). At the same time, its blunt rudeness, especially because it was delivered as an interpolation, dismissed my fear as not to be taken seriously,[6] so that it was just as reassuring as an explicit reassurance would have been. It functioned as positive facework, both in O'Driscoll's (2007, 2011) narrow sense and in Brown & Levinson's ([1978] 1987: 61–2) more general sense.

Apart from it being a nice illustration of the need to distinguish between (what I am calling) interactive face and other aspects of face (see section 2.2), the point of this anecdote is to highlight the fact that whether teasing is acceptable will always be radically situation-specific. No doubt the fictional tormenters of Barry in that test item, when called to account for their behaviour, will fall back on the 'just banter', no-harm-intended defence. There are two very clear indications in the rubric to the question which allow us to understand Barry is very unhappy about his colleagues' repeated derogatory allusions to his relatively advanced age – we are told he tries to "grin and bear it" (i.e. tolerate as best he can a situation which he finds unpleasant) but eventually decides he has "had enough and makes a complaint". With this information, it is easy to pick out choice A as one of the two correct answers required. The explanation given for why their behaviour can be classed as harassment also refers to Barry's feelings ("offensive or humiliating").

On the other hand, no explanation for the other correct answer is forthcoming. It is apparently self-evident ("certainly") that he is 'being ageist'. All we have to go on here to reach this judgement are quotes of the phrases used by his colleagues to characterize him. As my colleague implicated me as an 'old codger', by the same logic, s/he was 'being ageist' too. The significance of this assessment can be seen if we look again at the test rubric. The two incorrect choices offered either reluctantly exonerate the behaviour of Barry's colleagues ("unfortunate but acceptable") or blame Barry instead ("taking this too seriously"). We thus have a clear contrast between their behaviour being acceptable (the incorrect answers) or unacceptable (the correct answers). Accordingly, we infer that 'being ageist', identifiable merely by the use of certain characterizations which index advanced age, is unacceptable and prohibited. And yet I have just related an instance which, by the same criteria, can be labelled as 'ageism' but which was experienced as supportive and ultimately face-enhancing.

The argument is, then, that the charge of ageism in Barry's case is largely beside the point. His colleagues have been, it seems, disparaging him and making him feel very uncomfortable as a result. The fact that they have picked on his age to do this is incidental. The important thing is that they appear to have behaved at best insensitively and at worst cruelly. This example is one of the consequences of condemning behaviour as an instance of an 'ism', an institutionalized practice which ignores all situational contingencies.[7] In fact, as a not entirely tongue-in-cheek final observation, I cannot resist pointing out that the rubric and delivery of this test item has itself ignored one of these contingencies – the testers' interaction with the testee. I am a person of considerably more years than the fifty which caused Barry to be tormented about his age. How does this test item make somebody like *me* feel? Somebody so spectacularly ancient, it would seem, as to be not in the frame at all. If ageism is a practice to be condemned because it discriminates against or otherwise demeans those of an advanced age, the circumstances of my participation in this test have made me the victim of ageism!

Part Four

Reprise

Reporting offensive language

In all the cases examined in the last three chapters, the individual to whom blame might be attached for the offending utterance was transparent. This was because the roles of principal, author and animator of the utterance were united in the same person. This chapter addresses a thorny question. To what extent can the (re)animator of offensive language be held accountable for it? In terms of Goffman's (1981) production format, the answer would seem to be straightforward. The animator is no more than the person who gives words physical reality – who makes them manifest. If that person quotes someone else's words, they have neither chosen the words (author role), nor have they responsibility for the propositional content contained in those words (principal role).

However, if that person is more than just a mouthpiece – that is, if that animator is also principal and author of the text in which the quoted words are embedded – we have to face the fact that they have chosen to quote those words. It would, for example, be perverse not to hold Enoch Powell responsible for that quote of his constituent examined in section 10.1. Although the default position must be that if the author reports someone else as has having said something, then it is that other person, and not the author, who should in the first instance be held accountable for it, one could argue that the fact the author has chosen to relay what the other person said (whether by quoting or by some more indirect means) makes him/her accountable for its content too. After all, s/he could have chosen not to mention it at all. (In human history, an assumption to this effect has often been made, which is why, despite the maxim, the messenger sometimes *does* get shot.) In the context, for example, of me telling a student group about Goffman's notion of production format, it is clear that I can be held accountable for the ideas relayed to quite a large extent. By bringing them up at all, I signal that I think they are worthy of consideration and I can be held accountable for that opinion.

However, it is clear that we cannot *automatically* attribute the propositional content of what one person said to the person who reports what that person said. If we were to do this, everybody would be reluctant ever to report what somebody else said unless they agreed with or approved of it – and most debate and scholarship would grind to a halt. In a public medium such as newspapers, what the author of a text *is* accountable for is not the propositional content of what s/he reports as having been said but rather the *accuracy* of the reporting of that content. More generally, whether and to what extent we can justifiably judge the reporter to be aligning themselves with the propositional content of what they report requires close attention to co-text, to how the reported content has been packaged – to the *manner of embedding* of the embedded content.

To a degree, discourse presentation theory as developed within the discipline of stylistics can help here. This notion (see Leech & Short 2007: Chapter 10) identifies a spectrum along which a narrator represents the words of others, which goes from direct speech at one end (e.g. She said, "No, I won't") to a report of a speech act (e.g. She refused) at the other. However, the main concern in this theory is with the degree of narrator interference of, and therefore relative faithfulness to, the original words being reported. It does not tell us a lot about accountability for the propositional contents of what is reported. For this purpose, the distinction between attribution, by which a proposition is accredited to a person other than the writer, and averral, when the writer is its source, first made by Sinclair (1986, 1988) and developed by Hunston (2000), offers a little more help.[1] Hunston observes the possibility of what she calls 'hidden averral', often found in academic texts (such as when I wrote "one could argue" above), by which the author implies that the source for the proposition which follows is not him/herself when in fact it is. This distinction thus focuses a little more sharply on the extent to which the 'reporter' aligns with the embedded proposition, which is my main concern here.

11.1 Mel Gibson and the Jews

In 2006, the mass media reported an incident in which the Hollywood actor Mel Gibson was stopped for speeding and then arrested for drunken driving in California. At that time and later (serially, whenever he was reported as involved in another incident), reference to this incident included a quote of Gibson's words at the time taken from the police report. Here are three such references:[2]

> Gibson asked the officer if he was Jewish and said: "F**king Jews. The Jews are responsible for all the wars in the world."

> The foul-mouthed tirades [against his former partner] came after the Oscar-winner was arrested in California in 2006 after he was caught drink driving.

> Gibson, a devout Catholic, was alleged to have told the police officer that stopped him: "******* Jews. The Jews are responsible for all the wars in the world."

> Gibson's anti-Semitic tirade in 2006, when he told a police officer arresting him for drink-driving: "Are you a Jew? Jews are responsible for all the wars in the world."

All three articles contain words in quote marks which are thereby being attributed to someone other than the author at the time of writing. They belong, in Goffman's (1981: 147) words, "to the world that is spoken about, not the world in which the speaking occurs". But the authors of the articles have seen fit to relay these words, so it is legitimate to ask whether and to what extent they align with the words' propositional content.

The short answer is a straightforward 'no'. First, notice that in each case the relayed words are attributed in the reporting clause to a single identifiable person ("he" or "Gibson"), thereby emphasizing that the author is disowning not only the words (achieved through the use of quote marks) but also their propositional content. To see this more clearly, compare 'There has been a widespread opinion that "[proposition X]"', which could pass as hidden averral, allowing the inference that the author is possibly one of those who hold with the proposition X.

Second, notice that the reporting verb phrase is in the past tense ("told" or "said"). As has been widely observed (e.g. Kilby 1984, Leech 2004), the English past tense has the general effect of distancing. In this case, it causes the propositional content to be packaged as part of an event, as the expressing of an opinion at a certain particular time and to a particular interlocutor. The event is foregrounded at the expense of the propositional content, which therefore invites less serious consideration than if it were presented as a current opinion without situational information. The attention is drawn to what Gibson *did* and less to what he believes. To put this another way, attention is drawn to a particular act of animation – the author is merely the re-animator.

The authors (and so the newspapers they write for), then, have placed some clear blue water between themselves and the negative attitude towards Jews displayed in the propositional content of the quoted words. But still, they *have* chosen to re-animate this expressed attitude. An extremely offensive negative attitude to Jews *has* been displayed for readers to see. Perhaps the utterer of these words is being used as a cat's paw. Might we still be able to claim that what readers (could) take from this piece of text is a negative impression of Jews?

To answer this question, we have to examine how Gibson is represented in these articles. It is not impossible for a text to present an identified person in such a positive light that, event-packaging notwithstanding, readers are effectively invited to give serious consideration to the propositional content of that person's quoted words. However, from the little information we have in these short extracts, the opposite appears to be the case here. First, note that Gibson is quoted using a taboo word,[3] and that in its premodifying position this lexeme makes the noun phrase of which it is part ("Fucking Jews") a throwaway comment rather than a serious estimation. (Compare, for example, 'Bellicose Jews'). The propositional content of what follows, therefore, is framed as part of a foul-mouthed outburst, not the articulation of a considered opinion. Conclusion: this person's expressed view is not to be taken seriously (an impression bolstered, of course, by the exaggeration in the proposition itself – no group of people could realistically be held responsible for all wars).

Second, note the reporting of the situation of this person's utterance. He is presented uttering the words to a Jewish policeman. Only two possible impressions can be taken from this fact: either this person is aggressive and rude or, if he doesn't realize he's talking to a Jew, ignorant. Conclusion: this person is either deeply unpleasant or stupid. Finally, all these extracts are from articles which relate other examples of the outrageous things that Gibson has apparently said over the years. Moreover, they all appear in the magazine sections of the newspaper, under the heading 'people' or 'celebrity news', rather than in sober news sections, thereby presented more as gossip than as content for serious consideration.

Overall, then, the man to whom this view of Jews is attributed is portrayed in a very negative manner, and it is how *he* is represented, rather than how Jews are represented, which is foregrounded. It therefore becomes very unlikely that readers take away a negative impression of Jews. To do so, they would have to identify with the apparently unpleasant character whose utterance has been quoted, to represent *themselves* in their own minds as similarly unpleasant.

Admittedly, this is not impossible. They could perhaps, without subscribing to the specifics of the propositional content, identify with the general anti-Semitic *sentiment* expressed, in which case we would have to take this author's re-animation of Gibson's words as reinforcing whatever anti-Semitic feeling is already out there. After all, people's attitudes are not just composed, or even mainly composed, of considered opinion; there is a lot of feeling in there too. However, to allow for this possibility and accordingly censure this particular re-animation of an offending utterance would be to close off all speech about anything offensive.

11.2 The sacked bassoonist

This case is far less straightforward because presentation of direct speech is not involved. It avers not what somebody said on a particular occasion but rather what some *kinds* of people *typically* say. Rather than reporting an event, it reports habit. There is perhaps always an element of interpretation in the latter. For these reasons, the content of what is reported has greater focus than in the case above.

11.2.1 Background context

The Royal Academy of Music in London is a venerable institution of higher education in music. It has about 800 undergraduate and postgraduate students, about half of whom come from Britain, a quarter from mainland Europe and a quarter from elsewhere in the world. From 2017, as with other higher education institutions in England in the twenty-first century, part of the public funding received by the Academy is dependent on its rating in the 'Teaching Excellence Framework' (TEF), an external audit of its teaching provision. One element of this audit is an assessment of 'student outcomes', a measurement of the extent to which students achieve their goals. One factor with an effect on these outcomes is the quality of career advice and development provided by the institution.

In the summer of 2017, with a view to enhancing its provision in this area, the Academy hired two new part-time members of staff. One of these was Dr Francesca Carpos-Young, who was engaged to develop and deliver a module on the practicalities of making a career in the music profession. Part of the module was to include a series of five lectures to be delivered in October and November of that year and various other sessions. She was also encouraged by her line managers to circulate her lecture notes and other useful advice to all Academy students (not merely those who were attending her lectures).

11.2.2 Immediate context and data[4]

Accordingly, on 30 October, she sent an email to all students in the Academy with four attachments, one of which was entitled 'Networking Pathway ideas'. These were the notes for her first lecture, which she had already delivered, which had been billed as "networking and reputation building". It was a six-page document which largely comprised very general, sensible, even obvious, practical advice about overall approach and how to conduct oneself in the professional musical world. After a few quotes from musicians about how they describe those with good reputations, it reads:

> the implication is that building a reputation is about fitting in and be [sic] adaptable. Considering the way you look, the way you behave, a response to one another musically, what you say, and what you do not say. Everyone knows that having reputation is important. But how do you get one? At the very least you need to consider the following tips:

Below are extracts at which specific offence was taken.

> Become familiar with shared understanding of anecdote, caricature, stereotype and jokes. Google them and look them up on YouTube if this is not your culture. For example, you may hear terms like this: [fourteen terms, among which are] the boys = other orchestral musicians ... pond life (string players), gypos, short for gypsies = violinists specifically.

Among twenty-six bullet points of behavioural tips, are:

- Look young, up-together and cool in rehearsals, and smart in concerts; this is a superficial and ageist world
- Go to the pub, golf, play bridge, join Facebook, LinkedIn, Twitter, and be clubbable
- Joining in with sectional humour. Brass is pubs and pond life is tea queues

Later on the same day, the senior postgraduate tutor received an email (hereafter complaint 1) from a student which described the document as containing

> absurd suggestions, shameful stereotyping and ... descriptions of sexism and racism that are not acceptable under any circumstances.

Cited as examples were:

> 'gypos' [is] categorically racist [and] 'the boys': the idea that orchestras are made up only of males is not only damaging … but blatantly false and seemingly seeks to perpetuate a rapidly fading image.

The email also criticized the poor quality of presentation in the document, saying that it was similar in this respect to many other documents issued by the Academy.

The next day, two more student complaints were sent to the student union president. One (hereafter complaint 2) said that certain parts of the document were

> completely inappropriate and offensive [with] terminology of violins as gypos, look young, be clubbable

as examples. The other email (hereafter complaint 3) mostly ridiculed the advice, characterizing its list of tips as

> a manual for how to behave like an arsehole,

but also singled out the word 'gypos' as shocking, wondering how

> actual violinists who happened to be Sinti or Roma feel about it.

The following day, on the advice of her line manager, Dr Carpos-Young sent out an email to all students explaining that she did not intend to offend, and pointing out that the provocative terms "are those used by musicians", as evidenced in her recently completed PhD thesis, a study in inequality in the profession which included interviews with more than a hundred professional orchestral musicians. She observed that those who had attended her lecture would know this, and that the terms generated much lively discussion about how to deal with the things that get said in professional life by people "who may be in a position to hire or fire you".

The day after that, an open letter from the 'student body' to the Academy headed 'Our response' (hereafter complaint 4) was drawn up and then circulated to all students. It described the networking document as "unacceptable" and Dr Carpos-Young's follow-up email as "entirely inadequate". It condemned the document for encouraging antisocial behaviour and complicity in discrimination on the basis of various social categories (e.g. race, age, gender). It cites the "most egregious statements" in the document, asserting that

> 'boys = other orchestral musicians' [maintained] an environment in which anyone who is not a man is automatically an outsider,

commenting on the 'gypos' citation that

> it is shocking that such racist language would be accepted or implicitly encouraged by an official document sent out by the Academy

and labelling the 'Brass is pubs and pond life is tea queues' comment as the stereotyping of musicians. The open letter then went on to criticize the Academy more generally, describing Dr Carpos-Young's document as merely

> a symptom of [its] failure to live up to institutional aims regarding equality and diversity

and calling for student-led working groups on these matters. Students were asked to sign the letter. Fifty-eight did so. A few emailed the student union president to say that they disagreed with it. By the end of that day, complaint 4 had been posted on Facebook and Slipped Disc, the blog of a well-known music critic.

The next day Dr Carpos-Young was dismissed without notice for 'gross misconduct'. Her internal appeal against dismissal was rejected by the end of the month and soon afterwards she was asked to resign as a governor of the Royal Society of Musicians, a charity for musicians in need. About a year later, her appeal for wrongful dismissal was upheld by the Employment Tribunal and she was awarded compensation.

11.2.3 Analysis

It may be inferred from some of the detail above, and becomes clearer from additional facts recorded in the official appeal judgment in 2018, that a major factor in the Academy's decision to dismiss her was that managers regarded her as a difficult, argumentative character who, moreover, might delve into possible existing discriminatory practices at the Academy. But the stated reason, contained in a letter written to explain her dismissal was that

> sending [the document] to all students, without sufficient or relevant context, has resulted in numerous student complaints and caused significant damage to the relationship between the student body and the Academy [and] loss of confidence and trust between the student body and you [and has] brought the Academy into disrepute.

The reason, in other words, for offence being taken is that in the document Carpos-Young does not distance herself enough from the offensive views cited in it. As with the Gibson case above, we need to consider the extent to which Carpos-Young aligns with the references she cites to which exception was taken. And in doing so, we can begin to understand exactly what it was about the document that caused, among at least some of the students, offence severe enough for them to issue complaints to the management.

Context (of course!) has a role in answering this question. As regards background context, she sent the email in her capacity as someone whose specific role was to aid students' professional development (see section 11.2.1); that is, to help them take steps to progress in their careers. Moreover, she had every reason to assume that a student perception of sound, practical advice, with an emphasis on extant realities, plus actual 'student outcomes' over the years (see reference to the TEF above) were the criteria by which the institution would assess her performance as time went by. From this starting viewpoint, any advice she gives is framed as 'do A because of the existence of X' rather than 'do A in order to combat the existence of X'. However, this context may perhaps have been lost on those students who, not having attended her lecture or having registered internal publicity about her appointment, were not aware of her role.

The immediate context of the text itself (i.e. the co-text around which the particularly offending items appear) supports this background framing. Its style is the opposite of discursive. It contains a plethora of imperative predications in the service of how "you" can get a good reputation. Many of these are formatted as bullet points, and there is no attempt to relate one point to another (i.e. to offer an overall framework), both features emphasizing practical orientation rather than in-depth analysis. These are very clearly just "tips". The poor quality of presentation mentioned in complaint 1 also underlines this informal characteristic. As far as its author was concerned, this is not a document for publication in the conventional sense. However, the fact that two of the above-cited complaints link the document to practice in the Academy more generally suggests that this is not how they see it. Complaints 1 and 4 both refer to the document as sent "by the Academy", the latter referring to it as an "official" one. In our terms, they see the Academy as taking part in the principal role. The fact that it was emailed to all 800 students must have assisted in forming this impression.

The immediate co-text of the offending lexical items also distances the author from them. Most obviously, they are framed metalinguistically as "terms", the clause "you may hear terms like" having in speech act terms what Austin ([1962] 1975: 161–3) would call an expositive function, indicating the discoursal status of what is to follow (Oishi & Fetzer 2016). In this frame, and despite the lack of quotation marks, the lexical items themselves are a kind of what Fetzer & Weiss (2020) call 'canned quotations'; that is (in my terms), the re-animated speech of others without specifying time, place or individual source. They are, moreover, introduced as examples of non-serious representations ("anecdote, caricature, stereotype and jokes") with which readers are enjoined to "become familiar". Strictly speaking, they are only *examples* which "you may hear", so the students are not explicitly enjoined to become familiar with these particular terms, still less use them productively.

However, a reasonable inference is that these are the *best* examples with which to become familiar because they are the most frequently heard – the author has chosen to cite *them* rather than others. And of course she is clearly implicating her own familiarity with (but not necessarily use of) the particular terms she cites, and in the context of the presumed aim of an experienced practitioner inducting readers into a specific professional 'world', there is perhaps an element of imparting insider knowledge of which she implicitly approves, the more so because they are introduced as non-serious (i.e. insider jokes). The fact that none of the offending terms are framed by quote marks undermines somewhat the distancing effect of the quotative framing with which they are introduced. So does the fact that one of her bullet points refers to "pond life" as the bare subject of a sentence (i.e. without any metalinguistic framing). Moreover, the document's advice to "join[ing] in with sectional humour" carries the possible interpretation that these terms are not just for passive knowledge but also for use.

In summary, the author has owned to knowledge of the offending items but does not own them as part of her own productive use. However, she appears not to have done so in a manner which some students could pick up. They, it seems, would have needed explicit negative evaluations of the offending items to be inserted. The fact that these were introduced as "caricature, stereotype and jokes" was apparently not enough and/or not explicitly evaluative enough. This lack goes some way to explaining the offence they took.

But it goes further than that. Student complaints appear to have interpreted reference to the existence of something as acceptance of it. The citation itself is the cause of offence. All the above-cited complaints take issue with the appearance of 'gypos', with two of them describing it as 'racist'. Note that this word is used metaphorically; it is not used to refer to Roma people but rather to violinists, not in itself a derogatory referent. (See Padilla Cruz 2019 for this distinction between slur words and characterizing insults.) Both these features indicate that for these students it is a taboo word, and it was thought improper for a taboo word to appear in such a document, even quotatively, especially as a possible interpretation of the text is that they are being told to learn such words productively. (See the end of section 5.4.) Complaint 4 assumes this means its use is "accepted or implicitly encouraged". Likewise, the act of citing 'the boys' was deemed (complaints 1 and 4) to be supportive of male players as the norm and non-males as other. From this viewpoint, the document's explanation for the advice to "look young … and smart" – that "this is a superficial and ageist world" – can look, one presumes, like approval of ageism and superficiality too, notwithstanding the fact that to my knowledge the item 'ageist' (like 'racist' and 'sexist') is only ever used to indicate disapproval of the behaviour to which it refers.

It is odd that the most explicitly pejorative of the terms cited, the reference to string players as "pond life", is not singled out for condemnation. Instead, there is condemnation of the allusion to 'pond life' preferring tea to alcohol as stereotyping (complaint 4). In the light of this being explicitly introduced as "sectional humour", this criticism seems laboured. But it is possible that this comment is indicative of a broader, interactive reason for offence being taken at the document as a whole, as a result of the same stylistic features that signalled its informality. References in the letters of complaint to "absurd suggestions" (complaint 1), "manual for how to behave like an arsehole" (complaint 3) and (complaint 4) lack of professionalism in the document suggest that some students felt they were being talked down to. The obviousness of some of the tips and the unqualified directness of the discourse (all the bare imperatives) may have contributed to this impression. In this respect, the offending utterances discussed above were simply the last straw, and possibly the whole document was perceived as the tip of an iceberg which extended to relations between students, staff and managers at the Academy more generally (see complaint 4).

We learn from this case, then, that offence at specific utterances is sometimes not only taken but taken *up*, as a result of them being found symptomatic of a wider feeling of grievance. And while the aim of the analyses in this book has always been to find the cause of offence in the language of the offending utterance itself, this may sometimes be only the trigger – another reason why context in its widest sense must always be taken into account. (See also the Ebola case in section 8.3.) However, this case has again shown that context itself, being potentially variable among participants, is not entirely objective (see the cases in Chapter 9). Dr Carpos-Young's context for the offending document was not the same as the students', who themselves had different contexts, depending on whether or not they had attended her lecture and whether (among those who hadn't) they were aware of her role.

12

Social control and free speech

Several of the cases analysed in this book have instanced what I have referred to in Chapters 9–10 as social control; that is, the powerful sanctioning the social behaviour of the less powerful and thereby, through these examples, influencing that behaviour more generally. We have seen this control over what people say exercised by three powerful types of entity.

One of these is employers or their representatives: a multinational company (the Google internal memo – see section 6.1); a national government (the outcome of the incident at the Downing Street gates – see section 6.2); a sporting body (the English Football Association – see section 8.3); university authorities (the 'crap' email in section 8.2, the sacked lecturer in section 11.2 and the online workplace test in section 10.2). Another group comprises professional or occupational bodies, as in the suspensions imposed by political parties (see sections 6.1, 9.1.2 and 10.1). Such bodies sometimes have quasi-judicial status, as in the actions taken by the Dutch advertising standards authority (section 1.2.1) and the English Football Association against a football manager (section 8.4). Lastly, there are the judicial state authorities themselves, as in the various examples alluded to in section 6.1, the suspension imposed on Livingstone (section 6.2) and the internet messages examined in Chapter 9.

The licence of these groups to exercise this control, and the nature of the control itself, is of course subject to the influence of public opinion. But there is no doubt that the sanctions of the powerful also influence public opinion. One only has to think of the effect which the restrictions on smoking tobacco, imposed in most countries in the western world over the last couple of decades, have had on attitudes towards smoking in general. Moreover, the sanctions imposed have immediate, substantive effects on the perpetrators of offending utterances. In this book we have seen them take several forms. A couple have been mere workplace censure (of Pete's use of 'crap' – see section 8.2) or the threat of it (the reference to 'disciplinary procedure' in section 10.2.1). But we have also seen the imposition of financial penalties (on the football manager in section 8.4 and on Chambers for his tweet in section 9.2). There have been numerous cases of loss of position, not only of political role but also of employment (the Google employee in section 6.1, the football manager in 8.3 and the lecturer in 11.2). There has even been imprisonment (of the Facebook poster in 9.1.2 and the mock terrorists in 9.3). I therefore tend to think that, in the area of linguistic behaviour at least, the direction of influence from 'above' to 'below' is the greater. Most of the information needed for the case studies in this book was already in the public domain. The public learns about such cases – and their linguistic behaviour gets influenced.

Some of this control by the powerful is clearly to be appreciated. That those who publicly incite people to perpetrate extreme physical harm on others face legal sanction (as section 9.1), and that those in positions of power and influence face some kind of penalty if they do not consider the possible harmful effects of what they say (sections 8.3, 8.4 and 10.1), can only be a good thing. But the reader will have noticed cases in which the control has been exercised illogically (the reprimand to Pete in section 8.2), unwisely (the dismissal of the lecturer in section 11.2 which was later judged unfair), in a manner which is suspect (the online test of employees in section 10.2) or one which is either downright stupid or wilfully intimidating (the convictions of the tweeters in sections 9.2 and 9.3).

How is this control legitimized? How have so many of the offending utterances analysed in this book been deemed offensive enough to merit some kind of substantive sanction? I identify here two concurrent processes by which this is achieved, which I call taboo-ification and public-ization. These can be explained with reference to my definition of taboo language, which I repeat here:

> any (string of) words whose production is transgressive of polite social norms.

Taboo-ification relates in the first instance to the 'transgressive' description in this definition. Public-ization relates to when 'polite social norms' (see the definition in section 3.2) apply.

12.1 Taboo-ification

To taboo-ify an utterance is to place it within the inventory of words or strings of words which are deemed offensive in the abstract. A major way to do this, which has been witnessed repeatedly in the cases in this book, is to label it as some kind of 'ism'. The process is simple. We know that, for example, racism, sexism, ageism and terrorism are taboo. All that has to be done is to identify an utterance with one of these and it is – ipso facto – taboo too. The assessment "That's racist/ ageist/sexist" of an utterance is universally understood as a negative one. Now, if this assessment is understood to mean that the utterance (1) makes race, age or gender unwarrantedly salient and/or, more seriously, (2) can be interpreted in context as proposing or supporting some kind of unequal treatment of races, or ages or genders, quite right too. Of relevance here is Jacob Mey's (2012) interpretation of the notion of emancipatory pragmatics, which he avers is about "how to use language in a non-oppressive, even liberating way" so as to assist in "emancipating [people] from the bondage of false beliefs and societal oppression". He allies this notion to that of 'anticipatory pragmatics', whose task is to

> foresee and prevent such abuses, and enable the users to counteract abusive language (in the widest sense of the word), even before it starts being accepted as a normal way of dealing with the world. ('Politically correct' language may, despite its sometimes 'holier-than-thou' connotations, represent a step in the right direction.)
>
> (Mey 2012: 706)

I like to think that some of the analyses in this book (sections 8.3, 8.4, 9.1) have contributed to the identification of how even utterances which make no explicit reference to race or gender have effects which can contribute to societal oppression. And the fact that we are now being trained to consider carefully the effects which our words might have (see, for example, the online test in section 10.2) can help in the attempt to avoid various forms of social abuse.

However, I have also shown that when the assessment of 'racist/ageist/sexist' (and, indeed, 'terrorist') becomes interpreted as a blanket condemnation, the unfortunate effect is to shut down any further, deeper assessment, so that it becomes more difficult to distinguish between what is merely off-colour or shocking from what is genuinely nasty and/or dangerous. Mey goes on to caution that

> anticipating people's needs can be used to control those very people whose needs we intend to meet. The manipulative character of this kind of anticipation is clear: we may overstep the boundaries of other people's 'territories of information' … or we may impinge on the private sphere of people whose sufferings we want to empathize with … An emancipatory pragmatics with a proactive, anticipatory thrust should be aware of these dangers, and not fall back in the old groove of paternalistic colonialism, by which the poor natives were considered as unruly children, to be educated and formatted according to the principles and beliefs of the colonizers.
>
> (Mey 2012: 707)

It is ironic that the desire for particular groups of people not to be discriminated against on the basis of an ascribed attribute first came largely from below, from grass-roots movements, but, being now largely accepted in the western world, it can be used from above to control. Indeed, some features of the US presidential election campaign in 2016 – and its outcome – suggest that, in Anglo-American society at least, this 'politically correct' discourse has achieved so much that it is now widely perceived not so much as a movement to protect the vulnerable as an instrument of social control. How else can one explain the fact that some of the candidate Donald Trump's communicative behaviour appeared to work to his advantage rather than against it? During the campaign, he more than once exhorted or wished physical violence against any opponents at his rallies, insinuated that physical violence on his Democratic opponent might be a good idea, intimated that he might not accept the result of the election, made disparaging remarks about the family of a soldier who had been killed, and, at one rally, had recourse to spastic hand gestures and a mentally impaired facial expression when mock-quoting a disabled reporter to whose words he had taken exception. After this last incident, his supporters and Trump himself repeatedly claimed that his mockery on this occasion was not intended to mimic the reporter's disability. But it was interpreted that way by most people, and for good reasons. Trump introduced his performance with "you should see this guy" (rather than 'hear this guy'), thereby explicitly directing the attention of his audience towards the visible aspects of the performance. Moreover, the mock-quoted words themselves were devoid of context. They merely enacted incompetence.[1] Why did this last single incident alone not leave his campaign dead in the water? It can only be that there were enough voters in the United States (enough for him to be elected president[2]) who, even when they recognized the cruel, childish, jeering, playground-bully inanity of his behaviour, placed a higher value on their perception that this kind of behaviour heralded a candidate who refused to be constrained by the prevailing orthodoxy, someone who would not play by the rules of conduct they perceived as having been imposed on them – someone, in fact, who broke taboos.

12.2 Taboo-ification with public-ization

The other process, public-ization, involves extending the territory of domains deemed to be public or semi-public and within which, as a result, polite social norms are understood to apply. This way, strings of words deemed to be potentially offensive (i.e. taboo) become actually offending in a wider variety of situations. Of course, some of this public-ization is an inevitable reflex of present-day technological affordances: the presumed off-the-record remark of the football manager in section 8.4 turned out to be on the record and accessible to unlimited numbers of people; the intimations of violence in Chapter 9 whose producers assumed were being sent only to their associates were accessible to all and sundry. But the email cases in sections 8.2 and 10.2.1 also show an attempt to inscribe a canonically private medium as actually public. (See O'Driscoll 2013 for further discussion of the issue of public versus private.)

Significantly, this process, together with taboo-ification, is in evidence in the case cited at the end of section 5.4 (the complaints about the word 'negro') and the case examined in section 11.2 (the complaints about 'gypos' and other terms). In both cases, the people who objected to having words which they regarded as taboo directed at them (in one case through the spoken mode, in the other written), even though the offending words were issued quotatively, were students; that is, mostly younger adults, whose values and attitudes will become more mainstream as time passes. One might have assumed that the domain of higher education was a specialist domain, so that taboo words would not be an issue. But the students' reactions in both these cases suggest that they see it as a fully public domain.[3]

A different kind of public-ization can be gleaned from a series on British TV's Channel 4, which shows clips from programmes in decades past. Each programme shows clips from a particular decade. One example from the 1960s is the situation comedy *Till Death Us Do Part*, whose central character was Alf Garnett, a working-class reactionary, anti-immigrant, anti-feminist curmudgeon from London. He was portrayed as a ridiculous character. His extreme views were illustrated by his frequent disparaging references to, and opinions about, "sambos" or "coons" (taboo words denoting people with dark skins), "poofter(s)" (a taboo slur of gay men) and "Micks" (a semi-taboo word for the Irish). He referred to and addressed his son-in-law from Liverpool as a "scouse git". The utterances of this character, if taken seriously (i.e. if they are divorced from the context of a comedy about a horrible person to whom bad things happen), are highly offensive.

Fifty years on, there is disagreement about whether audiences laugh at Alf Garnett or laugh with him. Interestingly, the series which shows clips from this and other shows is called *It Was Alright in the [name of decade]*. The implicature derived from this title is, of course, that it is *not* 'alright' these days; that is, that it would not be acceptable for the things that get said in these clips to be broadcast today. In case there is any doubt about this, the clips are interspersed with shots of minor celebrities watching them in open-mouthed disbelief and offering accompanying horrified comments. The public-ization in this case, then, involves the stripping away of the embedding – what was a public portrayal of the utterances of a fictional figure of fun is now being assessed as if the utterances were addressed directly to the public, so that their mere animation is taboo.

As a final brief example of taboo-ification and public-ization in operation, consider the following case.[4] In the summer of 2019, a school student who had taken a religious studies exam set by a public body in England was initially disqualified for having committed a 'malpractice offence'. The offence was "obscene racial comments being made throughout an exam paper". The only example of such comments cited in the sources was the pupil's proposition that she found the idea of halal meat "absolutely disgusting". The disqualification decision was later overturned on appeal after the pupil's school pointed out that her negative opinion of halal meat stemmed from her strict vegetarianism and that no other stated opinion in her paper could be construed as racist. The exam board, OCR, apologized for the "upset and stress" caused by the original decision, which it described as "too harsh", and also accepted that its original letter "describing the frequency and severity of the comments" was "inaccurate". Note that OCR's re-evaluation of its decision was not that its assessment of the student's comment about halal meat was wrong but only that it was too harsh, implying thereby that it was only a little bit Islamophobic but Islamophobic nonetheless. This is an example of taboo-ification.

By way of explanation, the OCR statement added that "OCR takes all incidence [sic] of suspected offensive material against a religious group in exams very seriously and must apply rules which are set out for all exam boards in such cases". The 'rules' mentioned here refer to the 'examples of malpractice' by candidates set out by the Joint Council for Qualifications (JCQ), a body representing several public exam boards, in its policies and procedures document for dealing with suspected cases of malpractice for the academic year 2018–19 (hereafter JCQ 2018).[5] Among these is "the inclusion of inappropriate, offensive, obscene, homophobic, transphobic, racist or sexist material in scripts [and any other assessed work]" (JCQ 2018: 36). The same document contains a table (ibid.: 40–5) wherein the seriousness of such offences is graded. Incurring a mere warning are "isolated words or drawings, mildly offensive, inappropriate approaches or responses" (ibid.: 42), while "frequent mild obscenities or drawings; isolated strong obscenity; isolated mild obscenities or mildly offensive comments aimed at the examiner or member of staff" (ibid.) incur loss of marks. The most serious category is described as "offensive comments or obscenities aimed at a member of staff, examiner or religious group; homophobic, transphobic, racist or sexist remarks or lewd drawings" (ibid.). These incur disqualification from part or all of an assessment or even a whole series of assessments. As illustrations of malpractice, the document (ibid. 65–6) includes

> GCSE Mathematics: The examiner reported that the candidate had written a large number of offensive comments throughout their script. Upon review, the comments were found to contain inappropriate language and comments of an offensive nature. Outcome: The candidate was awarded a mark of 0 for the paper (penalty 4).
>
> GCSE Design Technology: The candidate's script contained several obscene comments including one specifically aimed towards the examiner, as well as a reference to drugs. Outcome: The candidate was disqualified from the qualification (penalty 7).

Nowhere in the document is there an attempt to define what constitutes "inappropriate, offensive, obscene, homophobic, transphobic, racist or sexist material" but the mention of "a reference to drugs" as part of the explanation for imposing the severest penalty quoted above suggests that the bar for acceptable language is set pretty high! It is worth noting here that for assessing ability in mathematics, "offensive comments" and "inappropriate language" cannot possibly have any relevance one way or the other. These are penalized, therefore, simply because they are deemed taboo.

As can be seen, the guidelines for rating the level of offence cite three criteria. Two of these are frequency ('isolated' versus 'frequent') and severity ('mild' versus 'strong'), neither of which require an offended party to be identified, a further pointer to taboo-ification. But the third criterion requires such a party. Comments 'aimed at' a member of staff, examiner or designated social group incur the severest penalties. This criterion at least recognizes that in order for an utterance to be offending, there has to be someone to be offended. And it is considerate of the exam boards to protect their examiners in this way. However, we should note that such examiners need no protection from personal attack, since exam candidates have no notion of who they might be. The only kind of offending utterance possible is one that denigrates a group with which an individual examiner tasked with marking the paper might identify. Moreover, these examiners are the only recipients of the language in these exam scripts. The matter of participation framework is made very explicit in the document, which makes reference to the 'confidentiality' and 'security' of the scripts. Only the handful of people authorized to see them may do so initially and permission has to be applied for and obtained before anybody else can see them.[6] Exam scripts, in other words, are not in the public domain, and are not destined for publication, so there is no possibility of overhearers coming across them. Language rated offensive which is 'aimed at' any of the other targets cited is sure to miss its mark because those targets are not part of the participation framework. Yet the document implies that they are.

This understanding of 'malpractice', then, is also an example of publicization. Together with the above-analysed taboo-ification, it is social control in action, which, because it involves young people in a gatekeeping situation, is of a particularly significant kind. The process of sitting an exam has been co-opted into their language socialization (see Ochs 1986).

12.3 Final word

Several of the cases examined in this book have pointed to what Goodwin & Duranti (1992: 4) aver as "the crucial importance of taking as a point of departure for the analysis of context the perspective of the participant(s) whose behavior is being analysed". In the analyses of these cases, in my desire to work 'from the outside in' (Mey 2001: 219 – see section 7.1), I have usually attempted an implicitly objective description of the relevant context. In reality, though, this has been at best an aggregate of the various contexts relevant to the participants involved. In more than one case, what the context 'is' depends on which participant's eyes we try to look out of. This realization is crucial for understanding how easily offending utterances occur, and sometimes the degree of their offensiveness. And for participants in interaction, it is a call for tolerance and empathy.

There is no doubt that TMC increases this tendency for different participants to perceive divergent contexts, perhaps especially Twitter. (See Chapter 9 and Terkourafi et al. 2018 for an in-depth case study.) TMC also explains the tendency for powerfully constituted bodies, including the state itself, to get involved. All of the cases of such involvement have taken place with TMC. It will be recalled that my definition of offensive language and offending utterances is couched in terms of the reactions of individuals. But the vast broadcast capacity of TMC helps to turn offences against the person into offences against the law. There is a fine line between taking up offence on someone's behalf, as the state and other bodies do, and taking it up for the purposes of control. To help counter the latter, "communities and workplaces that use CMC need to develop their own norms and guidelines [for] reduc[ing] offenses and misunderstandings" (Jay 2018: 121) rather than becoming subject to governmental intervention. It is also better, I think, to remain with the personal definition of offensive language offered in this work, as a reminder that an offending utterance is only such if a person or people *feel* offended. All of the cases of offending utterances analysed in this book can, mostly or entirely, be identified with reference to one or more of the negative felt reactions outlined in the definition: discomfited, insulted, hurt, frightened. It is worth mentioning that the last of these reactions has figured repeatedly, not just in the obvious cases in Chapter 9 and the 'Rivers of Blood' speech in section 10.1, but also as a contributory or background factor in the 'slap' remark in section 8.4 (causing fear among many of physical violence) and perhaps the employee's memo in section 6.1 (causing fear of discriminatory and intimidating practices). I hope thereby to have incorporated this aspect of offensive language into scholarship.

Most importantly, a personal, recipient-centred approach to offensive language forces us to examine its nature in a way which reference to a generalized proscription does not. The sociologist Christie Davies (2002, 2016) argues that jokes containing offensive or pejorative references to social groups have little or no effect on social outcomes, so that they are neither a cause nor a sign of marginalization, thereby calling into question their designation as 'hate speech' and their censoring in many domains. That utterances – serious utterances – which disparage particular social groups are to be deplored is without doubt. That in particular contexts they endanger the sense of wellbeing, and sometimes the safety, of the targeted group is also without doubt. Hateful speech does exist. But the particular contexts have to be identified first, before sweeping condemnation, and possible retaliation, is considered. Just as the appeal to 'banter' (as many cases in this book have shown) as a one-size-fits-all explanatory gloss for potentially offensive linguistic behaviour is dangerous, at best disingenuous and often cynical, so too is the move towards a blanket, context-spanning prohibition of that same linguistic behaviour.[7] Kate Burridge (2012: 67) has remarked that "[s]ince the 1980s, gender, sexuality, disability and race have become so highly-charged that speakers will shun anything that may be interpreted as discriminatory or pejorative". As a result, people increasingly feel the need to avoid reference to any kind of difference among them. (See O'Driscoll 2001 for a reflex of this regarding ethnicity.) Similarly, Tickoo (2010) demonstrates that 'verbal disempowerment' is frequently evident in twenty-first-century life.

Context-spanning prohibition of certain kinds of utterance constitutes part of an authoritarian undermining of relationships and an impoverishment of interpersonal interaction, leading to an interactive world which is not simply dry and boring but also full of fear. It attempts to relieve interactants of the responsibility for their interacting: instead of being engaged with what suits themselves, they are worried about what suits the authorities so that the relative acceptability of what is said, rather than being negotiated in situ by the interactants, become assessed with reference to a set of top-down rules.

These dangers to the tenor of human interaction, of desiccation and increased awkwardness, are reason enough for taboo-ification and its increasing reach through the attendant process of public-ization to be regarded with a high degree of suspicion. But I suggest there may be an additional reason. For while everyday discourse has become more circumspect and more controlled, political discourse on the part of populist leaders around the world has become more strident, more aggressive and therefore more divisive. The case of Donald Trump as analysed above suggests a relation between these two processes, that the latter is, at least in part, a grass-roots reaction to the former. If, therefore, we want to avoid the possible disastrous consequences of the latter, it may be wise to loosen the chains of the former.

Notes

Chapter 1

1   I would like to thank the person who first drew my attention to this advert. I think it was Kristy Beers Fägersten. But if it was not, my apologies to the person who actually did so.

2   I have been unable to determine exactly when the ad was made and how quickly it was banned. But it was sometime around the turn of the century and is still widely available for viewing, there having been numerous postings of it on YouTube. When I mentioned it to a seminar group recently, one of my students found it on her iPhone in 10 seconds. Just type in 'banned TV adverts fuck ass'. I believe the lyrics and music are to be attributed to The Outhere Brothers. As a matter of interest, this ad presents a valid reason for learning a global language which you can expect to be confronted with everywhere you go – get on top of it before it gets on top of you!

3   My apologies here to readers irritated by my belabouring of the obvious point that context matters. To linguists it may indeed be obvious, but as Jay (2009a) demonstrates, it does not appear to be obvious either in the legal domain or when appeals are made to 'common sense'.

Chapter 2

1   Both seem to credit the other with this term and the distinction between it and pragmalinguistics cited in the next paragraph. Leech (1983: 18, footnote 13) cites Thomas, while Thomas (1983: 99) cites Leech (1983: 10–11). Thanks to Maria Sifianou for drawing my attention to this conundrum.

2   This term denotes essentially the same as the general English 'implication'. But Grice invented it because he wanted to circumscribe *all* non-direct meanings. In general usage, 'implication' is used of a narrower set.

3   This criticism has hinged chiefly on the argued irrelevance of negative face to many cultures around the world: Polish (Wierzbicka 1985), Japanese (Matsumoto 1988, Ide 1989), Chinese (Gu 1990, Mao 1994), Igbo (Nwoye 1992), Greek (Sifianou 1992). Further references can be found in Watts (2003: 102–3).

4   Thanks to Sara Vilar Lluch for this observation. The material for this exercise is derived from the work of Gumperz on the 'CrossTalk' project (e.g. Cook-Gumperz & Gumperz 2002).

Chapter 3

1   By 'main heading' I mean that part of a title which appears before a break as indicated by a colon, question mark or full stop in citations. Items which appear in subheadings have only been included when the first part is obviously quotative. The list excludes unpublished theses, non-academic works and press articles. It also excludes individual chapter titles in the two edited volumes *Advances in Swearing Research* (Beers Fägersten & Stapleton 2017a) and *The Oxford Handbook of Taboo and Language* (Allan 2019a).

2   I am very grateful to Anne-Marie Simon-Vandenbergen and Maria Sifianou for information on these languages respectively. I only wish there was space here to do justice to their many perceptive observations on the subject. For similar information on many other languages, see Ljung (2011) and Beers Fägersten & Stapleton (2017b).

3   In the citing of examples of linguistic items, I have followed majority practice in using only items from the English language. This is for the sake of my own convenience and the widest accessibility. With more space, time and knowledge, I would quote items from other languages too. See also note 2.

Chapter 4

1   See https://www.independent.co.uk/news/uk/home-news/judge-uses-foul-mouthed-four-letter-response-to-racist-defendant-in-court-a7183056.html (dated 10/8/16) and http://www.independent.co.uk/news/uk/home-news/judge-patricia-lynch-qc-you-re-a-bit-of-a-ct-yourself-swearing-judge-britains-sweariest-judge-a7185526.html (dated 11/8/16), both accessed 19/2/20.

2   The word 'knackered' is used in many parts of the English-speaking world to mean 'extremely tired/worn out or damaged from overuse'. Dictionaries classify it as slang. Its mild taboo status comes from the fact the cognate form 'knackers' is also slang for testicles, hence a possible implication that the exhaustion has resulted from sexual exertion.

3   See https://www.theguardian.com/politics/2017/jul/26/bbc-apologises-after-tory-donor-insults-jeremy-corbyn (accessed 19/8/17), although the words quoted are as I heard them myself on the radio (not as in this report). There is, of course, in this example, an insult involved, which is one motivation for the apology issued. But note that the presenter apologized for the 'language', not the sentiment.

4   Interestingly, this explicit apology for bad language on the rugby field was not forthcoming on a previous occasion when a player from one side appeared to be remonstrating with a player from the other side about his actions and this latter then told the first to "Go fuck yourself". Again, it would have taken an alert TV

listener to pick up the precise wording of this utterance, but no more so than in the above-cited instance. This time, though, the commentator remarked, "Rona O'Gara, there, just politely telling X to go away". This time, then, instead of an apology there was an attempt at humorous understatement. The difference was that this latter commentator was not the main commentator. Traditionally in such sports coverage in Britain, there is one main commentator to give the running commentary and also one or two assistant commentators (usually cast as experts by virtue of their experience of and past achievements in the game). The main role of the former is to describe the action, of the latter to comment on it. In this latter case, then, the 'expert' did not feel the sense of responsibility for the presentation of the TV event apparently felt by the main commentator – an interesting case of different participant roles.

5   An amusing aside: *The Guardian* reported Keane's outburst in full as follows: 'He said: "Who the fuck do you think you are, having meetings about me? You were a crap player, you are a crap manager. The only reason I have any dealings with you is that somehow you are manager of my country and you're not even Irish, you English cunt. You can stick it up your bollocks". (*The Guardian*, 25/5/02). This facilitated the headline for the article, which read: 'Keane: A Tenuous Grasp of Anatomy'.

6   My thanks to Dan McIntyre for this observation. (And yes, the officer was indeed male.)

7   I am very grateful to Anne-Marie Simon-Vandenbergen for the information in this paragraph.

Chapter 5

1   My thanks to Mark Boardman for drawing my attention to the taboo-ness of this practice.

2   Perhaps unsurprisingly, the teachers were unable to help. They could not identify the student from Jim's description.

3   I last accessed a video of this encounter on 31/12/19 at https://www.bing.com/videos/search?q=Stephen+Fry+on+Parkinson&src=IE-SearchBox&ru=%2fsearch%3fq%3dStephen%2bFry%2bon%2bParkinson%26src%3dIE-SearchBox%26FORM%3dIENAD2&view=detail&mmscn=vwrc&mid=71F1B6926D244AC573B271F1B6926D244AC573B2&FORM=WRVORC. It is a clip of the show broadcast on 27/10/01. The dialogue represented below begins at 18:30.

4   See https://www.bbc.co.uk/news/uk-england-devon-50289553 (dated 4/11/19, accessed 5/11/19) and https://www.dailymail.co.uk/news/article-7838941/Plan-change-historic-ports-welcome-signs-featuring-nickname-Little-White-Town-scrapped.html (dated 31/12/19, accessed 3/1/20).

5   The only British media source I could find for this incident was https://www.
     dailymail.co.uk/news/article-7817647/The-University-York-forced-apologise-
     saying-negro-lecture-civil-rights-heros-book.html (dated 21/12/19, accessed
     24/12/19). The story was then reproduced and commented on with reference to the
     British source at https://legalinsurrection.com/2019/12/university-apologizes-to-
     students-after-lecturer-quotes-the-word-negro-in-material-from-black-writers/, a
     US website focusing on education, dated 31/12/19, accessed 3/1/20.

6   The word was employed frequently by the black civil rights campaigner Martin
     Luther King in the 1960s. Thirty-six thousand people self-identified as 'negro' in
     the 2010 US census, but the term has now been dropped from the census categories
     (*The Guardian*, 25/2/13).

Chapter 6

1   See, for example, http://www.smh.com.au/news/national/the-joke-that-bombed-
     before-takeoff/2005/07/06/1120329507199.html (accessed 1/12/16), which reports
     that in Australia "more than 70 passengers have been detained and questioned for
     making 'inappropriate comments' in airports and on board" in the space of three
     months since rules were introduced. For a more recent example, see https://www.
     thejakartapost.com/news/2018/06/05/no-laughing-matter-10-airplane-bomb-
     jokes-in-may.html (accessed 18/2/20) regarding such rules in Indonesia. The
     comments in https://www.theguardian.com/commentisfree/oliver-burkemans-
     blog/2012/nov/27/dynamite-advice-bomb-jokes-airports (accessed 18/2/20) have
     links to several such regulations in the United States.

2   See https://fot.humanists.international/download-the-report/ (dated 13/11/19,
     accessed 18/2/20).

3   See https://www.theguardian.com/politics/2016/apr/28/ken-livingstone-
     suspended-from-labour-after-hitler-remarks and https://www.bbc.co.uk/news/uk-
     politics-36160135 (dated 28/4/16), both accessed 18/2/20.

4   Information about this case comes from https://www.theguardian.com/
     world/2017/aug/06/google-staffers-manifesto-against-affirmative-action-sparks-
     furious-backlash and https://www.theguardian.com/technology/2017/aug/08/
     google-fires-author-anti-diversity-memo. The full text of the offending memo
     was found at https://gizmodo.com/exclusive-heres-the-full-10-page-anti-diversity-
     screed-1797564320 (dated 5/8/17). All these sources were accessed on 16/8/17.

5   The document from which this quote is taken was issued by the Speaker (i.e.
     the person who controls proceedings) and the Deputy Speakers of the House of
     Commons (i.e. the lower house of the bicameral legislalature, the one with most of
     the power) in November 2018. See https://www.parliament.uk/documents/media/
     Rules%20of%20behaviour%20and%20courtesies%20in%20the%20House%20
     of%20Commons%20November%202018.pdf (accessed 18/2/20).

6   My thanks to Anne-Marie Simon-Vandenbergen for this observation.
7   The transcript is that which appeared in *The Independent* newspaper, from which
    other information is also taken. See https://www.independent.co.uk/news/uk/
    politics/livingstone-suspended-for-four-weeks-over-nazi-gibe-6108274.html (dated
    25/2/06, accessed 14/1/20). See also https://en.wikipedia.org/wiki/Ken_Livingstone
    (accessed 18/2/20).

Chapter 7

1   In fact, Searle does not use the term 'felicity conditions', but I have used it here
    because that is how these criteria are generally glossed in scholarship in the field.
2   In any case, as Sifianou (2013: 98) argues and exemplifies, sincerity, and even more
    so insincerity, is a very slippery concept which cannot be pinned down.
3   The written text of this stanza is as it appears on page 196 of *Writings and Drawings
    by Bob Dylan* (Jonathan Cape 1973).
4   This one is so well known as to have become a cliché that can be satirized, as in
    the Monty Python sketch of a mafiosi pair entering the office of an army colonel
    and saying, "You got a nice army base here colonel. We wouldn't want anything to
    happen to it", whereupon the audience, recognizing the trope, immediately break
    into loud laughter. See https://www.youtube.com/watch?v=DNj1dXi-z0M from
    1:30 onwards (accessed 5/7/18).
5   This, of course, is the essence of the joke in the Monty Python sketch mentioned in
    the previous note. The colonel, with, we are told, several hundred tanks and several
    thousand armed soldiers at his disposal, cannot possibly believe that a civilian
    criminal gang is capable of causing harm to his army base.
6   I have followed Chovanec & Dynel (2015) in preferring this term to the conventional
    CMC (computer-mediated communication), both because I wish to include at the
    outset more traditional forms of technology (such as television) and also because, as
    they say, there are now many mobile internet devices which are not usually described
    as computers. To circumscribe in particular this internet communication regardless
    of the means, Graham & Hardaker (2017: 786–7) and Graham (2019: 326) suggest
    that 'digital' would be more accurate. I have followed this suggestion too.
7   My thanks to Hazel Price for this and the immediately above observation.

Chapter 8

1   See https://www.theguardian.com/football/2017/aug/21/eni-aluko-interview-
    race-difficult-situation (accessed 24/8/18). On the same day, the same paper
    published a news article https://www.theguardian.com/football/2017/aug/21/
    eni-aluko-england-manager-mark-sampson-ebola (accessed 21/1/20) from which
    information in the analysis here is also drawn.

2 See Magrath (2017: 115–17) for references and a discussion of the phenomenon in football. See also Clayton & Wolfers (2017).
3 See https://www.nhs.uk/conditions/ebola/ (accessed 19/8/19).
4 As seen on https://www.youtube.com/watch?v=UGCnNsPpQtE (accessed 19/12/19). Further information about the circumstance and outcome of the case was obtained from https://www.theguardian.com/football/2017/apr/03/sunderland-david-moyes-tells-reporter-get-slap-bbc-vicki-sparks (accessed 3/12/19) and https://www.bbc.co.uk/sport/football/40688969 (dated 21/7/17, accessed 21/1/20).

Chapter 9

1 Information taken from https://www.theguardian.com/technology/2010/nov/11/twitter-stoning-conservative-mp (accessed 2/12/16); https://www.theguardian.com/technology/2010/nov/11/tory-councillor-tweet-yasmin-alibhai-brown-arrested (accessed 22/1/17); http://www.bbc.co.uk/news/uk-england-birmingham-12343879 (dated 2/2/11, accessed 21/1/17).
2 See https://www.bbc.co.uk/news/uk-40574754 (dated 11/7/17) and https://www.bbc.co.uk/news/uk-40599992 (dated 13/7/17, both accessed 13/7/17), after having my attention drawn to this incident by Derek Bousfield, whom I thank. I also used https://www.theguardian.com/uk-news/2017/jul/11/man-jail-offering-money-run-over-gina-miller-rhodri-philipps-viscount-brexit (accessed 16/7/17).
3 The principal source for the information presented here is the official final judgment of the court, issued on 27/7/12 – see https://www.judiciary.gov.uk/wp-content/uploads/JCO/Documents/Judgments/chambers-v-dpp.pdf. Supplementary sources are items in the mass media, as follows: https://www.theguardian.com/uk/2010/may/10/tweeter-fined-spoof-message; http://www.independent.co.uk/news/uk/home-news/twitter-joke-led-to-terror-act-arrest-and-airport-life-ban-1870913.html (dated 18/1/10); https://www.theguardian.com/technology/2010/nov/12/iamspartacus-campaign-twitter-airport; http://www.bbc.co.uk/news/uk-england-19009344 (dated 27/7/12). All the above were accessed 2/12/16.
4 Information from http://www.theverge.com/2013/8/20/4641606/college-student-who-spent-six-months-in-jail-for-tumblr-post-caleb-clemmons-sentenced (accessed 1/12/16).
5 See https://www.amnesty.org/en/latest/news/2017/05/cameroon-thousands-worldwide-demand-release-of-students-jailed-for-sharing-boko-haram-joke/ and https://www.theguardian.com/global-development/2017/sep/21/no-laughing-matter-cameroon-students-face-10-years-in-jail-for-boko-haram-joke (both accessed 3/5/18).
6 My thanks to Sara Mills for drawing my attention to this possibility.

Chapter 10

1   Most of the historical facts outlined above and below are common knowledge. But I found the ITV news item, dated 20/4/18 (https://www.youtube.com/ watch?v=r3QC5_efQb0), accessed 8/1/20, helpful in filling in some of the gaps in my own knowledge.

2   The full text of the speech can be found at https://www.telegraph.co.uk/ comment/3643823/Enoch-Powells-Rivers-of-Blood-speech.html (dated 8/11/07, accessed 8/1/20).

3   I simply note in passing that this means of typification also ignores half of the population entirely!

4   My thanks to Lesley Jeffries for this and the immediately previous observation.

5   Thanks in particular to Emily Snell for articulating this argument.

6   For a discussion of the interactional sequential implications of both 'overdone' statements such as this and also laughter, see Holt (2011).

7   Apart from the presumed difference in relationship, another significant situational difference between my 'old codger' example and the Barry case, as Anne-Marie Simon-Vandenbergen has observed, is that of participation framework: private face-to-face dyadic conversation v. group against individual.

Chapter 11

1   My thanks to Charlotte Taylor for bringing this work to my attention.

2   These vary in their precise representation of the quote. The first is from https:// www.independent.co.uk/news/people/gary-oldman-defends-mel-gibson- s-anti-semitic-remarks-we-all-hide-and-try-to-be-so-politically-9557435. html (dated 23/6/14). The second is from https://www.telegraph.co.uk/news/ celebritynews/8208174/Winona-Ryder-claims-Mel-Gibson-called-her-an-oven- dodger.html (undated). The third is from https://www.telegraph.co.uk/news/ celebritynews/7887588/Mel-Gibson-is-a-bonehead-not-a-racist-says-Whoopi- Goldberg.html (dated 13/7/10). All were accessed 1/11/18.

3   And note it is a word with which the articles have editorially interfered – a further means of distancing themselves from the person to whom it is attributed. See section 4.2.

4   The main source of information for this background and the data below is the official judgment of an employment tribunal, which can be found at https://www. gov.uk/employment-tribunal-decisions/dr-f-carpos-young-v-royal-academy-of- music-2201614-2018 (last updated 7/3/19). Use was also made of the following newspaper articles: https://www.telegraph.co.uk/news/2017/11/06/royal-academy-

music-sacks-lecturer-student-guide-referred-string/; https://www.dailymail. co.uk/news/article-6320145/Royal-Academy-Music-professor-sacked-students-complained-used-offensive-word.html (dated 26/10/18); https://www.thesun. co.uk/news/7594516/bassoonist-gypo-email-tribunal-appeal/ (dated 26/10/18); https://www.independent.co.uk/news/uk/home-news/francesca-carpos-young-tribunal-royal-academy-music-violin-a8814351.html (dated 26/10/18), all accessed on 27/10/18, and https://www.telegraph.co.uk/news/2018/11/19/royal-academy-music-teacher-wrongfully-sacked-referring-violinists/ (accessed 12/1/20).

Chapter 12

1   For a forensic examination of this performance and strong argument that Trump knew exactly what he was doing when mimicking the disabled reported, see https://www.washingtonpost.com/news/the-fix/wp/2016/09/01/ann-coulter-says-she-can-prove-donald-trump-never-mocked-a-reporters-disability-she-cant/?tid=a_inl&utm_term=.c6f0d0e2813d (accessed 3/3/17). See also https://en.wikipedia.org/wiki/Donald_Trump_presidential_campaign,_2016#Controversies (accessed 5/1/20) for general information if needed.

2   In fairness to US voters, it should perhaps be pointed out that he actually received fewer votes than his opponent. It's just that votes for him were distributed more effectively under the electoral college system by which presidents of the United States (a federal state) are elected.

3   In England, where both these incidents occurred, it is tempting to suggest that this perception of university activities as part of a fully public domain is at least partly the result of the commodification of higher education which has taken place in this country over the last few decades. Students now pay for their courses, which are energetically marketed by the universities. This marketing is subject, like the advertising of any product, to legal constraints whereby universities can be sued if they do not deliver what their promotional material promises.

4   Information about this story was first accessed through articles in three newspapers, all accessed 20/8/19. These can be found at https://www.telegraph. co.uk/news/2019/08/17/gcse-student-disqualified-zealous-examiner-mistook-vegetarianism/; https://www.mirror.co.uk/news/uk-news/gcse-student-disqualified-after-examiner-18958743 (dated 18/8/19); https://www.standard.co.uk/news/uk/vegetarian-student-disqualified-from-gcse-paper-after-examiner-mistook-remarks-about-halal-meat-for-a4215746.html (dated 18/8/19).

5   This document was accessed at file:///C:/Users/Staff/Downloads/JCQ%20 Suspected%20Malpractice%2018-19.pdf on 20/9/19. It is no longer accessible, having been superseded by the 2019–20 version of the document, which uses

exactly the same quoted words and can at the time of writing be accessed at file:///C:/Users/Staff/Downloads/2020-03-27%20JCQ%20Suspected%20 Malpractice%2019-20.pdf.FN>

6   For further information on this matter, see https://www.ocr.org.uk/administration/ stage-5-post-results-services/access-to-scripts/ (accessed 20/9/19).

7   In this respect, the difference between praise and free speech on the one hand, and criticism and prohibition on the other, needs to be emphasized. It is a depressing fact that popular debate about such matters often neglects these distinctions. To take just one example, in an upcoming analysis of digital comments (and comments on comments) on the Greek pop song which translates as "Slut, I hate you", Sagredos & Nikolova (forthcoming) observe that its singer-songwriter defended himself against charges that his song legitimizes violence against women by arguing both that the lyrics are not sexist and, almost in the same breath, that every singer should have freedom of speech. Such an argument confuses two issues. To put it bluntly, free speech does not equate to good speech, just as bad speech should not automatically be banned.

References

Abrantes, Ana Margarida (2005), 'Euphemism and Co-operation in Discourse', in Eric Grillo (ed.), *Power without Domination: Dialogism and the Empowering Property of Communication*, 85–103, Amsterdam: John Benjamins.

Adams, Michael (2002), 'Teaching "Bad" American English: Profanity and Other "Bad" Words in the Liberal Arts Setting', *Journal of English Linguistics*, 30 (4): 353–65.

Adams, Michael (2016), *In Praise of Profanity*, Cambridge: Cambridge University Press.

Agyekum, Kofi (2002), 'Menstruation as Verbal Taboo among the Akan of Ghana', *Journal of Anthropological Research*, 58: 367–87.

Ainsworth, Janet (2016), 'Culture, Cursing, and Coercion: The Impact of Police Officer Swearing on the Voluntariness of Consent to Search in Police-Citizen Interactions', in Susan Ehrlich, Diana Eades and Janet Ainsworth (eds), *Discursive Constructions of Consent in the Legal Process*, 23–46, Oxford: Oxford University Press.

Allan, Keith (2015), 'When Is a Slur Not a Slur? The Use of Nigger in "Pulp Fiction"', *Language Sciences* 52: 187–99.

Allan, Keith (2016), 'The Reporting of Slurs', in Alessandro Capone, Ferenc Kiefer and Franco Lo Piparo (eds), *Indirect Reports and Pragmatics*, 211–32, Cham: Springer.

Allan, Keith, (ed.), (2019a), *The Oxford Handbook of Taboo Words and Language*, Oxford: Oxford University Press.

Allan, Keith (2019b), 'Taboo Words and Language: An Overview', in Keith Allan (ed.), *The Oxford Handbook of Taboo Words and Language*, 1–27, Oxford: Oxford University Press.

Allan, Keith and Kate Burridge (2006), *Forbidden Words. Taboo and the Censoring of Language*, Cambridge: Cambridge University Press.

Al-Owaidi, Muhtaram (2018), 'Investigating Speech Acts in English and Arabic Short News Interviews: A Cross-Cultural Pragmatic Study', unpublished PhD thesis, University of Huddersfield.

Anderson, Luvell and Ernie Lepore (2013a), 'Slurring Words', *Nous*, 47 (1): 25–48.

Anderson, Luvell and Ernie Lepore (2013b), 'What Did You Call Me? Slurs as Prohibited Words', *Analytic Philosophy*, 54 (3): 350–63.

Andersson, Lars (1985), *Swearing: A Report. Vol. 1*. Department of Linguistics, University of Göteborg.

Andersson, Lars and Peter Trudgill (1990), *Bad Language*, London: Penguin.

Andersson, Lars and Peter Trudgill (2007), 'Swearing', in Leila Monaghan and Jane Goodman (eds), *A Cultural Approach to Interpersonal Communication*, 195–9, Oxford: Blackwell.

Archard, David (2014), 'Insults, Free Speech and Offensiveness', *Journal of Applied Philosophy*, 31(2): 127–41.

Arundale, Robert (2013), 'Face as a Research Focus in Interpersonal Pragmatics: Relational and Emic Perspectives', *Journal of Pragmatics*, 58: 108–120.

Arundale, Robert (2020), *Communicating and Relating: Constituting Face in Everyday Interaction*, Oxford: Oxford University Press.

Austin, J. L. ([1962] 1975), *How to Do Things with Words* (2nd edn), Oxford: Oxford University Press.

Austin, Paddy (1990), 'Politeness Revisited: The Dark Side', in Allan Bell and Janet Holmes (eds), *New Zealand Ways of Speaking English*, 277–93, Philadelphia, PA: Multilingual Matters.

Avgerinakou, Anthi (2003), '"Flaming" in Computer-Mediated Interactions', in Colin B. Grant (ed.), *Rethinking Communicative Interaction: New Interdisciplinary Horizons*, 273–93, Amsterdam: John Benjamins.

Bailey, Lee Ann and Leonora A. Timm (1976), 'More on Women's and Men's Expletives', *Anthropological Linguistics*, 18: 438–49.

Balibar, Étienne (trans. G. M. Goshgarian) (2016). *Violence and Civility: On the Limits of Political Philosophy*. New York: Columbia University Press.

Baudhuin, E. Scott (1973), 'Obscene Language and Evaluative Response: An Empirical Study', *Psychological Reports*, 32 (2): 399–402.

Bayard, Donn and Sateesh Krishnayya (2001), 'Gender, Expletive Use, and Context: Male and Female Expletive Use in Structured and Unstructured Conversation among New Zealand University Students', *Women and Language*, 24 (1): 1–15.

Bayraktaroğlu, Arin (1991), 'Politeness and Interactional Imbalance', *International Journal of the Sociology of Language*, 92: 5–34.

Beers Fägersten, Kristy (2007), 'A Sociolinguistic Analysis of Swear Word Offensiveness', *Saarland Working Papers in Linguistics*, 1: 14–37.

Beers Fägersten, Kristy (2012), *Who's Swearing Now? The Social Aspects of Conversational Swearing*, Newcastle upon Tyne: Cambridge Scholars Publishing.

Beers Fägersten, Kristy (2014), 'The Use of English Swear Words in Swedish Media', in Marianne Rathje (ed.), *Swearing in the Nordic Countries*, 63–82, Copenhagen: Dansk Sprognævn Konferenceserie 2.

Beers Fägersten, Kristy and Karyn Stapleton, (eds), (2017a), *Advances in Swearing Research: New Languages and New Contexts*, Amsterdam: John Benjamins.

Beers Fägersten, Kristy and Karyn Stapleton (2017b), 'Introduction', in Kristy Beers Fägersten and Karyn Stapleton, (eds), *Advances in Swearing Research: New Languages and New Contexts*, 1–15, Amsterdam: John Benjamins.

Bergen, Benjamin (2016), *What the F: What Swearing Reveals about Our Language, Our Brains, and Ourselves*, New York: Basic Books.

Berger, Claudia (2003), *The Myth of Gender-Specific Swearing*, Berlin: Verlag für Wissenschaft und Forschung.

Bianchi, Claudia (2014), 'Slurs and Appropriation: An Echoic Account', *Journal of Pragmatics*, 66: 35–44.

Blakemore, Diane (2014), 'Slurs and Expletives: A Case against a General Account of Expressive Meaning', *Language Sciences*, 52: 22–35.

Blanco Salgueiro, Antonio (2010), 'Promises, Threats, and the Foundations of Speech Act Theory', *Pragmatics*, 20 (2): 213–28.

Blumberg, Frederick (2017), 'Obscenity and Marginality', *Law and Humanities*, 11: 7–23.

Booker, Christopher (2020), *Groupthink: A Study in Self Delusion*, London: Bloomsbury Continuum.

Bousfield, Derek (2008), *Impoliteness in Interaction*, Amsterdam: John Benjamins.

Bowers, Jeffrey S. and Christopher W. Pleydell-Pearce (2011), 'Swearing, Euphemisms, and Linguistic Relativity', *PLoS ONE*, 6 (7): e22341.

Brown, Lucien (2011), *Korean Honorifics and Politeness in Second Language Learning*, Amsterdam: John Benjamins.

Brown, Penelope and Steven C. Levinson ([1978] 1987), *Politeness: Some Universals in Language Usage*, Cambridge: Cambridge University Press. (Main body of which first published in Esther Goody, ed., *Questions and Politeness*, Cambridge: Cambridge University Press.)

Burridge, Kate (2006), 'Taboo, Euphemism and Political Correctness', in Keith Brown (ed.), *Encylopedia of Languages and Linguistics* (2nd edn), 455–62, Oxford: Elsevier.

Burridge, Kate (2010), 'Linguistic Cleanliness Is Next to Godliness: Taboo and Purism. An Overview of Prescriptivism in Relation to Public Perceptions of and Reaction to Language Use', *English Today*, 26 (2): 3–13.

Burridge, Kate (2012), 'Euphemism and Language Change: The Sixth and Seventh Ages', *Lexis: Journal in English Lexicology*, 7: 65–92.

Burridge, Kate and Réka Benczes (2019), 'Taboo as a Driver of Language Change', in Keith Allan (ed.), *The Oxford Handbook of Taboo Words and Language*, 180–98, Oxford: Oxford University Press.

Cameron, Deborah (2012), *Verbal Hygiene* (2nd edn), London: Routledge.

Cavazza, Nicoletta and Margherita Guidetti (2014), 'Swearing in Political Discourse: Why Vulgarity Works', *Journal of Language and Social Psychology*, 33 (5): 537–47.

Cheshire, Jenny (1982), *Variation in an English Dialect*, Cambridge: Cambridge University Press.

Chovanec, Jan and Marta Dynel (2015), 'Researching Interactional Forms and Participant Structures in Public and Social Media', in Marta Dynel and Jan Chovanec (eds), *Participation in Public and Social Media Interactions*, 1–26, Amsterdam: John Benjamins.

Christie, Chris (2013), 'The Relevance of Taboo Language: An Analysis of the Indexical Values of Swearwords', *Journal of Pragmatics*, 58: 152–69.

Clark, Herbert H. and Thomas Carlson (1982), 'Hearers and Speech Acts', *Language*, 58 (2): 332–72.

Clark, Herbert H. and Edward F. Schaefer (1992), 'Dealing with Overhearers', in Herbert H. Clark (ed.), *Arenas of Language Use*, 248–73, Chicago: University of Chicago Press.

Clayton, Daniel and Solvejg Wolfers (2017), 'Banter, Racism and Acculturation: Intercultural Dynamics in Team Sports', Sietar [Society for Intercultural Education, Training and Research] UK. Available at: https://sietar.co.uk/banter-racism-and-acculturation-intercultural-dynamics-in-team-sports/ accessed 21/1/20.

Colbeck, Katie L. and Jeffrey S. Bowers (2012), 'Blinded by Taboo Words in L1 but Not L2, *Emotion*, 12 (2): 217–22.

Cook-Gumperz, Jenny and John J. Gumperz (2002), 'Narrative Accounts in Gatekeeping Interviews: Intercultural Differences or Common Misunderstandings?', *Language and Intercultural Communication*, 2 (1): 25–36.

Coyne, Sarah, Mark Callister, Laura Stockdale, David Nelson and Brian M. Wells (2012), '"A Helluva Read": Profanity in Adolescent Literature', *Mass Communication and Society*, 15 (3): 360–83.

Cressman, Dale, Mark Callister, Tom Robinson and Chris Near (2009), 'Swearing in the Cinema: An Analysis of Profanity in US Teen-Oriented Movies, 1980–2006', *Journal of Children and Media*, 3 (2): 117–35.

Crisafulli, Edoardo (1997), 'Taboo Language in Translation', *Perspectives: Studies in Translatology*, 5 (2): 237–56.

Croom, Adam M. (2011), 'Slurs', *Language Sciences*, 33 (3): 343–58.

Croom, Adam M. (2014), 'The Semantics of Slurs: A Refutation of Pure Expressivism', *Language Sciences*, 41: 227–42.

Culpeper, Jonathan (1996), 'Towards an Anatomy of Impoliteness', *Journal of Pragmatics*, 25: 349–67.

Culpeper, Jonathan (2005), 'Impoliteness and Entertainment in the Television Quiz Show: The Weakest Link, *Journal of Politeness Research*, 1: 35–72.

Culpeper, Jonathan (2008), 'Reflections on Impoliteness, Relational Work and Power', in Derek Bousfield and Miriam A. Locher (eds), *Impoliteness in Language: Studies on its Interplay with Power in Theory and Practice*, 17–44, Berlin and New York: Mouton de Gruyter.

Culpeper, Jonathan (2011), *Impoliteness: Using Language to Cause Offence*, Cambridge: Cambridge University Press.

Culpeper, Jonathan (2012), '(Im)politeness: Three Issues', *Journal of Pragmatics*, 44(9): 1128–33.

Culpeper, Jonathan (forthcoming), 'Sociopragmatics: Roots and Definition', in Michael Haugh, Dániel Z. Kádár and Marina Terkourafi (eds), *Handbook of Sociopragmatics*, Cambridge: Cambridge University Press.

Culpeper, Jonathan and Michael Haugh (2014), *Pragmatics and the English Language*, Basingstoke: Palgrave Macmillan.

Culpeper, Jonathan and Michael Haugh (forthcoming), 'The Metalinguistics of Offence in (British) English', *Journal of Language Aggression and Conflict*. Available at: https://doi.org/10.1075/jlac.00035.cul

Culpeper, Jonathan, Derek Bousfield and Anne Wichmann (2003), 'Impoliteness Revisited: With Special Reference to Dynamic and Prosodic Aspects', *Journal of Pragmatics*, 35 (10–11): 1545–79.

Culpeper, Jonathan, Michael Haugh and Dániel Kádár (2017a), 'Introduction', in Jonathan Culpeper, Michael Haugh and Dániel Kádár (eds), *The Palgrave Handbook of Linguistic (Im)politeness*, 1–8, London: Palgrave Macmillan.

Culpeper, Jonathan, Paul Iganski and Abe Sweiry (2017b), 'Linguistic Impoliteness and Religiously Aggravated Hate Crime in England and Wales', *Journal of Language, Aggression and Conflict*, 5 (1): 1–29.

Culpeper, Jonathan, Michael Haugh and Valeria Sinkeviciute (2017c), '(Im)politeness and Mixed Messages', in Jonathan Culpeper, Michael Haugh and Dániel Kádár (eds), *The Palgrave Handbook of Linguistic (Im)politeness*, 323–55, London: Palgrave Macmillan.

Daly, Nicola, Janet Holmes, Jonathan Newton and Maria Stubbe (2004), 'Expletives as Solidarity Signals in FTAs on the Factory Floor', *Journal of Pragmatics*, 36: 945–64.

Davies, Bethan (2018), 'Evaluating Evaluations: What Different Types of Metapragmatic Behaviour Can Tell Us about Participants' Understandings of the Moral Order', *Journal of Politeness Research*, 14 (1): 121–51.

Davies, Christie (2002), *The Mirth of Nations*, New Bruswick, NJ: Transaction Publishers.

Davies, Christie (2016), 'The Rise and Fall of Taboo Comedy in the BBC', in Chiara Bucaria and Luca Barra (eds), *Taboo Comedy: Television and Controversial Humour*, 21–40, London: Palgrave Macmillan.

Davis, Hayley (1989), 'What Makes Bad Language Bad?', *Language and Communication*, 9 (1): 1–9.

de Klerk, Vivian (1992), 'How Taboo Are Taboo Words for Girls?', *Language in Society*, 21: 227–89.

Dewaele, Jean-Marc (2004a), 'Blistering Barnacles! What Language Do Multilinguals Swear In?', *Estudios de Sociolinguistica*, 5 (1): 83–105.

Dewaele, Jean-Marc (2004b), 'The Emotional Force of Swearwords and Taboo Words in the Speech of Multilinguals', *Journal of Multilingual and Multicultural Development*, 25 (2–3): 204–22.

Dewaele, Jean-Marc (2005), 'The Effect of Type of Acquisition Context on Perception and Self-Reported Use of Swearwords in the L2, L3, L4 and L5', in Alex Housen and Michel Pierrard (eds), *Investigations in Instructed Second Language Acquisition*, 531–59, Berlin: Mouton de Gruyter.

Dewaele, Jean-Marc (2010), '"Christ Fucking Shit Merde!" Language Preferences for Swearing among Maximally Proficient Multilinguals', *Sociolinguistic Studies*, 4: 595–614.

Dewaele, Jean-Marc (2016a), 'Self-Reported Frequency of Swearing in English: Do Situational, Psychological and Sociobiographical Variables Have Similar Effects on First and Foreign Language Users?', *Journal of Multilingual and Multicultural Development*, 37 (4): 330–45.

Dewaele, Jean-Marc (2016b), 'Thirty Shades of Offensiveness: L1 and LX English Users' Understanding, Perception and Self-Reported Use of Negative Emotion-Laden Words', *Journal of Pragmatics*, 94: 112–27.

Dewaele, Jean-Marc (2017), '"Cunt": On the Perception and Handling of Verbal Dynamite by L1 and LX Users of English', *Multilingua: Journal of Cross-Cultural and Interlanguage Communication*, 37 (1): 53–82.

Drange, Eli-Marie Danbolt, Ingrid Kristine Hasundi and Anna-Brita Stenström (2014), '"Your Mum!" Teenagers' Swearing by Mother in English, Spanish and Norwegian', *International Journal of Corpus Linguistics*, 19 (1): 29–59.

Dutton, Edward (2007), '"Bog Off Dog Breath! You're Talking Pants!" Swearing as Witness Evangelism in Student Evangelical Groups', *Journal of Religion and Popular Culture*, 16 (1).

Dynel, Marta (2010), 'Not Hearing Things – Hearer/Listener Categories in Polylogues', *MediAzioni*, 9. Available at: http://mediazioni.sitlec.unibo.it, ISSN 1974-4382.

Dynel, Marta (2012). 'Swearing Methodologically: The (Im)politeness of Expletives in Anonymous Commentaries on YouTube', *Journal of English studies*, 10: 25–50.

Eelen, Gino (2001), *A Critique of Politeness Theories*, Manchester: St Jerome.

Evans, Matthew, Lesley Jeffries and Jim O'Driscoll (eds) (2019), *The Routledge Handbook of Language in Conflict*, Abingdon: Routledge.

Feinberg, Joel (1983), 'Obscene Words and the Law', *Law and Philosophy*, 2 (2): 139–61.

Fetzer Anita and Daniel Weiss (2020), 'Doing Things with Quotes: Introduction', *Journal of Pragmatics*, 157: 84–8.

Finkelstein, Shlomit R., Rob Poh and Jorge L. Juncos (2016), 'Swearing: Language for Feeling. Lessons from Tourette Syndrome', *Cognitive Semantics*, 2: 237–61.

Fishman, Joshua A. (1972), 'Domains and the Relationship between Micro- and Macro-Sociolinguistics', in John J. Gumperz and Dell Hymes (eds), *Directions in Sociolinguistics: The Ethnography of Communication*, 435–53, Oxford: Basil Blackwell.

Fleming, Luke and Michael Lempert (2011), 'Introduction: Beyond Bad Words', *Anthropological Quarterly*, 84: 5–13.

Fraser, Bruce (1990), 'Perspectives on Politeness', *Journal of Pragmatics*, 14 (2): 219–36.

Fry, Stephen (2011), *Moab Is My Washpot*, London: Soho Press.

Fyfe, Nicholas, John Bannister and Ade Kearns (2006). (In)civility and the City. *Urban Studies* 43 (5–6): 853–861.

Garcés Blitvich, Pilar and Maria Sifianou, (eds) (2013–), *Journal of Language Aggression and Conflict*.

Garcia, Ofelia and Richard Otheguy, (eds), (1989), *English across Cultures: Cultures across English*, Berlin: Mouton de Gruyter.

Ginsburg, Harvey J., Shirley Ogletree and Tammy Silakowski (2003), 'Vulgar Language: Review Of Sex Differences in Usage, Attributions, and Pathologies', *North American Journal of Psychology*, 5 (1), 105–16.

Goddard, Cliff (2015), '"Swear words" and "curse words" in Australian (and American) English. At the Crossroads of Pragmatics, Semantics and Sociolinguistics', *Intercultural Pragmatics*, 12 (2): 189–218.

Goffman, Erving (1959), *The Presentation of Self in Everyday Life*, Harmondsworth: Penguin.

Goffman, Erving (1963), *Behavior in Public Places: Notes on the Social Organization of Gatherings*, New York: The Free Press.

Goffman, Erving (1964), 'The Neglected Situation', *American Anthropologist* 66 (6), Part II (special issue): 133–6.

Goffman, Erving ([1955] 1967a), 'On Face-Work', in E. Goffman (collection), *Interaction Ritual: Essays on Face-to-Face Behavior*, 5–45, Harmondsworth: Penguin. (Originally in *Psychiatry: Journal for the Study of Interpersonal Processes*, 18 (3): 213–31.)

Goffman, Erving (1967b), 'Mental Symptons and Public Order', in Erving Goffman (collection), *Interaction Ritual: Essays on Face-to-Face Behavior*, 137–48, Harmondsworth: Penguin.

Goffman, Erving (1974), *Frame Analysis: An Essay on the Organization of Experience*, New York: Harper and Row.

Goffman, Erving (1981), *Forms of Talk*, Oxford: Blackwell.

Gonzalez-Regiosa, Fernando (1976), 'The Anxiety Arousing Effect of Taboo Words in Bilinguals', in Charles D. Spielberger and Regiosa Diaz-Guerrero (eds), *Cross-Cultural Anxiety*, 89–105, Washington, DC: Hemisphere.

Goodwin, Charles and Alessandro Duranti (1992), 'Introduction', in Alessandro Duranti and Charles Goodwin (eds), *Rethinking Context: Language as an Interactive Phenomenon*, 1–42, Cambridge: Cambridge University Press.

Graham, Sage L. (2007), 'Disagreeing to Agree: Conflict, (Im)politeness and Identity in a Computer-Mediated Community', *Journal of Pragmatics*, 39 (4): 742–59.

Graham, Sage L. (2008), 'A Manual for (Im)politeness? The Impact of the FAQ in an Electronic Community of Practice', in Derek Bousfield and Miriam Locher (eds), *Impoliteness in Interaction: Studies on its Interplay with Power in Theory and Practice*, 281–304, Berlin: Mouton de Gruyter.

Graham, Sage L. (2019), 'Interaction and Conflict in Digital Communication', in Matthew Evans, Lesley Jeffries and Jim O'Driscoll (eds), *The Routledge Handbook of Language in Conflict*, 310–28, Abingdon: Routledge.

Graham, Sage L. and Claire Hardaker (2017), '(Im)politeness in Digital Communication', in Jonathan Culpeper, Michael Haugh and Dániel Kádár (eds), *The Palgrave Handbook of Linguistic (Im)politeness*, 785–814, London: Palgrave Macmillan.

Grice, H. Paul (1975), 'Logic and Conversation', in Peter Cole and Jerry L. Morgan (eds), *Speech Acts, Syntax and Semantics 3: Speech Acts*, 41–58, New York: Academic Press.

Griffith, Phoebe, Will Norman, Carmen O'Sullivan and Rushanara Ali (2011). *Charm Offensive: Cultivating civility in 21st century Britain*. London: The Young Foundation.

Griffith, Tom (1996), 'Dirty Words', *Perspectives*, 22: 135–7.

Grimshaw, Allen D., ed. (1990), *Conflict Talk: Sociolinguistic Investigations in Conversations*, Cambridge: Cambridge University Press.

Gu, Yueguo (1990), 'Politeness Phenomena in Modern Chinese', *Journal of Pragmatics*, 14 (2): 237–57.

Gumperz, John J. (1982), *Discourse Strategies*, Cambridge: Cambridge University Press.

Hagen, Sverre H. (2013), *Swearwords and Attitude Change: A Sociolinguistic Study*, unpublished MA thesis, University of Bergen.

Haigh, Matthew, Andrew J. Stewart, Jeffrey S. Wood and Louise Connell (2011), 'Conditional Advice and Inducements: Are Readers Sensitive to Implicit Speech Acts during Comprehension?', *Acta Psychologica*, 136: 419–24.

Halvorsen, Kristin and Srikant Sarangi (2015), 'Team Decision-Making in Workplace Meetings: The Interplay of Activity Roles and Discourse Roles', *Journal of Pragmatics*, 76: 1–14.

Harris, Catherine L., Ayse Ayçiçeği and Jean Berko Gleason (2003), 'Taboo Words and Reprimands Elicit Greater Autonomic Reactivity in a First Language than in a Second Language', *Applied Psycholinguistics*, 24 (4): 561–79.

Harrison, Saul and Mark Hinshaw (1968), 'When Children Use Obscene Language', *Medical Aspects of Human Sexuality*, 2 (12): 6–11.

Haugh, Michael (2007), 'The Discursive Challenge to Politeness Research: An Interactional Alternative', *Journal of Politeness Research*, 3 (2): 295–317.

Haugh, Michael (2013), 'Im/politeness, Social Practice and the Participation Order', *Journal of Pragmatics*, 58: 52–72.

Haugh, Michael (2015a), *Im/politeness Implicatures*, Berlin: Mouton de Gruyter.

Haugh, Michael (2015b), 'Impoliteness and Taking Offence in Initial Interactions', *Journal of Pragmatics*, 86: 36–42.

Haugh, Michael (2016), '"Just Kidding": Teasing and Claims to Non-Serious Intent', *Journal of Pragmatics*, 95: 120–36.

Haugh, Michael and Valeria Sinkeviciute (2019), 'Offense and Conflict Talk', in Matthew Evans, Lesley Jeffries and Jim O'Driscoll (eds), *The Routledge Handbook of Language in Conflict*, 196–214, Abingdon: Routledge.

Haugh, Michael, Dániel Z. Kádár and Sara Mills, (eds), (2013), *Journal of Pragmatics*, 58 (special issue on Interpersonal Pragmatics).

Haugh, Michael, Dániel Z. Kádár and Marina Terkourafi, (eds), (forthcoming), *Handbook of Sociopragmatics*, Cambridge: Cambridge University Press.

Hedger, Joseph A. (2012), 'The Semantics of Racial Slurs: Using Kaplan's Framework to Provide a Semantic Theory of Derogatory Epithets', *Linguistic and Philosophical Investigations*, 11: 74–84.

Hedger, Joseph A. (2013), 'Meaning and Racial Slurs: Derogatory Epithets and the Semantics/Pragmatics Interface', *Language and Communication*, 33 (3): 205–13.

Herbert, Robert K. (1997), 'The Sociology of Compliment Work in Polish and English', in Nikolas Coupland and Adam Jaworski (eds), *Sociolinguistics: A Reader*, 487–500, London: Macmillan.

Herring, Susan (2007), 'A Faceted Classification Scheme for Computer-Mediated Discourse', *Language@Internet*, 4 (1).

Hinze, Carl G. (2012), 'Chinese Politeness Is Not about "Face": Evidence from the Business World', *Journal of Politeness Research*, 8 (2): 11–27.

Hoeksema, Jack and Donna Jo Napoli (2008), 'Just for the Hell of It: A Comparison of Two Taboo-Term Constructions', *Journal of Linguistics*, 44 (2): 347–78.

Holmes, Janet (1988), 'Paying Compliments: A Sex-Preferential Politeness Strategy', *Journal of Pragmatics*, 12: 445–65.

Holt, Elizabeth (2011), 'On the Nature of "Laughables": Laughter as a Response to Overdone Figurative Phrases', *Pragmatics*, 21 (3): 393–410.

Holt, Elizabeth (2013), '"There's Many a True Word Said in Jest": Seriousness and Nonseriousness in Interaction', in Phillip Glenn and Elizabeth Holt (eds), *Studies of Laughter in Interaction*, 69–89, London: Bloomsbury.

Holt, Elizabeth and Jim O'Driscoll (forthcoming), 'Participation and Footing', in Michael Haugh, Dániel Z. Kádár and Marina Terkourafi (eds), *Handbook of Sociopragmatics*, Cambridge: Cambridge University Press.

Holzknecht, Susanne (1988), 'Word Taboo and its Implications for Language Change in the Markham Family of Languages, PNG', *Language and Linguistics in Melanesia*, 18: 43–69.

Horgan, Mervyn (2019), 'Everyday Incivility and the Urban Interaction Order: Theorizing Moral Affordances in Ritualized Interaction', *Journal of Language Aggression and Conflict*, 7 (1): 32–55.

Hughes, Geoffrey (1998), *Swearing: A Social History of Foul Language, Oaths, and Profanities in English*, Oxford: Blackwell.

Hughes, Geoffrey (2006), *An Encyclopedia of Swearing: The Social History of Oaths, Profanity, Foul Language, and Ethnic Slur in the English-Speaking World*, New York: Sharpe Inc.

Hughes, Susan E. (1992), 'Expletives of Lower Working-Class Women', *Language in Society*, 21: 291–303.

Hunston, Susan (2000), 'Evaluation and the Planes of Discourse: Status and Value in Persuasive Texts', in Susan Hunston and Geoff Thompson (eds), *Evaluation in Text: Authorial Stance and the Construction of Discourse*, 176–207, Oxford: Oxford University Press.

Hymes, Dell (1974), *Foundations in Sociolinguistics: An Ethnographic Approach*, Philadelphia: University of Pennsylvania Press.

Ide, Sachiko (1989), 'Formal Forms and Discernment: Two Neglected Aspects of Universals of Linguistic Politeness', *Multilingua*, 8: 223–48.

Janschewitz, Kristin (2008), 'Taboo, Emotionally Valenced, and Emotionally Neutral Word Norms', *Behaviour Research Methods*, 40 (4): 1065–74.

Jay, Timothy (1980), 'Sex Roles and Dirty Word Usage: A Review of the Literature and a Reply to Haas', *Psychological Bulletin*, 88 (3): 614–21.

Jay, Timothy (1992), *Cursing in America. A Psycholinguistic Study of Dirty Language in the Courts, in the Movies, in the Schoolyards and on the Streets*, Amsterdam: John Benjamins.

Jay, Timothy (1996), 'Cursing: A Damned Persistent Lexicon', in Douglas Herrmann, Cathy McEvoy, Christopher Hertzog, Paula Hertel and Marcia Johnson (eds), *Basic and Applied Memory Research: Practical Applications*, 301–13, Mahwah, NJ: Erlbaum.

Jay, Timothy (2000), *Why We Curse: A Neuro-Psycho-Social Theory of Speech*, Amsterdam: John Benjamins.

Jay, Timothy (2009a). 'Do Offensive Words Harm People?', *Psychology, Public Policy, and Law*, 15 (2): 81–101.

Jay, Timothy (2009b), 'The Utility and Ubiquity of Taboo Words', *Perspectives on Psychological Science*, 4: 153–61.

Jay, Timothy (2018), 'Swearing, Moral Order, and Online Communication', *Journal of Language Aggression and Conflict*, 6 (1): 107–26.

Jay, Timothy B. (2019), 'Taboo Language Awareness in Early Childhood', in Keith Allan (ed.), *The Oxford Handbook of Taboo Words and Language*, 96–107, Oxford: Oxford University Press.

Jay, Timothy and Kristin Janschewitz (2008), 'The Pragmatics of Swearing', *Journal of Politeness Research*, 4: 267–88.

Jay, Timothy and Kristin Janschewitz (2013), 'The Science of Swearing', *Psychological Science*. Retrieved from www.psychologicalscience.org/index.php/publications/observer/2012/mayjune-12/the-science-of-swearing.htm

Jay, Timothy, Catherine Caldwell-Harris and Krista King (2008), 'Recalling Taboo and Nontaboo Words', *American Journal of Psychology*, 121 (1): 83–103.

Jay, Kristin and Timothy Jay (2013), 'A Child's Garden of Curses: A Gender, Historical, and Age-Related Evaluation of the Taboo Lexicon', *American Journal of Psychology*, 126 (4): 459–75.

Jay, Kristin and Timothy Jay (2015), 'Taboo Word Fluency and Knowledge of Slurs and General Pejoratives: Deconstructing the Poverty-of-Vocabulary Myth', *Language Sciences*, 52: 251–9.

Jay, Timothy, Krista King and Tim Duncan (2006), 'Memories of Punishment for Cursing', *Sex Roles*, 55 (1–2): 123–33.

Jefferson, Gail, Harvey Sacks and Emanuel Schegloff (1987), 'Notes on Laughter in the Pursuit of Intimacy', in Graham Button and John R. E. Lee (eds), *Talk and Social Organisation*, 152–205, Clevedon, UK: Multilingual Matters.

Jeffries, Lesley (2010), *Opposition in Discourse*, London: Continuum.

Johnson, Danette and Nicole Lewis (2010), 'Perceptions of Swearing in the Work Setting: An Expectancy Violations Theory Perspective', *Communication Reports*, 23 (2): 106–18.

Johnson, Fern and Marlene Fine (1985) 'Sex Differences in Uses and Perceptions of Obscenity', *Women's Studies in Communication*, 8 (1): 11–24.

Kádár, Dániel Z. and Michael Haugh (2013), *Understanding Politeness*, Cambridge: Cambridge University Press.

Kapoor, Hansika (2016), 'Swears in Context: The Difference between Casual and Abusive Swearing', *Journal of Psycholinguistic Research*, 45 (2): 259–74.

Kaye, Barbara and Barry Sapolsky (2004), 'Offensive Language in Prime-Time Television: Four Years after Television Age and Content Ratings', *Journal of Broadcasting and Electronic Media*, 48 (4): 554–69. doi:10.1207/s15506878jobem4804_2

Kaye, Barbara and Barry Sapolsky (2009), 'Taboo or Not Taboo? That Is the Question: Offensive Language on Prime-Time Broadcast and Cable Programming', *Journal of Broadcasting and Electronic Media*, 53 (1): 22–37.

Kecskés, István (2010), 'The Paradox of Communication: Socio-Cognitive Approach to Pragmatics', *Pragmatics and Society*, 1 (1): 50–73.

Keesing, Robert M. and Jonathan Fifiʔi (1969), 'Kwaio Word Tabooing in its Cultural Context', *Journal of Polynesian Society*, 78 (2): 154–77.

Kehayov, Petar (2009), 'Taboo Intensifiers as Polarity Items: Evidence from Estonian', *Sprachtypologie und Universalienforschung*, 62 (1–2): 140–64.

Kelsey, Darren and Lucy Bennett (2014), 'Discipline and Resistance on Social Media: Discourse, Power and Context in the Paul Chambers "Twitter Joke Trial"', *Discourse, Context and Media*, 3: 37–45.

Kilby, David (1984), *Descriptive Syntax and the English Verb*, London: Routledge.

Kinney, Terry A. (1994), 'An Inductively Derived Typology of Verbal Aggression and its Association to Distress', *Human Communication Research*, 21: 183–222.

Krajewsky, Sabine and Hartmur Schröder (2008), 'Silence and Taboo', in Gerd Antos and Elija Ventola (eds), *Handbook of Interpersonal Communication*, 595–622, Berlin: Mouton de Gruyter.

Kushner, Howard I. (1999), *A Cursing Brain? The Histories of Tourette Syndrome*, Cambridge, MA: Harvard University Press.

Lachenicht, Lance (1980), 'Aggravating Language: A Study of Abusive and Insulting Language', *International Journal of Human Communication*, 13 (4): 607–88.

Lakoff, Robin Tolmach (1973), 'The Logic of Politeness: Or, Minding Your P's and Q's', *Papers from the Ninth Regional Meeting of the Chicago Linguistic Society*, 292–305.

Landau, Sidney I. (2001), *Dictionaries. The Art and Craft of Lexicography*, Cambridge: Cambridge University Press.

LaPointe, Leonard (2006), 'Profanity', *Journal of Medical Speech-Language Pathology*, 14 (1): vii.

Leaver, James (2011), 'Swear Like a Victorian: Victoria's Swearing Laws and Similar Provisions in NSW and Queensland', *Alternative Law Journal*, 36: 163–5.

Leech, Geoffrey ([1980] 1977), *Language and Tact*, Trier: Linguistic Agency, University of Trier, Paper No. 46. (Reprinted with revisions as Chapter 4 of Leech (1980), *Explorations in Semantics and Pragmatics*, Amsterdam: John Benjamins.)

Leech, Geoffrey (1983), *Principles of Pragmatics*, London: Longman.

Leech, Geoffrey (2004), *Meaning and the English Verb* (3rd edn), London: Routledge.

Leech, Geoffrey (2014), *The Pragmatics of Politeness*, Oxford: Oxford University Press.

Leech, Geoffrey and Mick Short (2007), *Style in Fiction* (2nd edn), Harlow: Pearson.

Levinson, Stephen C. ([1992] 1979), 'Activity Types and Language', *Linguistics*, 17: 365–99. (Also appearing in Paul Drew and John Heritage (eds), *Talk at Work*, 66–100, Cambridge: Cambridge University Press.)

Levinson, Stephen C. (1981), 'The Essential Inadequacies of Speech Act Models of Dialogue', in Herman Parret, Marina Sbisà and Jef Verscheuren (eds), *Possibilities and Limitations of Pragmatics: Proceedings of the Conference on Pragmatics, Urbino, July 8–14, 1979*, 473–492, Amsterdam: John Benjamins.

Levinson, Stephen C. (1988), 'Putting Linguistics on a Proper Footing: Explorations in Goffman's Concepts of Participation', in Paul Drew and Anthony Wootton (eds), *Erving Goffman. Exploring the Interaction Order*, 161–227, Cambridge: Polity Press.

Lim, Tae-seop and John Waite Bowers (1991), 'Facework: Solidarity, Approbation, and Tact', *Human Communication Research*, 17 (3): 415–50.

Limberg, Holger (2009), 'Impoliteness and Threat Responses', *Journal of Pragmatics*, 41: 1376–94.

Ljung, Magnus (2011), *Swearing: A Cross-Cultural Linguistic Study*, Basingstoke: Palgrave Macmillan.

Locher, Miriam A. and Richard J. Watts (2005), 'Politeness Theory and Relational Work', *Journal of Politeness Research*, 1 (1): 9–33.

Locher, Miriam A. and Richard J. Watts (2008), 'Relational Work and Impoliteness: Negotiating Norms of Linguistic Behaviour', in Derek Bousfield and Miriam Locher (eds), *Impoliteness in Interaction: Studies on its Interplay with Power in Theory and Practice*, 77–99, Berlin: Mouton de Gruyter.

Locher, Miriam A. and Sage Lambert Graham, (eds), (2010), *Interpersonal Pragmatics*, Berlin: Mouton de Gruyter.

Mabry, Edward (1975), 'A Multivariate Investigation of Profane Language', *Communication Studies*, 26 (1): 39–44.

Macafee, Caroline (1989), 'Qualitative Insights into Working-Class Language Attitudes', *York Papers in Linguistics*, 13: 191–202.

Magrath, Rory (2017), 'Footballing Masculinities: The Changing Nature of the Football Academy', in Daniel Kilvington and John Price (eds), *Sport and Discrimination*, 109–21, Abingdon: Routledge.

Mao, LuMing Robert (1994), 'Beyond Politeness Theory: "Face" Revisited and Renewed', *Journal of Pragmatics*, 21: 451–86.

Márquez-Reiter, Rosina (2009), 'How to Get Rid of a Telemarking Agent? Facework Strategies in an Intercultural Service Call', in Francesca Bargiela-Chiappini and Michael Haugh (eds), *Face, Communication and Social Interaction*, 55–77, London: Equinox.

Marsilli-Vargas, Xochitl (2014), 'Listening Genres: The Emergence of Relevance Structures through the Reception of Sound', *Journal of Pragmatics*, 69: 42–51.

Matsumoto, Yoshiko (1988), 'Re-examination of the Universality of Face: Politeness Phenomena in Japanese', *Journal of Pragmatics*, 12: 403–26.

McEnery, Tony (2006), *Swearing in English: Bad Language, Purity and Power from 1586 to the Present*, London: Routledge.

McEnery, Tony and Zhonghua Xiao (2004), 'Swearing in Modern British English: The Case of Fuck in the BNC', *Language and Literature*, 13 (3): 235–68.

Mercury, Robin-Eliece (1995), 'Swearing: A "Bad" Part of Language; a Good Part of Language Learning', *TESL Canada Journal*, 13 (1): 28–36.

Merrison, Andrew John, Jack J. Wilson, Bethan L. Davies and Michael Haugh (2012), 'Getting Stuff Done: Comparing "E-mail Requests" from Students in Higher Education in Britain and Australia', *Journal of Pragmatics*, 44: 1097–8.

Mey, Jacob L. (2001), *Pragmatics* (2nd edn), Oxford: Blackwell.

Mey, Jacob L. (2006), 'Pragmatic Acts', in Keith Brown (ed.), *Encyclopedia of Language and Linguistics* (2nd edn), Oxford: Elsevier.

Mey, Jacob L. (2010), 'Reference and the Pragmeme', *Journal of Pragmatics*, 42 (11): 2882–8.

Mey, Jacob L. (2012), 'Anticipatory Pragmatics', *Journal of Pragmatics*, 44 (5): 705–8.

Mills, Sara (2003), *Gender and Politeness*, Cambridge: Cambridge University Press.

Millwood-Hargrave, Andrea (2000), *Delete Expletives?: Research Undertaken Jointly by the Advertising Standards Authority, British Broadcasting Corporation, Broadcasting Standards Commission and the Independent Television Commission*, London: ASA, BBC, BSC and ITC.

Mirus, Gene, Jami Fisher and Donna Jo Napoli (2012), 'Taboo Expressions in American Sign Language', *Lingua*, 122 (9): 1004–20.

Mohr, Melissa (2013), *Holy Sh*t: A Brief History of Swearing*, Oxford: Oxford University Press.

Montagu, Ashley ([1967] 2001), *The Anatomy of Swearing* (3rd edn), Philadelphia: University of Pennsylvania Press (1st edn published in London: Rapp and Whiting).

Mulac, Anthony (1976), 'Effects of Obscene Language upon Three Dimensions of Listener Attitude', *Communication Monographs*, 43: 300–7.

Murphy, Brona (2009), '"She's a Fucking Ticket": The Pragmatics of FUCK in Irish English – An Age and Gender Perspective', *Corpora*, 4 (1): 85–106.

Murray, Thomas (2012), 'Swearing as a Function of Gender in the Language of Midwestern American College Students', in Leila Monaghan, Jane Goodman and Jennifer Meta Robinson (eds), *A Cultural Approach to Interpersonal Communication: Essential Readings*, 233–41, Hoboken, NJ: John Wiley and Sons.

Mursy, Ahmad and John Wilson (2001), 'Towards a Definition of Egyptian Complimenting', *Multilingua*, 20 (2): 133–54.

Napoli, Donna Jo and Jack Hoeksema (2009), 'The Grammatical Versatility of Taboo Terms', *Studies in Language*, 33 (3): 612–43.

Napoli, Donna Jo, Jami Fisher and Gene Mirus (2013), 'Bleached Taboo-Term Predicates in American Sign Language', *Lingua*, 123: 148–67.

Nelson, Marie (2014), '"You Need Help as Usual, Do You?": Joking and Swearing for Collegiality in a Swedish Workplace', *Multilingua*, 33 (1–2): 173–200.

Nishimura, Yukiko (2010), 'Impoliteness in Japanese BBS Interactions: Observations from Message Exchanges in Two Online Communities', *Journal of Politeness Research*, 6 (1): 35–55.

Norrick, Neal R. (2015), 'Narrative Illocutionary Acts Direct and Indirect', *Journal of Pragmatics*, 86: 94–9.

Nwoye, Onuigbe G. (1992), 'Linguistic Politeness and Sociocultural Variation of the Notion of Face', *Journal of Pragmatics*, 18 (4): 309–28.

Ochs, Elinor (1986), 'Introduction', in Bambi B. Schieffelin and Elinor Ochs (eds), *Language Socialization across Cultures*, 1–13, New York: Cambridge University Press.

O'Driscoll, Jim (1996), 'About Face: A Defence and Elaboration of Universal Dualism', *Journal of Pragmatics*, 25: 1–32.

O'Driscoll, Jim (2001), 'Hiding Your Difference: How Non-Global Languages Are Being Marginalised in Everyday Interaction', *Journal of Multilingual and Multicultural Development*, 22 (6): 475–90.

O'Driscoll, Jim (2007), 'Brown and Levinson's Face: How it Can – and Can't – Help Us to Understand Interaction across Cultures', *Intercultural Pragmatics*, 4 (4): 463–92.

O'Driscoll, Jim (2011), 'Some Issues with the Concept of Face: When, What, How and How Much?', in Francesca Bargiela-Chiappini and Dániel Z. Kádár (eds), *Politeness across Cultures*, 17–41, London: Palgrave Macmillan.

O'Driscoll, Jim (2013), 'Situational Transformations: The Offensive-izing of an Email Message and the Public-ization of Offensiveness', *Pragmatics and Society*, 4 (3): 369–87.

O'Driscoll, Jim (2017), 'Face and (Im)politeness', in Jonathan Culpeper, Michael Haugh and Dániel Z. Kádár (eds), *The Palgrave Handbook of Linguistic (Im)Politeness*, 89–119, London: Palgrave Macmillan.

O'Driscoll, Jim (2018), 'Dances with Footings: A Goffmanian Perspective on the Soto Case', *Journal of Politeness Research*, 14 (1): 39–62.

Oishi, Etsuko and Anita Fetzer (2016), 'Expositives in Discourse', *Journal of Pragmatics*, 96: 49–59.

Oliver, Marion and Joan Rubin (1975), 'The Use of Expletives by Some American Women', *Anthropological Linguistics*, 17: 191–7.

O'Neil, Robert (2002), 'Sexual Profanity and Interpersonal Judgement', *Dissertation Abstracts International: The Humanities and Social Sciences*, 63 (2): 781.

Ouidade, Sabri and Carl Obermiller (2012), 'Consumer Perception of Taboo in Ads', *Journal of Business Research*, 65 (6): 869–73.

Padilla Cruz, Manuel (2019), 'Qualifying Insults, Offensive Epithets, Slurs and Expressive Expletives', *Journal of Language Aggression and Conflict*, 7 (2): 156–81.

Parks, Tim (1992), *Italian Neighbours: An Englishman in Verona*, London: Vintage Books.

Pedraza, Andrea Pizarro, ed. (2018), *Linguistic Taboo Revisited. Novel Insights from Cognitive Perspectives*, Berlin: Mouton de Gruyter.

Peetz, Vera (1977), 'Promises and Threats', *Mind*, 86 (344): 578–81.

Pérez-Reverte, Arturo (2019), *Una historia de España*, Madrid: Alfaguara.

Pinker, Steven (2007), *The Stuff of Thought. Language as a Window into Human Nature*, New York: The Penguin Group.

Pinker, Stephen (2011), *The Better Angels of Our Nature: A History of Violence and Humanity*, London: Penguin.

Pinker, Stephen (2018), *Enlightenment Now: The Case for Reason, Science, Humanism, and Progress*, London: Penguin.

Pope, Rob (1995), *Textual Intervention: Critical and Creative Strategies for Literary Studies*, London: Routledge.

Quirk, Randolph and Sidney Greenbaum (1973), *A University Grammar of English*, London: Longman.

Rassin Eric and Peter Muris (2005), 'Why Do Women Swear? An Exploration of Reasons for and Perceived Efficacy of Swearing in Dutch Female Students', *Personality and Individual Differences*, 38: 1669–74.

Rathje, Marianne (2014), 'Attitudes to Danish Swearwords and Abusive Terms in Two Generations', in Marianne Rathje (ed.), *Swearing in the Nordic Countries*, 11–36, Copenhagen: Sprognaevnets Konferenceserie 2.

Rosenberg, Patricia, Sverker Sikström and Danilo Garcia (2017), 'The A(ffective) B(ehavioral) C(ognitive) of Taboo Words in Natural Language. The Relationship between Taboo Words' Intensity and Frequency', *Journal of Language and Social Psychology*, 36 (3): 306–20.

Sagredos, Christos and Evelin Nikolova (forthcoming), '"Slut I Hate You": A Critical Discourse Analysis of Gendered Conflict on YouTube', *Journal of Language Aggression and Conflict*.

St André, James (2013), 'How the Chinese Lost "Face"', *Journal of Pragmatics*, 55: 68–85.

Salmani Nodoushan, Mohammad Ali (2016), 'On the Functions of Swearing in Persian', *Journal of Language Aggression and Conflict*, 4 (2): 234–54.

Sanders, Robert E. (2013), 'The Duality of Speaker Meaning: What Makes Self-Repair, Insincerity, and Sarcasm Possible', *Journal of Pragmatics*, 48: 112–22.

Sapolsky, Barry and Barbara Kaye (2005), 'The Use of Offensive Language by Men And Women in Prime Time Television Entertainment', *Atlantic Journal of Communication*, 13 (4): 292–303.

Sarangi, Srikant and Stefaan Slembrouck (1996), *Language, Bureaucracy and Social Control*, London: Longman.

Schmitt, Christian and Rosina Márquez-Reiter (2019), 'Leadership in Conflict: Disagreement and Conflict in a Start-up Team', in Matthew Evans, Lesley Jeffries and Jim O'Driscoll (eds), *The Routledge Handbook of Language in Conflict*, 286–309, Abingdon: Routledge.

Scollon, Ron (1996), 'Discourse Identity, Social Identity, and Confusion in Intercultural Communication', *Intercultural Communication Studies*, 6 (1): 1–16.

Scott, Kate (2015), 'The Pragmatics of Hashtags: Inference and Conversational Style on Twitter', *Journal of Pragmatics*, 83: 8–20.

Searle, John R. (1969), *Speech Acts. An Essay in the Philosophy of Language*, Cambridge: Cambridge University Press.

Searle, John R. (1975), 'A Classification of Illocutionary Acts', *Language in Society*, 5: 1–23.

Searle, John R. and Daniel Vanderveken (1985), *Foundations of Illocutionary Logic*, Cambridge: Cambridge University Press.

Seizer, Susan (2011), 'On the Uses of Obscenity in Live Stand-up Comedy', *Anthropological Quarterly*, 84: 209–34.

Selnow, Gary (1985), 'Sex Differences in Uses and Perceptions of Profanity', *Sex Roles*, 12 (3–4): 303–12.

Shakiba, Nooshin (2011), *Swearing: A Cross-Cultural Linguistic Study*, Houndmills, Basingstoke: Palgrave Macmillan.

Sidiropoulou, Maria (1998), 'Offensive Language in English-Greek Translation: Perspectives', *Studies in Translatology*, 6 (2): 183–99.

Sifianou, Maria (1992), *Politeness Phenomena in Greek and in English*, Oxford: Clarendon Press.

Sifianou, Maria (2001), '"Oh! How Appropriate!" Compliments and Politeness', in Arin Bayraktaroglu and Maria Sifianou (eds), *Linguistic Politeness across Boundaries: The Case of Greek and Turkish*, 391–427, Amsterdam: John Benjamins.

Sifianou, Maria (2013), 'The Impact of Globalisation on Politeness and Impoliteness', *Journal of Pragmatics*, 55: 86–102.

Simons, Gary F. (1982), 'Word Taboo and Comparative Austronesian Linguistics', in Amran Halim, Lois Carrington and Stephen A. Wurm (eds), *Papers from the Third International Conference on Austronesian Linguistics, Vol. 3: Accent on Variety*, 157–226, Canberra: Pacific Linguistics.

Sinclair, John M. (1986), 'Fictional worlds', in Malcolm Coulthard (ed.), *Talking about Text*, Birmingham: University of Birmingham ELR.

Sinclair, John M. (1988), 'Mirror for a Text', *Journal of English and Foreign Languages* (Hyderabad), 1: 15–44.

Smith, Philip, Timothy L. Phillips and Ryan D. King (2010), *Incivility: The Rude Stranger in Everyday Life*, Cambridge: Cambridge University Press.

Spender, Dale (1980), *Man Made Language*, London: Routledge and Kegan Paul.

Spencer-Oatey, Helen (2000), 'Rapport Management: A Framework for Analysis', in Helen Spencer-Oatey (ed.), *Culturally Speaking: Culture, Communication and Politeness Theory*, 11–47, London: Continuum.

Spencer-Oatey, Helen (2005), '(Im)politeness, Face and Perceptions of Rapport: Unpacking Their Bases and Interrelationships', *Journal of Politeness Research*, 1 (1): 95–119.

Spencer-Oatey, Helen (2007), 'Theories of Identity and the Analysis of Face', *Journal of Pragmatics*, 39: 639–56.

Stapleton, Karyn (2003), 'Gender and Swearing: A Community Practice', *Women and Language*, 26 (2), 22–33.

Stapleton, Karyn (2010), 'Swearing', in Miriam A. Locher and Sage L. Graham (eds), *Interpersonal Pragmatics*, 289–305, Berlin: Mouton de Gruyter.

Stapleton, Karyn (2019), *Swearing and Perceptions of the Speaker: Online Responses to Celebrity Swearing*, abstract from The 6th Swearing in Scandinavia Symposium, Stockholm, Sweden.

Stenstrom, Anna-Brita (1991), 'Expletives in the London-Lund Corpus', in Karin Aijmer and Bengt Altenberg (eds), *English Corpus Linguistics: Studies in Honour of Jan Svartvik*, 239–53, London: Routledge.

Stenström, Anna-Brita (2006), 'Taboo Words in Teenage Talk: London and Madrid Girls' Conversations Compared', *Spanish in Context*, 3 (1): 115–38.

Stephens, Richard and Claudia Umland (2011), 'Swearing as a Response to Pain – Effect of Daily Swearing Frequency', *The Journal of Pain*, 12 (12): 1274–81.

Stepka, Daniel (1997), 'Obscenity Online: A Transactional Approach to Computer Transfers of Potentially Obscene Material', *Cornell Law Review*, 82: 905–46.

Stone, Geoffrey (2007), 'Origins of Obscenity', *NYU Review of Law and Social Change*, 31: 711–31.

Stone, Teresa E. and Mike Hazelton (2008), 'An Overview of Swearing and its Impact on Mental Health Nursing Practice', *International Journal of Mental Health Nursing*, 17: 208–14.

Stone, Teresa E., Margaret McMillan and Mike Hazelton (2015), 'Back to Swear One: A Review of English Language Literature on Swearing and Cursing in Western Health Settings', *Aggression and Violent Behaviour*, 25: 65–74.

Strub, Whitney (2013), *Obscenity Rules: Roth v. United States and the Long Struggle over Sexual Expression*, Lawrence: University Press of Kansas.

Tayebi, Tahmineh (2016), 'Why Do People Take Offence? Exploring the Underlying Expectations', *Journal of Pragmatics*, 101: 1–17.

Terkourafi, Marina (2001), 'Politeness in Cypriot Greek: A Frame-Based Approach', unpublished PhD thesis, University of Cambridge.

Terkourafi, Marina (2002), 'Politeness and Formulaicity: Evidence from Cypriot Greek', *Journal of Greek Linguistics*, 3: 179–201.

Terkourafi, Marina (2005), 'Pragmatic Correlates of Frequency of Use: The Case for a Notion of "Minimal Context"', in Sophia Marmaridou, Kiki Nikiforidou and Eleni Andonopoulou (eds), *Reviewing Linguistic Thought: Converging Trends for the 21st Century*, 209–233, Berlin: Mouton de Gruyter.

Terkourafi, Marina (2008), 'Toward a Unified Theory of Politeness, Impoliteness and Rudeness', in Derek Bousfield and Miriam Locher (eds), *Impoliteness in Interaction: Studies on its Interplay with Power in Theory and Practice*, 45–74, Berlin: Mouton de Gruyter.

Terkourafi, Marina, Lydia Catedral, Iftikhar Haider, Farzad Karimzad, Jeriel Melgares, Cristina Mostacero-Pinilla, Julie Nelson and Benjamin Weissman (2018), 'Uncivil Twitter: A Sociopragmatic Analysis', *Journal of Language Aggression and Conflict*, 6 (1): 26–57.

Thelwall, Mike (2008), 'Fk Yea I Swear: Cursing and Gender in MySpace', *Corpora*, 3 (1): 83–107.

Thiranagama, Sharika, Tobias Kelly and Carlos Forment (2018). Introduction: Whose civility? *Anthropological Theory* 18 (2–3): 153–174 (special issue on civility).

Thomas, Jenny (1983), 'Cross-Cultural Pragmatic Failure', *Applied Linguistics*, 4 (2): 91–112.

Thomas, Jenny (1995), *Meaning in Interaction*, London: Longman.

Tickoo, Asha (2010), 'On Assertion without Free Speech', *Journal of Pragmatics*, 42 (6): 1577–94.

Traugott, Elizabeth C. and Richard B. Dasher (2001), *Regularity in Semantic Change*, Cambridge: Cambridge University Press.

Trudgill, Peter (1983), *Sociolinguistics: An Introduction to Language and Society* (2nd edn), Harmondsworth: Penguin.

Tsiplakou, Stavroula and Georgios Floros (2013), 'Never Mind the Text Types, Here's Textual Force: Towards a Pragmatic Reconceptualization of Text Type', *Journal of Pragmatics*, 45: 119–130.

Valdeón, Roberto A. (2015), 'The (Ab)use of Taboo Lexis in Audiovisual Translation: Raising Awareness of Pragmatic Variation in English-Spanish', *Intercultural Pragmatics*, 12 (3): 363–85.

Vallée, Richard (2014), 'Slurring and Common Knowledge of Ordinary Language', *Journal of Pragmatics*, 61: 78–90.

Vandergriff, Ilona (2013), 'Emotive Communication Online: A Contextual Analysis of Computer-Mediated Communication (CMC) Cues', *Journal of Pragmatics*, 51: 1–12.

Van Dijk, Teun (1977), *Text and Context. Explorations in the Semantics and Pragmatics of Discourse*, London: Longman.

Vangelisti, Anita L. and Stacy L. Young (2000), 'When Words Hurt: The Effects of Perceived Intentionality on Interpersonal Relationships', *Journal of Social and Personal and Social Relationships*, 17 (3): 393–424.

Van Lancker, Dianna and Jeffrey L. Cummings (1999), 'Expletives: Neurolinguistics and Neurobehavioral Perspectives on Swearing', *Brain Research Reviews*, 31: 83–104.

Verschueren, Jef (1999), *Understanding Pragmatics*, London: Arnold.

Vingerhoets, Ad J. M., Lauren M. Bylsma and Cornelis de Vlam (2013), 'Swearing: A Biopsychosocial Perspective', *Psychological Topics*, 22 (2): 287–304.

Wajnryb, Ruth (2005), *Expletive Deleted. A Good Look at Bad Language*, New York: Free Press.

Watts, Richard J. (1989), 'Relevance and Relational Work: Linguistic Politeness as Politic Behavior', *Multilingua*, 8 (2–3): 131–66.

Watts, Richard J. (1992), 'Linguistic Politeness and Politic Verbal Behaviour: Reconsidering Claims for Universality', in Richard J. Watts, Sachiko Ide and Konrad Ehlich (eds), *Politeness in Language: Studies in its History, Theory and Practice* 43–69, Berlin: Mouton de Gruyter.

Watts, Richard J. (2003), *Politeness*, Cambridge: Cambridge University Press.

Werkhofer, Konrad T. (1992), 'Traditional and Modern Views: The Social Constitution and the Power of Politeness', in Richard Watts, Sachiko Ide and Konrad Ehlich (eds), *Politeness in Language: Studies in its History, Theory and Practice*, 155–99, Berlin: Mouton de Gruyter.

Wierzbicka, Anna (1985), 'Different Cultures, Different Languages, Different Speech Acts: Polish vs. English', *Journal of Pragmatics*, 9: 145–78.

Wierzbicka, Anna (1987), *English Speech Act Verbs: A Semantic Dictionary*, New York: Academic Press.

Yule, George (2010), *The Study of Language* (4th edn), Cambridge: Cambridge University Press.

Ziewitz, Malte and Christian Pentzold (2014), 'In Search of Internet Governance: Performing Order in Digitally Networked Environments', *New Media and Society*, 16 (2): 306–22.

Zimmerman, Daniel J. and Theodore A. Stern (2010), 'Offensive Language in the General Hospital', *Psychosomatics*, 51 (5): 377–85.

Index

For reasons of space, this index does not include the names of authors which appear only in the tables in chapter 3 and/or the list of references